Network Analysis: Studies in Human Interaction

CHANGE AND CONTINUITY IN AFRICA

MONOGRAPHS UNDER THE AUSPICES OF

THE AFRIKA-STUDIECENTRUM - LEIDEN

MOUTON · THE HAGUE · PARIS

Network Analysis
Studies in Human Interaction

edited by

JEREMY BOISSEVAIN and J. CLYDE MITCHELL

MOUTON · THE HAGUE · PARIS

Library of Congress Catalog Card Number: 72-77471

Jacket-design by Jurriaan Schrofer

Printed in the Netherlands

FOREWORD

This book is the outcome of one of the symposiums which are annually organized by the Afrika-Studiecentrum at Leiden.

The purpose of this particular symposium was to discuss theoretical aspects of the network approach in the social sciences, as well as the merits of this approach to actual field work in Africa.

Scholars associated with the Departments of Anthropology of the Universities of Edinburgh and Manchester and with various Dutch universities and research associates of the Afrika-Studiecentrum delivered papers at the conference, for the greater part based on field work, and participated for one week in discussions on the basis of these contributions.

Though we do not expect this book to be acclaimed as an example of rapid publication of conference proceedings (the symposium was held in September 1969) and though the discussions were in many respects inconclusive, we feel confident that the importance of the theme amply justifies publication of the contributions in book form.

G. W. Grootenhuis
General Secretary Afrika-Sudiecentrum
September 1972

Preface *

JEREMY BOISSEVAIN

This collection of articles presents some of the insights into social relations and processes which can be gained by making use of network analysis. This form of analysis has only very recently become an accepted part of the social sciences, and this book represents the proceedings of the fourth symposium to be held on the subject in the past few years.[1]

As the contributions of Noble and Mitchell indicate, the study of social networks has arisen out of the dissatisfaction of a number of social anthropologists with the conventional form of structural-functional analysis. Structural-functional analysis by definition views societies as essentially static, moral corporations whose members' behaviour is explicable in terms of, if not determined by, jural rules. The behaviour of persons is explained in terms of their roles, that is, the rights and duties devolving upon them as the result of the formal positions they occupy in various institutions. These institutions are explained, in their turn, in terms of the contribution they make to the maintenance of the social structure. Conflict is usually regarded as dysfunctional, although some view certain conflicts as salutory as they foster the formation of groups and the demarcation of structural boundaries. Thus conflict is regarded as dysfunctional when it brings about change and functional when it helps preserve the *status quo*. Behaviour which does not conform to the prevalent norms is regarded as deviant. Change is seen as coming from outside, as impinging upon a system in equilibrium. Hence change, too, is regarded as dysfunctional, for it disturbs the postulated harmonious balance. It is viewed as something of secondary importance (*cf.* Barth, 1967: 661).

The structural-functional framework used by anthropologists, developed primarily through the study of slowly changing tribal and simpler societies, is inadequate to cope with the study of rapidly changing complex societies,

* Anton Blok, Clyde Mitchell and Bonno Thoden van Velzen provided helpful criticism of an earlier version of this preface, which was sent to all contributors for comment.

in both the western and the third worlds. The concept of change contradicts the basic structural-functional assumptions of balance, complementary opposition and continuity of the existing order. Indeed, it is legitimate to ask if structural-functional analysis is in fact an adequate instrument for the study of primitive societies. Mitchell, following Srinivas and Béteille (1964), suggests that it is. This was an issue that gave rise to a lively but inconclusive debate at the Leiden meeting.

Network analysis is thus first of all an attempt to reintroduce the concept of man as an interacting social being capable of manipulating others as well as being manipulated by them. The network analogy indicates that people are dependent on others, not on an abstract society. This is a concept which was rendered all but superfluous by the concentration on culture, rules, belief systems, and groups which made up the moral order that anthropologists reared in the structural-functional tradition sought to analyse. This moral order was seen as impinging upon persons, moulding them and determining their behaviour. Secondly, network analysis seeks to place again in the foreground of social analysis the notion of internal process and the inherent dynamics in relations between interdependent human beings. This concept was banished following the overreaction to the simplistic turn of the century evolutionary theories.

This is a large and ambitious order and the instruments available to accomplish it are at the moment rather limited. The basic postulate of the network approach is that people are viewed as interacting with others, some of whom in their turn interact with each other and yet others, and that the whole network of relations so formed is in a state of flux. The approach makes no explicit assumptions about the nature of the interactions (linkages) though those who use this concept are constantly seeking patterns and formulating and testing hypotheses regarding such patterns and their effects on behaviour. This approach has many possibilities but also faces many problems, a considerable number of which are discussed in the lively collection of essays which follows.

The articles are divided in three major categories. The contributions of Noble, Mitchell, Banck and Niemeijer discuss a series of theoretical and methodological problems which are of crucial importance to this new field of analysis. The other articles, all of which are based on empirical material, reflect the two ways that social networks have been viewed: 1) as a system of relations which impinge upon individuals and influence their behaviour, and 2) as a series of relations which persons use to achieve their ends. The contributions of Cubitt, Kapferer, Trouwborst and myself reflect the first orientation and deal essentially with the comparison of ego-centred networks (or 'first order zones' in the vocabulary of network analysis) and the way in which these and certain of their structural features, such as density, affect the behaviour of the individuals at the centre of the network. The contributions of Blok, Jongmans and Thoden van Velzen, on the other hand, deal more specifically with the manipulation of others by persons competing for power in Sicily, Tunesia, and Tanzania.

The articles raise a number of important issues. They resolve many of them, but leave others unanswered. That this should be so is not surprising considering that all the authors are working in what may be called a frontier area of the behavioural sciences. Each has had to develop some of the instruments used to deal with the analytical problems faced. Many of these are rough-and-ready methods which may be refined or discarded. The data presented in the empirical studies are by and large rich and varied and will permit reanalysis by others interested in this new approach.

The authors have made a number of methodological as well as theoretical contributions. The concepts of density and clustering have been subjected to sharp criticism by Rudo Niemeijer among others. He suggests ways in which these concepts can be refined and tested and also proposes an ingenious technique whereby comparative data on networks could be collected by means of a sampling procedure. Cubitt and I examine some of the problems related to collecting data on total personal networks or first order zones and present some of our findings. Cubitt and Kapferer examine critically and refine a number of Elizabeth Bott's hypotheses and assumptions. Finally, Jongmans presents an application of balance theory to the analysis of a political dispute in a Tunesian mountain village. Jongmans and Kapferer also make extensive use of matrices to analyse their data. These provide a rewarding method for systematically analysing social relations, for they impose a discipline which ensures that the data are fully presented, hence making it possible for others to re-analyse them.

Besides a number of important refinements to the rather esoteric methodology of network analysis, the articles also make contributions of a more general nature. Kapferer provides a well argued demonstration of the need to apply theory to network analysis. He does this by applying Blau's (1964) exchange theory. He notes, and I think rightly, that network analysts have placed far too much emphasis on the task of classification and definition without giving enough attention to the basic theoretical assumptions which should guide this work. Only by operating with a clearly delineated body of theory will it be possible to formulate and test hypotheses. The fruitfulness of an approach which combines network analysis with exchange theory is also demonstrated by Thoden van Velzen's study of conflict groups in

Tanzania, by the data provided by Jongmans on the way in which Tunesian village leaders recruit support, and finally by Blok's analysis of how *mafiosi* and bandits in Sicily form coalitions.

Thoden van Velzen attempts to apply the concepts of network analysis and exchange theory to the study of competing coalitions. He describes the 'interest coalition' formed by the local establishment of wealthy peasants and government personnel and the 'levelling coalition' of anti-establishment elements. He suggests that these are basic forms of conflict which are found in all societies. He concludes that while network analysis enables him to set out the exchange circuit linking the members of the interest coalition, the concepts of the network approach are of little use to the analysis of the levelling coalition, whose members acknowledge no one as their leader and are not linked in an exchange circuit. It may be noted, however, that the greater sensitivity to the interaction and exchange relationships between people which derive from the network approach has permitted him to set out the structural attributes of both these coalitions.

In my own contribution I compare the total personal networks of a townsman and a countryman to trace the influence of the macro-environment via their personal networks on their behaviour and personality. The greater gregariousness of the countryman and the more important place of kinsmen in his network as compared to the townsman is explained in terms of the structure of their networks, which, in turn, is related to the difference of environment between town and country. These findings, which build on the work of Elizabeth Bott in 1957, suggest that in addition to establishing the more obvious bridges between social anthropology and communication and graph theory, network analysis can also construct bridges between social and development psychology if not psychiatry. These interdisciplinary bridges are badly needed if social anthropology is to find a way off the structural-functional island on which it has been marooned for the past 30 years, and improve our understanding of human behaviour.

The theoretical articles in this collection, and particularly those of Mitchell and Banck, raise a number of very important issues. Mitchell and Banck both explore the relation between network and group. Mitchell argues that the opposition between network and corporate groups is a 'false dichotomy' as they are social phenomena at different levels of abstraction. He argues that 'social networks are in no way distinct from corporate groups'. In his contribution, which deserves serious consideration, he also attempts to set out a conceptual framework in which networks are related to norms, roles and eventually institutions. Banck is less optimistic. He argues that, while group and network analysis should be kept conceptually distinct, the changes in groups can be understood by using propositions relevant to networks and coalitions, but that this dynamic process cannot be understood by only using propositions relevant to groups.

The related problem of just how far it is permissible to analyse partial networks, such as kinship, religious or economic relations, in isolation from other partial networks was also raised but not resolved. At one level of abstraction these partial networks may be conceived of as providing a set of systematic relationships out of which the analyst constructs institutions. At yet another level, providing criteria can be developed to isolate them, these institutions can be viewed as partial networks. Yet, as Trouwborst, Cubitt, Mitchell, Blok and I explicitly, and the others implicitly, indicate, treating these relations independently of other relations poses a grave methodological problem. It has for long been a basic assumption of anthropology that where relations are multiplex, that is where the relations between two persons derive from their activities in several institutional fields, the different types of relations impinge on and influence the actors in the various roles they play. Indeed it is a basic assumption of those ascribing to the network approach that behaviour cannot be explained in terms of any one single activity field. Thus the problem of handling multiplex or many stranded relations remains, in spite of the increasingly sophisticated analytical apparatus provided by network analysts.

Finally, although the basic attraction of the network approach is that it promises a way of studying the problems of social change and process, very little theoretical progress has been made in this direction.[2] This is due chiefly to the point Kapferer makes: without an input of theory there can be no set of derived hypotheses relating to change. Many of the studies, although they indicate that relations are continually shifting, provide little empirical backing. Exceptions are the articles of Blok, Thoden van Velzen and Jongmans. Jongmans' material is particularly interesting, for it compares a network of social relations over a period of four years. In fact, he notes that of the relations recorded in 1965, fully 50% had changed content by 1969. It is important, therefore, that in future studies using the network approach a conscious effort is made to build in a time perspective. Detailed diachronic studies will presumably always show that the relations between people are constantly shifting. Yet these shifts – both the realignments of coalition members as well as the changes that take place in the content of the relations between people not in conflict – must, somehow, be isolated, explained, and brought into a general theory which will permit the development of hypotheses regarding the processes, forces and directions of change.

What is badly needed now is the development of a theory which presents a real alternative to structural-functionalism; this last has been discredited but it has not yet been replaced. Until a rival theory is developed that resolves all the anomalies of structural-functional analysis, the theoretical crisis in social anthropology will continue.[3] Network analysis, exchange theory and cultural ecology (*cf.* Harris, 1968) are reactions which express dissatisfaction with structural-functionalism. They all lead away from it, yet, as Kapferer has shown, they can in part be made to converge. What is needed now is a greater degree of synthesis to bring the various alternative theories, as it were, together, to combine them into a unified theory which can enlarge our understanding of human behaviour and the patterns which it forms. The configurational theory of Norbert Elias, to which Blok draws attention, may be able to play a part in any such synthesis. Elias has worked out a development model which shares much with network analysis, for it is premised upon the interdependence of human beings. The shifting configurations they form are both interrelated institutional complexes as well as networks. Moreover, the notion that people strive to achieve a superordinate position in terms of exchange and transaction, which as we have seen is a concept underlying many of the studies in this collection as well as the work of Homans (1961), Barth (1966) and Blau (1964), figures implicitly in Elias' model. In short, Blok's advice to consider Elias' framework must be examined seriously.

However, in continuing to develop our own conceptual apparatus, we should also note the warning sounded by Blok about not separating the individual from the total pattern of interactions of which he forms a part. If structural-functionalism was characterized by its inflexibility and static approach, network analysis may be characterized by its flexibility and the scope which it gives to the study of individual manipulation. As Noble has perceptively noted, we must be careful that the pendulum does not swing too far in the direction of the manipulating individual. Whereas people are freer than classic structural-functionalists would have us believe, they are not as free as optimistic action theorists would like to believe, for structural and moral constraints on their behaviour remain.

Emancipation, revolution and the questioning of the right of those who wield established power to exact obedience are themes which are dominant in the societies in which network analysts live and work. We must make sure that our theorizing and analysis are based on fact and not merely wishful thinking.

These introductory remarks scarcely do justice to the insights and detailed treatment of the material as well as the problems raised by the various authors. They are meant merely to signal some of the issues raised, and to alert the reader to their background and wider implications. He must now see for himself which insights can be gleaned from this new approach.

NOTES

1. Others are Mitchell (1969), Aronson (1970) and the symposia held during the 69th and 70th annual meetings of the American Anthropological Association in 1970 and 1971. For general introductions to the concept and uses of social networks the reader is referred to J. Clyde Mitchell's contribution to the papers he edited in 1969, and to the detailed theoretical and methodological inventory on the subject prepared by Whitten and Wolfe (n.d.).

2. Whitten and Wolfe (n.d.) and Anderson (1970) also note that the network approach has not lived up to its promises, especially in the field of social change.

3. *Cf.* Kuhn (1970: esp. Chap. 7 and 8). Kuhn's description of the professional insecurity and the proliferation of new theories that accompany the awareness of the anomalies of an old scientific theory and precede the development of a new one, provides an analysis of the situation now prevailling among social anthropologists and sociologists.

Table of contents

PREFACE VII

PART I THEORY AND METHODOLOGY

MARY NOBLE, Social network: Its use as a conceptual framework in family analysis 3
J. CLYDE MITCHELL, Networks, norms and institutions 15
GEERT A. BANCK, Network analysis and social theory 37
RUDO NIEMEIJER, Some applications of the notion of density 45

PART II NETWORKS COMPARED

TESSA CUBITT, Network density among urban families 67
BRUCE KAPFERER, Social network and conjugal role in urban Zambia: Towards a reformulation of the Bott hypothesis 83
A. TROUWBORST, Two types of partial networks in Burundi 111
JEREMY BOISSEVAIN, An exploration of two first-order zones 125

PART III NETWORK AND COALITIONS

ANTON BLOK, Coalitions in Sicilian peasant society 151
D. G. JONGMANS, Politics on the village level 167
H. U. E. THODEN VAN VELZEN, Coalitions and network analysis 219

BIBLIOGRAPHY 251

BIBLIOGRAPHICAL DATA OF AUTHORS 256

INDEX 258

Part 1

Theory and methodology

Social network: Its use as a conceptual framework in family analysis

MARY NOBLE

In this paper the intention is to follow the pattern set by Nye and Berardo in their book *Emerging Conceptual Frameworks in Family Analysis* (1966). In that book they put forward the following model:

1. A note on the historical development of the framework;
2. Foci of content;
3. Concepts;
4. Basic assumptions;
5. Product, or impact on the study of the family;
6. Value orientation of scholars;
7. A re-statement of the framework;
8. An evaluation of its contributions, contradictions and inadequacies;
9. An annotated bibliography.

At the present state of family studies involving the network approach it is not suggested that this paper will provide a definitive statement. For one thing, a groundwork of empirical studies is necessary to indicate more clearly the difficulties and disadvantages of this approach. Both at Edinburgh and at Manchester Universities, and possibly elsewhere, field studies are in progress or being completed. When the results have been published there will be a substantial body of data available which will enable us to evaluate the approach more adequately. Nevertheless, it is precisely because this area is so uncharted that a succession of sign-posts is needed. It is hoped that this paper will provide one of the initial guides.

1. THE HISTORICAL DEVELOPMENT

The use of the concept of network in a specifically theoretical context rather than as a vague analogy is comparatively new. Radcliffe-Brown in *Structure and Function in Primitive Society* (1952) states 'But direct observation does reveal to us that these human beings are connected by a complex network of social relations. I use the term "social structure" to denote this network of actually existing relations' (p. 190).

The use of social network as a conceptual tool of analysis has emerged as a response to a growing doubt as to the adequacy of the structural-functional approach in the study of complex societies. This doubt arises from four sources. The first is from the basic structural assumption that what is studied is a social structure, that is to say a system of social relations of the same kind as a natural system, existing as a social fact and characterised by fixed boundaries. Firth (1951), for example, states that 'a culture is a unity in so far as it is tied to a bounded social structure' (p. 53). But as Nagel (1961) points out, it is difficult to designate unambiguously the system which is to be investigated except perhaps in the case of non-literate societies.

Levy (1949) points out a second source of doubt in the logical fallacy of 'functional teleology'. 'It is not, however, permissible to observe that the existence of a given phenomenon is the result of its being a functional prerequisite of the phenomenon of which it is a part'.

A third source of doubt lies in the static quality of the extreme structural-functional approach. Change is not taken into account in its philosophical background. If change is not admitted, neither are the processes or agents of change admissible as subjects of study. Yet we have incontrovertible evidence all around us that change does take place.

A final source of doubt lies in the feeling that the individual as a factor in the situation has been largely ignored by the structural-functionalists. While not accepting the extreme psychological position that nature, not nurture, could explain all behaviour, it was generally felt that the extreme anthropological thesis that 'Custom is King' is a distortion of the situation. It was even more true when the anthropologist turned to the study of heterogeneous societies where a larger proportion of the social roles available are achieved rather than ascribed and where, even in the case of ascribed roles, the way in which, say, a parent's role is fulfilled may be a question of preference and selection. More scope then should be given to the interplay of the individual with others and with the environment.

One of the first to use 'social network' in a more systematic way was Barnes (1954) in his study of a Norwegian fishing village. His main interest was the analysis of social class and he wished to select a model which would avoid the limitations of the structuralist approach by positing neither a bounded group nor a static equilibrium. The concepts he used were social network and set. He conceived of social network as a field of social relations. The network was essentially concerned with interpersonal links rather than with the definition and analysis of group membership. He distinguished between the unbounded social network and the bounded social network, centred on a single person, ego. The latter he called 'set'.

Redfield (1955) in a Huxley Memorial Lecture stressed the importance of the idea of social network but one of the first to use it analytically was Elizabeth Bott in her book *Family and Social Network* (1957). One of her aims was to establish the existence of a diversity of patterns of conjugal role relationships and to investigate the possibility of a relationship of such patterns with extra-familial factors. Her use of the term social network follows that of Barnes except that she does not consistently make the distinction between the social field and the ego-centred relations.

Epstein (1961) tends to follow Bott in failing to distinguish between network and set, a distinction which is, I think, an important methodological one. Epstein distinguishes between effective and extended networks. The effective network is made up of those people known to ego who also are known to each other. The extended network includes people who are known to ego but not to other members of ego's network and who in turn know other people. He suggests that the effective network is where there are most continuous and intense relations and where through gossip the norms and values are defined and affirmed. Where the effective network comprises those in the upper reaches of the prestige system the norms and values established amongst them will be promulgated through the extended network to the rest of the community. At this point he is clearly approaching the concept of reference group, both normative and comparative, advanced by Merton and Rossi (1957). Epstein is perhaps the first person to discuss the question of variation in different parts of a network according to the amount of interaction. This particular point has been taken up by Boissevain (1968) and Barnes (1969).

2. FOCI OF CONTENT

The foregoing description has shown that the original foci of study were not in all cases the family. One of the main interests centred on the processes of interaction, especially in the formation and dissemination of norms and values. Barnes, Epstein and Mayer have concentrated on 'political', that is class or 'influential', networks. The value of network theory as a tool in the analysis of family interaction was, however, central to Bott's work. Her work aroused the interest of social anthropologists and this combined with the basic anthropological orientation towards the family and kinship. Firth

(1956) points out, 'The study of kinship is a perennial theme for social anthropology. An understanding of the kinship system in any society is essential as clues to the working of some of the most fundamental relationships – sexual, marital, economic – in that society. It also may be of prime importance in the process of socialisation, in developing patterns of reaction to authority and in providing important symbols for the moral evaluation of conduct'.

It may be that network theory will also provide a bridge between the sociological analysis of human behaviour and the personal or motivational aspect. Much of human activity is directed towards the realisation of personal aims and ambitions, especially in terms of marriage, the maintenance of the home and the establishment of a family. Yet for long sociological analysis has interpreted social behaviour in terms of jural and economic systems. The implicit assumption seems to have been that man works and inter-relates in society to maintain the social and economic system. It would seem a much more valid interpretation that man works to eat and to provide a living for his dependants and that much of his youthful effort is devoted to acquiring such dependants. Talking to informants reveals that to them work is a means to an end – in youth courtship and marriage; in adulthood the maintenance of a family. Work is valued for itself in very few cases.

3. CONCEPTS

There is as yet no fully accepted and definitive body of concepts. The central term, social network, has not yet lost its ambiguities as will be shown in section 8. The other concepts used are those regularly accepted by the social anthropologist: relationship, role, kinship, descent, etc.

4. BASIC ASSUMPTIONS

Hill and Hansen (1960) point out that 'Perhaps the most significant elements in differentiating one framework from another are the underlying assumptions which each makes about the nature of man, the family and society'. Because we are at the present feeling our way in the use of the term there has been little explicit discussion of the assumptions basic to the concept of social network. Nevertheless we can perhaps explore the most apparent at this point.

In the first place there is no assumption that man is either a working or an acquisitive creature, an assumption which tends to be implicit in much of sociological theory. Methodologically the network theorist is interested in the relations set up between and among individuals and families. If an assumption *is* made it is a return to Locke (n.d.) that man is by nature a social creature experiencing an innate need to establish relations with others of his kind. The nature of the relationship is not predicated.

Secondly, no assumption is necessarily made about the place of the family in society. Although social anthropologists are traditionally orientated towards the view-point that the family is the basic and most significant social unit, network theory itself can be applied to a study of the relations between any grouping of men and women, whatever the nature of the bond.

One of the advantages of this theoretical framework lies in the assumptions made about the nature of society. The structural-functional approach sees society as a bounded group existing over time for a period long enough to enable the group to evolve its own characteristic culture. This approach immediately raises the problem of defining the boundaries of the group and indeed much anthropological discussion has been devoted to resolving this problem. The network approach does not suffer from this defect. The network model enables one to conceptualise both an infinite series of interconnecting relationships and also bounded groups. Again, while the network approach seems to accept that there do emerge foci of relationships over time which may be studied from a structural point of view it does not assume that such a static framework is a necessary condition for the proper study of social relationships. It therefore lends itself much more freely to the analysis of urban mobile societies without the theorist becoming involved in the distortions which result from the use of a static and rigid model. In addition, this flexibility – together with a lack of any basic notion of social equilibrium, as is implicit in structural theory – enables the conceptual framework to be applied to the study of social change.

This leads us back in full circle to a consideration of the nature of man. The model of society is not that of a static bounded group sub-divided into a variety of types of sub-groups – the lineage, the unit of economic production, the political unit, the cult-group or congregation – each clearly delimited and membership ascribed or achieved according to clearly defined criteria. Instead, in any situation, there is a finite number of possible relations available to the individual. It is accepted that the field of social relationships provides a social and cultural environment within which the individual operates but he is not completely constrained by this environment. Culture is no longer King. By eschewing any assumption about standardisation of behaviour patterns through cultural conditioning, network theory enables one to take into account personal choice and possible manipulation of relations in the interest of self. It enables the field-worker to observe and analyse the operation of what Malcolm Ruel (1968) has called the 'Opportunist Society', without the philosophical gymnastics which a strict adherence to the structural-functional framework necessitates.

5. PRODUCTS OF THE APPROACH

The social network approach is still at an early stage. Thus its impact on the study of the family has not yet been fully felt. Nevertheless a great deal of work has been initiated, particularly by Bott's book on the relationship between family and social network. Some of this work has reached the stage of publication. There is Udry and Hall (1965) whose work gave a limited support to Bott's thesis. Aldous and Strauss (1965/66) on the basis of their field-work conclude that their findings tend to disprove Bott, although they do point out that the nature of their sample was such that it did not provide a fully adequate test. Turner (1967) has also used Bott's hypothesis to examine his own material and points out that a crucial variable is geographical mobility – a point of which Bott herself was not unaware. At Edinburgh University a number of studies are in progress or have been completed – Margaret Whiteley and Tessa Cubitt on different populations within the Edinburgh area; Barbara Bond and Christine Oppong in Sierra Leone and Ghana respectively; myself in a small town in the central belt of Scotland. In Manchester too the network concept is in the process of being tested as a tool in the analysis of social relations.

In general, published results have so far been indecisive as far as the validity of Bott's hypothesis is concerned. It would appear that it may be applied to fairly stable working class communities but that its applicability to geographically and socially mobile and to middle-class populations is by no means certain. More work is necessary. Little if any work is being undertaken in non-urban and non-industrial areas. I examined my own Nigerian field-work material in the light of Bott's hypothesis (Noble, 1964). Although the data had not been collected within a framework of the network concept a cursory examination seems to show that they accorded with Bott. Research in peasant and tribal communities might yield valuable comparative material which could illuminate the question of the universality or otherwise of the thesis that there is a correlation between the kind of social network and familial relationships.

6. VALUE-ORIENTATIONS

The analysis of family organisation in terms of social network is as yet in its infancy and the concepts and basic assumptions have not yet been clearly formulated. It is difficult therefore to do anything more than to indicate the value judgements or objectives of the scholars using this approach. Because the approach is, in Britain, largely confined to social anthropologists the value orientations will obviously be largely influenced by those generally accepted by British social anthropologists. Paradoxically the value orientation of such scholars is a commitment to the avoidance of value-judgements. Nevertheless because of the reaction in the early part of the century against evolutionary doctrine in social theory there was a general swing against a dynamic approach incorporating ideas of social change and social progress. There now appears to be another reaction, against the static, equilibrium, approach. This, however, is not accompanied by any return to an acceptance of a uniform and determinant process of change. Instead there appears to be more adherence to a belief in the right of man to select that way of life which is most appropriate to his own circumstances and to his attainment of the basic 'rights of man'. The Opportunist Society must provide opportunities for the individual to manipulate his environment to his own advantage, given always that he does not thereby impinge too severely on the rights and opportunities of others. It may be that implicit in the network approach is the value of self-identification and self-fulfilment by a proper (i.e. restricted by the rights of others) manipulation of the opportunities afforded by the environment – self progress rather than either social progress or an ordered but static society.

7. THE FRAMEWORK – A RE-STATEMENT

The social network approach has emerged from a dissatisfaction with a strictly structural approach. It is an attempt to develop a conceptual framework which will be more adequate in tackling problems of urban societies and of changing peasant and tribal communities. Wolf (1966) analyses the contexts in which kinship, friendship and patron-client relations are respectively dominant in complex societies. In discussing work in this field he concludes, 'Yet it is possible that complex societies in the modern world differ less in the formal organisation of the economic or legal or political systems than in the character of their inter-personal sets' (p. 19). Clyde Mitchell (1966) in an essay in the same book develops this point in respect of changes in the social system and of 'situational change', that is where the individual himself is translated into a situation which is to him new. In dealing with both these types of change Mitchell emphasises the importance of studying 'the network of personal links which individuals have built around themselves in towns' (p. 54) and goes on to suggest that the study of networks may show 'the way in which norms and values are diffused in a community, and how the process of "feed-back" takes place' (p. 56).

8. EVALUATION

The network approach then appears to offer a deeper understanding of human behaviour. But both at the theoretical and at the practical levels there are certain contradictions and inadequacies which must be resolved. One of the first relates to the ambiguity in the term network which has already been mentioned. For example, the distinction made by Barnes between unbounded and bounded has not been fully developed although Adrian Mayer (1966) is concerned to clarify the different kinds of networks and action-sets.

A second point which requires clarification is concerned with the focus of the network. Clyde Mitchell (1966) discusses the 'networks of personal links which individuals have built around themselves in towns' (p. 54) and Adrian Mayer (1966) mentions 'ego-centred entities such as action-sets and quasi-groups' (p. 119). But in spite of this apparently clear indication that the focus of the network is ego or the individual, many field-workers use the family as the focus. The familial network, the separate networks of the parents, the children's networks – these may be largely congruent. On the other hand they may not. Indeed the existence of a 'total' family network as a social reality is subject to question. This problem is not unnoticed. Jay (1964) states that 'the units . . . may be individuals, families, communities or other social aggregates'. But there has been no evidence produced to elucidate whether there are differences in character between fields of interaction where the focus is the individual or the family.

Yet a third difficulty is raised by the question of density. Epstein (1961) points out that within a social network there may be differences of density – in Bott's terms a network may in some areas be loose-knit and in others close-knit. Barnes (1969) has sought to clarify the notions of close-knit and loose-knit by distinguishing between connectedness, connectivity and density. Boissevain (1968) also discusses this problem. One of my colleagues, Tessa Cubitt, is contributing a paper in which she reviews some of the discussion.

A fourth point which needs clarification is the question of what Adrian

Mayer (1966) has called complex action-sets. Here he is referring to 'A combination of relationships linking people directly to ego, and of those linking people to intermediaries who are themselves in direct contact with ego' (p. 109). If one is examining the set of a wife, one may distinguish between *her* set and that of her husband. She may never herself be in direct contact with her husband's employer; the latter may not be a member of her set but may in fact exert a great deal of influence on her life. Mayer contrasts the complex action-set with the simple action-set, that in which people are all directly linked with ego.

Turning to the more practical aspects, many difficulties are immediately apparent. One of these is the question of charting the ramifications of a network. Even when one is restricting one's attention to a simple bounded network or action-set, the numbers of individuals in direct contact with ego may be large. As soon as one turns to the study of the family network then obviously the ramifications are even greater. Even in a network where the density is low and where one is looking at the network only from the point of view of ego's contacts the amount of work involved in charting the individuals concerned will be high. With an increase in density the work will correspondingly increase. But the increase will be astronomical when the research worker proceeds to the next necessary stage – the charting of contacts among the component members of the network apart from those they share with ego. The matter is further complicated by the fact that frequency of contact must also be considered.

There is also the temporal aspect. As has been mentioned above there is at present in social anthropology a reaction against the equilibrium approach with its accompanying notion of the 'anthropological present' as a hypothetical stage in time when a society is in a perfect state of balance. There is also therefore a movement towards the study of behaviour as forming ongoing patterns of social relationships (Gluckman, 1967), typified among others by van Velsen's (1967) 'situational analysis'. Within the framework of network analysis it is obvious that the relations of ego with his contacts and the relations among the contacts themselves must take place over a period of time. This raises difficulties at two levels. At the interpretive level one may have to evaluate the relationship of time and frequency with the other factors which may be involved – geographical and social distance, economic factors and so forth. At the practical level there are the usual difficulties. Has the research worker enough time and money to remain in the field a sufficient time to observe the full range of contacts? Even if he can remain he cannot expect to be in a position to observe all contacts directly. What tools will he select – diary, formal schedule for informants to complete? And can he rely on his informants' honesty, reliability and intelligence? If he employs one or more research assistants he must ensure some standardisation of procedure and interpretation. If he is relying on retrospective information from informants then the difficulties proliferate. Memories are unreliable. The informant may forget or may be selective in his recollections: or may suppress certain facts which he sees as shameful, degrading or even as impolite to the questioner. All such factors may lead to distortions and inaccuracies.

In addition there is the question of duration of contact. Is a visit of an hour a week by a mother to the home of her married daughter equivalent to a daily visit of the same duration? And should place and initiation of contact be ignored? Is a mother's visit to her daughter equivalent to the daughter's visit to her mother? Is it significant or even relevant who first initiated the contact? This kind of question leads to a consideration of motivation. Why did the daughter visit her mother or conversely why did she invite her mother to visit her? If we are interested in individual choice and action then surely we must take motivation into our evaluation. This subject has for a time been under discussion among psychologists. Do we venture into the realms of motivation and if so how can we ensure that we deduce the motives correctly or that our informant informs us honestly? On the other hand do we yield to the difficulties and accept the behaviouristic doctrines, thus leaving a significant gap in our data? Recent developments in the field of linguistics would suggest that the latter alternative would be retrogressive. Chomsky (1967) has initiated a revolution in linguistic studies by diverting interest away from the 'surface structure' of languages to the 'deep structure'. He suggests that all languages share a common deep structure. Attention therefore becomes focused not on the overt behaviour patterns but on inner mental processes. As a result of his new approach Chomsky has been said to have routed behaviourism. If one of the basic postulates of the network approach is that man can make a choice in his relationships, the question of *how* he arrives at this choice is a basic one.

The philosophical problem of what is inside man and its relevance to network theory confronts us once again when we turn to consider the quality of relations. One suggestion is that each type of institution – economic, legal, political, religious and kin – has a dominant set of characteristic norms and values. Adrian Mayer (1966) distinguishes between transactional and non-transactional links. Epstein's discussion of the differential densities of separate areas of interaction is relevant here. But it is doubtful whether this provides an adequate solution to the problem. Such areas of interaction are not necessarily discrete nor is each itself necessarily homogeneous qualitatively. If one looks at kinship one can perceive circles of intimacy (Firth, 1956) and members of different circles may have very different types of relation with ego. Even if one selects one relationship, such as that between mother and daughter, for investigation one may see the actual behaviour between different individuals is not constant within a single society, although all may conform in general to the accepted reciprocal pattern of the relationship within that society. One of the difficulties then is that in complex societies wide variations are possible in interpreting the correct fulfilment of the rights and obligations inherent in a particular relationship. One cannot equate behaviour and effect.

What emerges is an approach which at a methodological level appears capable of providing a satisfactory analysis of the family in complex societies. Undoubtedly much refining of the concept is needed. The most fundamental difficulties seem to lie in the gathering of field data. We seem to be faced with a basic contradiction, that the theoretical framework seems adequate to be developed into a satisfactory model but that the practical drawbacks restrict its application to small numbers. Up till now there seems to be little effective answer to the problem of how to gather and to assess the qualitative data, although the developments in linguistic philosophy may once again provide a lead to social anthropologists. Some answer to the quantitative problem of the magnitude and complexity of the data may be sought in statistical procedures (Mitchell, 1967).

2

Networks, norms and institutions

J. CLYDE MITCHELL

1. NETWORKS AND STRUCTURAL ANALYSIS

The recent increase of interest in social networks appears to be due in part to dissatisfaction with conventional modes of structural analysis. In fact, the introduction of the notion of the social network into social analysis seems to have arisen out of exactly such circumstances. When Barnes (1954) studied the social structure of the small Norwegian island parish of Bremnes he isolated three separate 'fields' or types of social relationships, which, he argued, subsumed most of the interactions of the people in the parish. Two of these fields could be fitted into the set of categories conventionally used by sociologists. The first were the sets of relationships the islanders were involved in in their working life – the industrial system. The second embraced the relationships people became involved in by reason of their occupying a place in a territorial system of social relationships. But in addition to these there was a set of personal relationships which interfused and cross-cut the set of relationships in the industrial and territorial systems. These were the relationships based on friendship, kinship and neighbourliness and the particular feature of them was that they were likely to be distinctive for each person in the community, being based as they were to a large extent on the personal choices of the individual concerned. Barnes was induced to take account of these personal relationships, I presume, because he found that there were a large number of actions of the people he was studying which could not be understood in terms of the more formal industrial and territorial systems of social relationships. Subsequently he explained his position thus: 'My aim in making these divisions was to discriminate between those relationships which were subsumed by the framework of bounded institutionalized groups or categories, such as the hamlet, the parish, the factory workshop, the missionary society, and the ship's crew, and those relationships deriving from the ever-ramifying web of cognitive kinship, affinity and friendship' (Barnes, 1969a: 72).[1]

The personal networks of individuals, however distinct they might be from the point of view of who was or was not involved in them, could nevertheless be studied in a systematic way. Thus Barnes was interested in drawing the distinction between the *structure* of the interpersonal relations in general in simple small-scale societies, for example, as against more complex large-scale societies. The behaviour of individuals therefore, could be understood in terms of the pattern of inter-personal relationships they were involved in outside the normal aspects of the industrial and territorial systems.

This approach was extended and specified by Bott in her now classical study of twenty families in London. Initially she set out to explain variations in the pattern of the allocation of tasks in the household in terms of social class and the neighbourhood, that is in what we would call institutional factors, but inconsistencies in her data forced her to look for a more effective explanation. It is for this reason that she turned to the structure of interpersonal relationships or 'social networks'. Bott adopted a definition of the social network which was identical with Barnes's. She saw the social network as being made up of friends, neighbours and kinsfolk and she contrasted the relationships her couples had with these with the relationships derived from involvement in what she called 'organized groups', particularly those relating to work or local government, medical services and schools. In a way which closely paralleled Barnes's approach she implicitly contrasted personal relationships with relationships deriving from organized groups and then went on to draw the distinction between large-scale urban situations and small-scale village situations.

In the small-scale society, she argues, nuclear families are encapsulated in local groups (Bott, 1957: 99). In these circumstances she argues: 'The division of labour in small-scale societies is relatively simple; the division of labour in an industrial society is exceedingly complex. In a small-scale relatively closed society, most of the services required by a family can be provided by the other families in the local group and in the kin group. In an urban industrialized society, such tasks and services are divided up and assigned to specialized institutions. Whereas a family in a small-scale relatively closed society belongs to a small number of groups each with many functions, an urban family exists in a network of many separate unconnected institutions each with a specialised function. In a small-scale relatively closed society the local group and the kin group mediate between the family and the total society; in an urban industrial society there is no single encapsulating group or institution that mediates between the family and total society'. (Bott, 1957: 100). The immediate environment in Bott's analysis therefore was the set of personal contacts which members of the family had with others – the friends, neighbours and kinsfolk. Bott conceptualized these net-work' relationships as an intervening variable between what she called organized groups, in other words, institutional structures, and the conjugal behaviour of the spouses she was studying. She saw the factors of social class and neighbourhood as contextual variables which influenced but did not determine the 'connectedness' of the network the couples were involved in, and this and the structure of the network in turn influenced the allocation of domestic tasks between husband and wife. The position can be represented in a pseudo-causal[2] diagram as follows:

Diagram 1

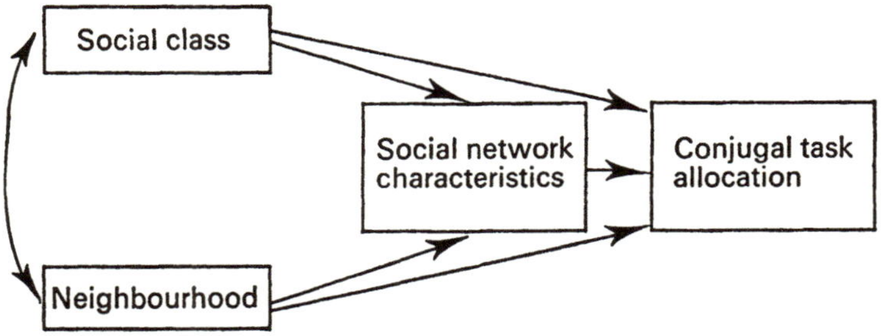

But when Bott specifically discusses the influence of institutional factors on network structure and role segregation she implies more than simply contextual effects for she speaks of elementary families being contained within organized groups that control many aspects of their daily activities in small-scale societies with a simple division of labour. This she contrasts with the situation in urban families where 'although individuals may belong to organized groups the family itself may be controlled in some aspects by a doctor, by a church, by a local borough council or by some other government bodies.' She contrasts this situation with that of the nuclear family in small-scale society by pointing out that: in large-scale societies 'there is no organized group that regulates all aspects of a family's life, informal activities as well as formal' (Bott, 1957: 217). The implication of the expression 'organized group that regulates all aspects of a family's life' here seems to be that of functional integration, the mechanism of which, in Bott's thinking, is the transmission of norms and pressures along the links of the connected or closed networks (and hence in small-scale societies) or not, in the case of 'open' networks (and hence in urban communities).

The distinction between social networks on the one hand and organized groups, corporate groups or institutional structures on the other has continued to be discussed by writers since Barnes and Bott. Harumi Befu, who was influenced by Barnes's 1954 paper, has recently discussed the matter in connection with an analysis of data relating to rural Japan. Befu draws the distinction between networks on the one hand defined in terms of Barnes's notion and corporate structures on the other, though he makes the important point that for analytical purposes the networks traced by kinship should be considered separately from that by friendship or by neighbourliness and not as a single field as Barnes conceived it (Befu, 1963: 28). Corporate groups, he argues, are characterized by a clear-cut boundary membership, composition in terms of a plurality of individuals no one of which forms the centre of the structure and by durability and persistence of the structure. In the Japanese rural community he is analysing he gives as examples the administrative structure, which subsumes component substructures of the prefecture, the village and the hamlet, and the educational structure which subsumes the Ministry of Education, the prefectural Department of Education, the Board of Education and the elementary schools. Other corporate-structured social systems he mentions are the agricultural cooperative association, the irrigation cooperative and the Shinto institution. Befu describes how cultivators seek help in agricultural activities and house construction from kinsfolk recruited bilaterally, who are drawn from hamlets five or six miles away. He describes also how some of the people who grow up in the same area and attend the same elementary school utilize this early companionship to provide the basis for later financial aid. He defines neighbours as those who live in the same hamlet and to whom a person may turn for help. It is clear that the members of a hamlet may be in each other's networks as kinsfolks, friends or neighbours. Members in more distant hamlets may be friends or kinsfolk or the friends or kinsfolk of neighbours. Members of yet more distant hamlets may fall into these categories or into the category of friends or kinsfolk of friends or kinsfolk. Befu talks of a network structure with heavy density of relationships in and around the hamlet gradually fading out as one goes outward in all directions but embracing dozens of neighbouring hamlets (Befu, 1963: 34).[3] The relationships with the external world of people in the hamlets Befu studied therefore could be mediated through personal networks or through corporate structures.

The point I wish to take up in this presentation of material is the epistemological basis of the separation of kinship, friendship and neighbourliness links from those arising out of membership to corporate groups. The distinction between networks and groups or institutions has been drawn by several writers. Bott, it will be recalled, drew a contrast between situations where a family could be thought of as a unit within a corporate structure, such as a lineage and those where the family could be thought of as a link to several different institutional forms without being encapsulated in any of them. Befu on the other hand although he recognizes that kinship links as in a lineage system may constitute part of a corporate structure in the sort of social situation he was concerned with, that is where bilateral kinship predominated, felt that kinship links, like friendship links, could be thought of as relationships which were separate from and cross-cut corporate structures.

Boissevain (1968) in a recent discussion of the place of non-groups in sociological analysis makes the same basic distinction between networks and groups of the corporate kind and much of his argument is directed towards correcting what he argues is an undue emphasis on structural relationships in modern sociology and social anthropology. Basically he conceives of social relationships as lying along a continuum at one pole of which would be personal networks. Ranged ordinally along the continuum would be quasi-groups, factions, interactional groups, corporate groups (and what he calls 'institutional complexes') and finally society itself.[4] Obviously the validity of this formulation must depend upon the nature of the heuristic dimension along which these types of interactional pattern are ranged. Unfortunately this is by no means clear from Boissevain's paper. He talks of 'social forms' which individuals generate in social interaction and points out how existing social forms are used and modified by individuals in various ways and concludes that 'individuals and the loose coalitions they form are thus logically prior to groups and society'. (p 545). Social forms, however, are left undefined and could imply different things. Later, when discussing the difference between social networks and quasi-groups he talks of the degree of the quasi-group's exhibiting patterned interaction and organization and defines patterned interaction as 'regular and purposive contact between at least some of the members' (p. 550). Here the dimension underlying the continuum seems partly to be the duration of the relationship and partly its purposive nature. The aggressive action of a number of children in a play-group may be a regular aspect of their behaviour and it is clearly purposive in at least one sense of the word, but obviously the children characterized by this behaviour could not be for this reason considered to be a quasi-group. Clearly Boissevain implies by purposive, 'directed towards a common or shared end'. Furthermore the pattern is presumably derived from the *organization* of the activities of the members of the quasi-groups – that is that there is some rationally understandable coordination of activities directed towards some end.

An attempt to specify the parameter of the continuum along which social networks, quasi-groups, factions and corporate groups may be arranged must involve a prior question: whether a single dimension underlies the continuum or could the arrangement of the social phenomena Boissevain refers to be considered as an ordering derived from a projection on to a single axis of the position of these phenomena along several divergent dimensions? In less abstract terms, quasi-groups and factions for example, may be distinguished in different ways such as in terms of the division of activities within them on the one hand and the duration of the relationships among the members on the other. At present the exact nature of the parameters underlying the continuum are unspecified and must emerge by implication only.

Some years ago Epstein (1962) and I (1959, 1966) independently of each other suggested the conceptual separation of three types or orders of social relationships which were significant in the analysis of the behaviour of people in town. As set out more recently (Mitchell, 1969: 9) these were:

a. the *structural order* by means of which the behaviour of people is interpreted in terms of actions appropriate to the position they occupy in an ordered set of positions, such as in a factory, a family, a mine, a voluntary association, a trade union, a political party or similar organization.
b. the *categorical order* by means of which the behaviour of people in unstructured situations may be interpreted in terms of social stereotypes such as class, race, ethnicity, 'Red' or 'School' among the Xhosa migrants to East London and so on.
c. the *personal order* by means of which the behaviour of people in either structured or unstructured situations may be interpreted in terms of the personal links individuals have with a set of people and the links these people have in turn among themselves and with others such as the social networks of the families in Bott's study.

These three orders of social relationships, however, should not be looked upon as three different *types* of actual behaviour, but rather as three different ways of making abstractions from the same actual behaviour so as to achieve different *types of understanding and explanation.* By this argument, therefore, there can be no opposition of structural and personal links but only different ways of subsuming the data into explanatory frameworks.

The matter is clarified particularly in a paper which in my opinion represents a considerable advance in theoretical sophistication in respect of the relationship between networks and corporate groups or institutional structures. It is the paper published by Srinivas and Béteille in 1964. Srinivas and Béteille start with the observation that 'the model of social structure which bases itself on enduring groups and categories and their interrelations has been developed largely by social anthropologists engaged in the study of primitive societies' (Srinivas and Béteille, 1964: 165). The typical example of this type of approach is Evans-Pritchard's study of the Nuer. But in more complex social systems or in social systems undergoing social changes 'Boundaries between groups tend to be blurred or broken down, there is greater circulation of personnel and an increasing degree of interpretation between different systems of groups, classes and categories.' (Srinivas and Béteille, 1964: 165). Opportunities thus arise for persons to become involved in contractual relationships outside and beyond those of the formal categories and groups of the traditional social system. As Srinivas and Béteille put it: 'The individual is progressively being drawn into networks and interpersonal relations which cut across the boundaries of village, sub-caste and lineage' (p. 166). Srinivas and Béteille isolate two particular discriminating characteristics of groups and networks: that groups are bounded whereas networks are not and that groups are objective whereas networks are not. To say that a group in bounded implies a distinct discontinuity of the quality of social relationships between those who are considered members of the group (or category as well, in Srinivas and Béteille's words) and those who are not. Furthermore the concept of boundedness would seem to contain within it also the notion of finiteness for Srnivas and Béteille contrast the bounded group with a network 'which ramifies in every direction, and, for all practical purposes stretches out indefinitely' (p. 166). Clearly however, a criterion of boundedness to distinguish groups from networks could be awkward to apply in practice for we know that even such an apparently formal (hence bounded) group as a political party may expand and contract in response to the issue that is being raised. I refer here to social action, of course, and not to the formal or legal definition of membership in the party, i.e., whether the member has paid his dues and carries a card or not.

The solution of the difficulty is contained within Srinivas and Béteille's second feature by which they distinguish between groups and networks. Here they talk of the 'objective' existence of the group in the sense that its boundaries are the same for the 'outsider' as for the 'insider' whereas the character of a network on the other hand, they argue, varies from one individual to another. What is implied by this somewhat elliptical formulation becomes clear later in Srinivas and Béteille's paper. They describe a social network as 'a set of concrete individuals who are members of diverse systems of enduring groups and categories. Here we represent the network from the point of view of the actor and there are as many networks as there are actors in the social system' (p. 166). The anthropologist, they argue, sets about making a study by mapping out the concrete networks of the interpersonal relations of individual actors. But this mapping they insist 'in itself does not fully meet the needs of his analysis. At best it can provide him with a broad idea of the linkage between the groups and systems of groups in a society. For a deeper understanding it is necessary not only to chart the concrete networks of different individuals but to relate these different networks to one another, to draw up, so to say, a master chart, in a coherent and systematic manner. This involves abstraction and synthesis'.

They proceed then to argue that the actual relationships between individuals will usually be multifarious in nature that is, they will be multiplex or multistranded or as they put it 'composite and multi-bonded'. For the purpose of analysis one single aspect of the relationship may, by an act of intellect, be abstracted and correlated with the actions and behaviour of other pairs of individuals linked by a conceptually equivalent relationship. Out of this set of abstracted relationships a pattern may be constructed which can be formulated as a structure, an institution or a group. It is at this step, Srinivas and Béteille argue, that the shift from 'the subjective network of the actor to the objective one of the observer takes place'.

This formulation of the connection between social networks and institutional structures provides a way of handling some of the problems which have arisen in the presentations of Barnes, Befu and Boissevain we have been considering. Basically the social network is thought of as the actual set of links of all kinds among a set of individuals and not as Barnes, Bott and Befu argue only of the links of kinship, friendship and neighbourliness. These rather are only specific aspects of the linkages among individuals which may be abstracted from the amalgam of all linkages in which pairs of individuals may be involved.

It is here that a new development by Barnes is relevant. In a recent paper (1969a) Barnes has extended and clarified his earlier paper on networks (1954). In 1954 he had spoken of the total network as all the social links that exist in any given community. Presumably he implies that these are all the links which are observable rather than all links observed and unobserved, but this is not clear. This total network, says Barnes, is a first-order abstraction from reality (1969: 56). Barnes then defines what he calls a partial network as 'an extract of the total network based on some criterion applicable throughout the whole network' (1969a: 57) and gives as examples of partial networks the cognatic web of kinship, networks of marriage, political networks and religious networks as described in the works of Cohn and Marriott and by A. Mayer. Thus out of the set of multiplex links connecting a number of individuals the observer may select, say, those he perceives as 'kinship' and present them as a partial network.[5] It is out of the partial networks that the observer constructs groups, institutions or social categories.[6].

2. THE CONTENT OF LINKS

Before we can pursue this relationship between social networks and social structures further we need to consider more fully what I consider to be a crucial point in the analysis. Thus far we have been writing about links between individuals in a network in a general unspecific way. In these terms the social network is little more than a metaphor and not of much use for analytical purposes. We may represent the set of observed social relationships existing within a specified collectivity of individuals as lines (standing for the relationships) connecting points (standing for individuals) or alternatively as entries in a matrix at the intersection of rows and columns representing relationships between individuals. We could now go on to draw conclusions about the pattern of social relationships directly from these representations, or alternatively by matrix manipulation, about the degree to which there appears to be a clique in the collectivity or to what extent every individual is linked to every other individual in the collectivity. But the diagram or the matrix, like a sociogram, is in fact merely a symbolic representation of an abstract set of relationships and in order to use it analytically we need to be able to specify what the lines actually represent and in what way they are deemed to be isomorphic with reality.

There are at present it appears three rather different ways in which the contents of the links of social networks may be appreciated.

a) *Communication content; i.e., information*

One of these relates to the passage of information of some kind from one person to another. The sort of information will differ from one observer to another and will be relevant presumably to the sort of proposition that the observer wishes to establish. The sort of study I am referring to here is that dealing with, for example, the diffusion of rumour or gossip through a community. The use of networks in this way probably lies more in the field of social psychology than in sociology but the study from Coleman, Katz and Menzel (1957) on the way in which a new drug is taken up by the physicians in an American town is an example of this sort of study. Here the network is seen primarily as a set of communication links relating physicians to one another in a particular manner.

Note, however, that in a study such as this the basic proposition is that the communication network is determined largely by the structure of interpersonal relationship so that the analysts in fact, are here working with two networks: the network conceived of in terms of communication links and the network conceived of in terms of friendship, professional links and so on. This is one of the interesting points that emerge from Epstein's analysis of gossip in an African town (1969). Epstein examines the flow of information along a personal network among a set of relatively high status African residents of a suburb in Ndola. The people in the network are all connected by friendship, having been school fellows, and perceived membership of an 'elite' category. Epstein's point is that the norms in terms of which the information passing through the networks is evaluated influences and modifies the information accordingly. Thus the fact that co-members of an elite group are passing on information about the peccadilloes of one of their number with a person of lower social status enables them to discuss the matter in terms which reinforce their own self-identity as an elite. The distinctiveness of the social network established on the basis of the flow of information from that established on the basis of the normative content of the links is well illustrated by a study of the process by which women find out in America about how to contact an abortionist. (Lee, 1969: 123-146). Lee finds that 'communication concerning abortion tends to occur within the framework of the acquaintance network rather than through formal channels', the 'acquaintance network' here being similar to what we have distinguished below as networks based on normative contents. But the important thing is that there are certain parts of the social network of the women which were effectively excluded from the information network. Examples of the categories of such persons are mothers and parents, friends who disapprove (e.g., Catholics) and neighbours (Lee, 1969: Table 50: 142) Lee generalises this to argue that 'barriers to free flow of information are located (1) within the kinship area of the acquaintance universe, particularly across generational lines; (2) across authority lines, exemplified where women mentioned employers, teachers, school authorities, and subordinates such as pupils and employees; and (3) at some social distance, barring communication with people with whom the woman does not have an intimate relationship, such as neighbours or 'someone you work with' (Lee, 1969: 141-2). The point that is relevant to the discussion here is that it is clear that in the particular study Lee was making while the acquaintanceship and information network may have overlapped to some degree there were significant categories of persons where the two different networks were mutually exclusive. The content of the network selected for emphasis must be chosen in accordance with the problem being examined: there is no way of defining a network relevant for all purposes.

b) *Exchange contents*

A somewhat different but equally important way of conceptualizing the links between individuals in personal networks is by means of the exchange content of these links. In this approach individuals are related to each other by sets of transactions which have implications for the actors wider than the simple act of exchange itself. This seems to me to be the basis of Adrian Mayer's notion of the action-set (1964). Here a number of actors are involved in a number of transactions which bind them to one another in a series of expectations and obligations. In the example that Mayer uses the actors are the candidate in a municipal election on the one hand and a set of his potential electoral supporters on the other. Mayer then traces a series of offers of services in exchange for support during the election. The electors are connected by links to the candidate by their expectations of his patronage such as for example the improvement of a road near the elector's house or the employment of the elector (or his kinsman) in an office over which the candidate has control, or his brokerage that is by introducing the elector to business contacts or government officials in order to further his private ends.

Mayer is at pains to point out that the action-set may be recruited on the basis of a number of different criteria. He gives a diagram of the links connecting the candidate to various electors or categories of electors, in which thirty-eight links are shown. Of these ten are in terms of kinship, kin factions or ritual kinship; seven in terms of economic links; five in terms of Party membership; four in terms of caste and the rest in terms of a wide range of characteristics: the State, a wrestling club, trade union membership, occupational links, village links and so on. Here then we have three networks: an exchange network, a communication network and a 'social network'. As with communication networks some of the propositions that could have been developed from Mayer's material could have been related to the inter-relationships among the exchange network, to the communication network and the 'social' networks.

A more specific examination of an exchange network in terms of the categories in terms of which the links have been forged has been made by Kapferer (1969) in a study of the work relationships in an ore-processing plant in Broken Hill, Zambia. Kapferer's interest is in examining the way in which a 'rate-buster' is subjected to pressures from his colleagues to conform to their expectations about productivity. The workers in the plant share several attributes such as membership in tribal categories, fictional and clan kinship, age and so on which constitute the basis of the recruitment to personal linkages in the plant. In addition they perform a number of services for each other both in relation to work tasks and on a more personal basis which form the elements of exchange among them. Kapferer then goes on to explore the relationship between different combinations of attributes to the exchange relationships among the workers in the plant and is able to show, in a detailed quantitative analysis of his material, how alignments in the two networks coincide to a considerable degree.

c) *Normative content*

The third type of content which the observer may single out as relevant in the construction of social networks has been implied by the brief discussion of communication and exchange contents of networks. This refers to that aspect of the relationship between two individuals which can be referred to the expectations each may have of the other because of some social characteristic or social attribute the other may possess. Thus when Barnes referred to the social network he was concerned with a limited content, that is with 'kinship', 'neighbourliness' or 'friendship'. These are in fact, the actors' perceptions which the observer uses in order to abstract from the behaviour of the individual those aspects which are relevant for his analysis. These perceptual categories exist as frameworks for evaluating the behaviour of people in the appropriate situations and it is for this reason that I have referred to the content here as 'normative'.

What we observe in any social situation is in fact a series of social actions in which people perform activities and undertake tasks, pass information among themselves and enter into arrangements with one another with regard to the alliances and oppositions among themselves. They do this in terms of their perceptions of the attributes of one another which have meaning for one another in terms of the set of beliefs, values and ideas they share.[7] What we distinguish then as communication, exchange or normative networks are the ways of abstracting analytically meaningful aspects of behaviour from social reality for the purpose of establishing regular connections among them. Communication, exchange and normative contents of the linkages in social networks are all intermingled in real social institutions for all social interaction involves communication, explicit or implicit, some exchange and evaluation of behaviour in terms of social norms. Whichever aspect we choose to emphasise in our analysis will depend upon the sort of problems we are interested in.

3. THE PROBLEM OF MEANING IN NETWORK CONTENTS

Several rather difficult problems have been glossed over, however, in this presentation of the different contents which form the basis of networks. Here I wish to explore more fully those problems which impinge on the relationship between networks and corporate groups or institutional structures. In particular I wish to concentrate upon the normative content of networks and how they are connected with corporate groups and institutional structures. Special problems related to communication and exchange networks I leave to others to handle.

The observer as theoretician, I assume, finds it necessary, as I have said, to refract the actual behaviour of people in specified social situations into conceptually 'pure' elements which are amenable to manipulation in terms of his explanatory scheme. The actors in the social situations are engaging in a similar and parallel procedure at a somewhat different level of operation. They are operating with 'common sense' formulations of observable aspects or behaviour which are related to the body of norms and beliefs associated with these perceptions. An African townsman, for example, learns by chance that a woman whom he has known for a long time by a series of oblique connections through some remote kinsfolk stands as a classificatory mother-in-law to him. Whatever the relationship before, the new perception of the link between them will impose a restriction upon their behaviour towards each other by the common expectations of normal behaviour of sons-in-law and mothers-in-law. These expectations here exist as 'meanings' which the actors attribute to the relationship and these 'meanings' serve as a reference though not as a firm injunction for the appropriate behaviour between the couple. The analyst must take into account these 'common sense' meanings, for they are very real from the point of view of the actors. For them the situation is now so defined as to make these particular values and beliefs salient where they were not before. But at this level of abstraction they are merely data: the analyst will presumably want to move to a somewhat more abstract level of generalisation where he relates these common-sense meanings to one another in a way which brings out their interconnections – a set of interconnections which are as likely as not to be completely beyond the comprehension and grasp of the people themselves.

We are here face to face with a problem familiar in all sociological analysis: the phenomenological problem of the meanings which actors attribute to actions and attributes and how these may be integrated into logically related theoretical propositions. The participant perceives a set of role-signs displayed by the other protagonists – a set of symbols which predicate appropriate behaviour on the part both of the perceiver and the perceived. Thus the social attributes that people exhibit can be looked upon as role-signs which have significance for the behaviour of actors in social situations. Sex and age, for example, have social meaning in the sense that they signify certain expectations of behaviour and attitude-orientations to the actors. Even more so attributes such as 'ethnicity' and 'race' can be looked upon as perceptions on the part of actors which have distinct consequences for their behaviour towards people exhibiting these attributes. The selection of attributes to serve as role-signs, however, is not mechanical or automatic. Which of the variety of potential role-signs that an actor is assumed to be displaying in a given social situation will be determined to a considerable extent by the way in which the actors in that situation define it. In our attempt to understand the behaviour of participants in a set of social actions then we need to work with the perceptions of the persons as they are presenting them.

The contents of the links in a social network, therefore, are not immediately apparent but exist in the understandings that the actors have of the implications of the relationships among them for their behaviour. To label a link as 'friendship' or 'clanship' or as any other type of social relationship means that the actors construe the behaviour to be expected in relation to that link as that indicated by the label they give to it. This means that an observer whose raw data are the actions of people in a variety of social situations is in some difficulty in abstracting elements from actual behaviour in the form of partial networks. He must be sufficiently familiar with the implicit meanings in social behaviour to be able to appreciate the behaviour in terms of the perceptions of the actors. Not only that but he must also know the actors well enough to be able to appreciate the influence on them of people who may be significant for their action but who are not physically part of the ongoing social activity.

The members of an African family in a town in Central Africa for example gathered to propitiate ancestor spirits in connection with the illness or misfortune of one of their number will be involved in a set of links with absent members in the rural areas or in other towns whose existence may well affect the behaviour of the participants in the ceremony. Some of the links, in other words, may be latent and become activated as observable links only in special circumstances.

This leaves the problem of methods to be used in the study of social networks undistinguished from that in ordinary sociological fieldwork. Thus far the use of formal techniques of data collection, as for example by self-completed questionnaires such as used by sociometrists or even of schedules completed by relatively skilled interviewers, has not been very successful precisely, I suspect, because the basic phenomenological problem involved in adequately distinguishing the content of the links in networks has remained unsolved. Bott's work was done by means of extensive interviewing and the limited amount of observation she could employ while she was in the company of her research families. Barnes, Befu, Boissevain and Srinivas and Béteille seem to have relied mainly upon participant observation. The implication I draw from this is that in participant observation the analysts are able to use 'verstehen' to make the initial abstractions from the actual behaviour and this in turn leaves it open to them to be able to distinguish the partial networks they wish to use in their theoretical synthesis.

4. INSTITUTIONS, ROLES AND GROUPS

The appreciation of the process of abstraction by which the observer moves from the actual behaviour of individuals to social networks to partial networks helps, I think, to clarify the connection between networks on the one hand and groups and institutions on the other. The notion of multiplexity enables us to conceive of the relationship between any one person and someone else to whom he is addressing himself as involving several analytically separable normative elements. The actor himself may be consciously aware of these elements particularly if the normative elements are potentially incompatible as a medical practioner would be, for example, if he has an ailing child. The actor may then be able to state quite explicitly what sort of behaviour or actions other people would expect of him in terms of these links. Other relationships such as being a neighbour or a friend, for example, may be general norms and difficult for the actor to express clearly in words. Here the sociologist may have to analyse the value-orientations of the actors to obtain a clear notion of exactly what the expectations are.

Insofar as the expectations are collectively recognized in a defined population we can begin to summarize these general expectations into the notion of institutions as it is commonly defined in sociology: a set of interwoven folkways, mores and laws built round one or more functions (Davis, 1952: 70). The point being emphasized here is that the term 'institution' is applied to a set of norms and values which relate to a phenomenologically distinct aspect of social relationships. These norms and values are interwoven in two respects, therefore, first in that they refer to a conceptually separate area of social life and second in that the norms are related to one another to form a system of norms and values around the pivotal theme. The institution of marriage which Davis uses as an example included the folkways surrounding mating such as courting behaviour and wedding: norms regarding pre- and post-marital chastity and laws defining the rights of the spouses to each other. 'All of these norms taken together,' he writes, 'form a definite structure which has meaning as a whole and which when operative in behaviour results in the performance of certain social and individual functions such as reproduction and child rearing on the social side and social gratification and affection on the individual side'. (Davis, 1952: 70). From the network point of view the basic elements in the appreciation of the institution, therefore, could be represented as the links in a partial network which have been abstracted from actual behaviour because they possess a sociologically relevant common component such as kinship or friendship. This can only be the first stage in the delimitation of an institution since the interconnectedness of the norms in some logically intelligible way is an essential part of the notion of a social institution. A second stage of abstraction from the partial network must therefore be made so that in Srinivas and Béteille's words they 'can be put together' (p. 167). In other words the analyst must relate the norms subsumed in the partial network to one another in a 'structure' or 'pattern'.

It is at this stage that the notion of 'role' can be related to the idea of social network. If we accept definition of a role as 'a set of expectations applied to an incumbent of a particular position' and a position as 'the location of an actor or class of actors in a system of social relationships' (Gross, Mason and McEachern, 1968: 67) it is clear that the notion of role emerges at the level of abstraction of the partial network and involves pairs of elements in the network only. The implication of this is that the content of the links selected for the construction of a partial network relates to the expectations applicable to a theoretically coherent and distinguishable set of actions. We wish to deal with kinship relations only, for example, and intellectually to isolate these relationships from all other relationships which a number of people may have with one another. Both the observer and the people involved perceive these relationships primarily as normative expectations. The relationship between two arbitrarily chosen individuals in the partial network so created can now be referred to the specific set of expectations which are summarized by the concept of position. So that if one stands in the relationship of father-in-law, the other stands in the relation of daughter- or son-in-law. Social roles therefore are an abstraction from the partial network and are derived from empirical data by considering the expectations of persons linked in a partial network to others of a designated social 'position'. It follows from this that the notion of a role-set equally emerges at the level of the partial network occupying different social positions and linked in dyadic relationships to the centre-point of the network.

Note that in dealing with role expectations we are ignoring the effect of the *de facto* structure of the network on the observed behaviour of the individual concerned. If we turn our attention from the role expectation to role behaviour then we will find it essential to measure the actual behaviour of the actor against what we would expect the behaviour to be in the light of the social positions he occupies. It is here that the utility of the network approach becomes apparent for as sociologists we would look for the explanation of any discrepancies we observe in the structure of network links not only between the person who is the centre of enquiry and others who are in direct contact with them, but also possibly in the structure of relationships among persons at two more steps away from him. It is in this way that the departure and deviations from the standardized behaviour presumed by a structural analysis and which van Velsen (1954, 1967) argues must be taken account of in any sociological analysis are dealt with in network studies.

We are now in a position to re-examine the connection between social networks and social groups. As with so many other terms used in sociology the word 'group' has a number of different connotations. Insofar as the discussion of social networks is concerned the ideal-typical notion of group seems to have been the corporate group from which the quasi-group has been distinguished, and from both in turn, the network (or action-set). But even with the corporate group different analysts are likely to emphasize different aspects as being the crucial characteristics. The point I wish to make, however, is that all definitions of a group, whether corporate or not, imply a good deal more than merely a set of social interactions, and that this necessarily implies a fairly high level of abstraction. This may be illustrated by the definition which Lucy Mair gives for a corporate group; viz. '*a corporate body with a permanent existence*: a collection of people recruited on recognized principles with common interests and rules (*norms*) fixing rights and duties of the members in relation to one another and to those interests' (quoted by Boissevain 1968: 546). In this definition the phrase 'corporate body' seems to be a tautology since the implication of the word 'corporate', I take it, is common action, that is, action as a body. The implication of the existence of rights and duties, I assume, is that there is some division of labour among the various members of the group. There then appear to be at least six basic criteria to the notion of the corporate group:

1. A criterion of membership recognized by both members and non-members;
2. Common aims and interests of the members;
3. Norms and rules commonly accepted by the members;

4. Capability of joint action by the members;
5. A division of labour between members in terms of their common aims and interests – i.e., organization;
6. The persistence of relationships of positions beyond the incumbency of individual occupants of these positions.

These criteria are not wholly independent of one another. The relationship among them might be represented in a pseudo-causal diagram in the following way:

Diagram 2

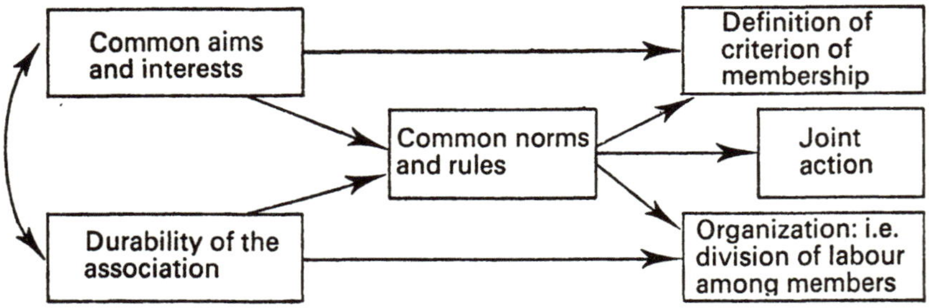

The existence of common aims and interests among a set of people is presumably independent of the duration of the relationships amongst them since a quasi-group with a short expectancy of continued existence would clearly share aims and interests albeit of a transitory kind. The persistence of common aims and interests presumably leads eventually to the formulation of commonly accepted rules and norms which in turn implies the allocation of who will and who will not be accorded the rights that members who occupy designated positions within the group will have on the others and their obligations towards them. That is they specify the organization of the group. The organization of the group by coordinating the activities of its members makes joint action possible.

In line with the argument I have presented about the relationship of social networks to institutions and roles, I would argue in the same way that a group, whether corporate or not, is an abstract construct of both the participants and the sociologist who is observing them, the former in terms of their appreciation of symbols, values and cues which align their social action, the latter in terms of the interrelationship of role expectations and role behaviour. The common interests and aims of the set of people and their incorporation in norms and values form the basis of strands in the links of a social network. These strands arise out of the way in which in the first instance the actors construe their own actions and the actions of relevant others. The recognition of common aims and interests in this way provide the basis for the criterion of membership of the group. The sets of expectations among those who share these common interests insofar as they allow a coordinated set of actions constitute the roles of pairs of persons in the network. The coordination of activities arises in turn out of the rules and norms of the group and provides an additional criterion in the eyes of the observer for the existence of the group.

The upshot of my argument then must be that the distinction between social relationships seen as social networks as against corporate groups (or as quasi-groups) is primarily a matter of the level of abstraction at which we are able to operate in summarising the regularities that we can discern in social relationships as a whole. Social networks are in no way distinct from corporate groups for as Barnes has pointed out: 'It may be useful to look at the networks of relationships within a religious cult, or between participants in a system of exchange in isolation from relationships of other kinds. Likewise the bounded partial networks found within groups provide an essential part of the data needed for a study of the working of these groups' (Barnes, 1969a: 74). I would go further than this and say that the networks of relationships are the starting point in the analysis of group behaviour and that they exist as analytical constructs which the observer erects partly by taking the participants' perceptions into account and by fitting together observations not available to the participants themselves. The constructs may be at differing levels of abstraction and when, at a fairly high level of abstraction, certain necessary conditions obtain which enable the observer to subsume a large part of the behaviour in terms of a few compact formulations he will be dealing with institutions and structured groups.

But this is not the only way in which abstractions of regularities can be made from social networks. Conceptualizing the structure of social relationships in terms of institutions and groups implies that the initial abstraction must always be made from the content of the links in the network and higher order abstractions built up from the partial network so obtained. An alternative procedure is to accept the inherent multiplexity of social relationships and to examine the configuration of the links *per se* at one, two or more steps from the person on whom the network is centred, with the object of establishing regularities in the way in which the social behaviour of individuals is affected by their indirect links of differing content with one another. At present this seems to be an inviting possibility before us. Adrian Mayer's study of the election provides an example of this procedure. The content of the outgoing links are varied while that of the incoming links is political support. But the configuration of links traced by whatever content is what determines the amount of support the candidate gets. This seems to be the procedure adopted by those who use networks in connection with exchange theory where they trace the consequences of transactions of different sorts among a set of actors.

In summary then, my argument is that the opposition of networks and corporate groups (or institutions) must be a false dichotomy: they are social phenomena at different levels of abstraction. It may well be that we are able to subsume most of the actions of a collectivity in terms of highly abstract statements such as Evans-Pritchard was able to do for the Nuer. Srinivas and Béteille point out that he was able to 'provide a fairly comprehensive account of Nuer social struction while confining himself to three systems of groups' (Srinivas and Béteille, 1964: 165). But this is not a matter of the opposition of corporate groups and networks but fundamentally a matter of the simplicity or complexity of social systems. Some types of field data may lend themselves to summarization in terms of a few general abstract principles based on what we have called the 'content' of social links, while others may be only inadequately encompassed in highly abstract statements such as in terms of corporate groups and institutions. This is, of course, the familiar problem in sociology of the distinction between large-scale and small-scale societies. We will probably find it necessary to make more use of the notion of social network to explain social behaviour in large-scale societies than in small-scale societies but all that this means is that in the face of greater complexity we cannot work at very high levels of abstraction, starting from the content of social links. Commensurately high levels of abstraction based on other aspects of social networks may yet be developed, as for example, along the lines of configurations of multiplexity of links. If they are, they may have the explanatory power for large-scale societies that institutional analysis has for small-scale societies at present. But it is too early to say: network analysis is still in its infancy.

ACKNOWLEDGEMENTS

This paper is an extension and development of some of the points raised in my introductory essay 'The concept and use of social networks' in Mitchell, J. C. (Ed.) *Social Networks in Urban Situations* (Manchester, Manchester University Press for Institute of Social Research, Zambia, 1969: 1-50). I am grateful to the participants of the Seminar on Network Approaches,

Leiden, 22-26 September 1969 for the points they raised in connection with this paper; Dr. Kingsley Garbett and Dr. Bruce Kapferer, Mr. G. Banck, Prof. Howard S. Becker and Prof. M. N. Srinivas, all of whom have suggested useful improvements. The responsibility for the points of view expressed, of course, remains mine.

NOTES

1. It is interesting to note, however, that later he seems to have moved from this position for he writes; 'These empirical findings suggest that the non-institutional third field may not be a useful category, in that action-sets may seldom if ever be systematically confined to it... the non-institutional field may be a redundant category' (Barnes, 1969a:73). This point becomes the main topic of discussion in the text.

2. That is setting out the 'causal' relationships among the variables without giving numerical values to the paths between pairs.

3. Befu leaves the notion of density undefined. He could mean by density 'completeness' in graph theory (Barnes, 1969a, 1969b) that is the extent to which every person in the set is in fact connected by some link or another to every other person. He could also mean by it 'multiplexity' in the sense that the links near at hand could be thought of partly as those involving the rights and obligations of neighbourliness as well as those of kinship and friendship. Third, he could have meant single-step links as against two-step or three-step links. Probably all three elements were intended.

4. At one part of his paper (p. 544) he says that the continuum has two poles: the interacting individual and the group. Later he talks of points beyond the interacting individual and the quasi-groups indicating 'the range of groups institutional complexes and at the other pole society itself' (pp. 553). I am not clear what is implied by the word 'society' here. Commonly it is used to indicate the sum total of all social relationships at all levels of abstraction in a defined population, but obviously this could not be the intention here. Here it seems to imply the national State.

5. It is important to realise that the links in the partial network need not necessarily be single-stranded: they may still be multiplex within the compass of the content of the partial network as for example when a person marries a cross-cousin he may be linked by both consanguineal and affinal relationships to the same *person.*

6. Note the difference of Boissevain's approach here for he speaks of the group being 'a product of individual action and drives' and of 'building the individual into our view of society in his own right and not just as a member of groups or as a variable dependent on an institutional complex' (p. 544). I take it from this that he looks upon individual behaviour as something which is qualitatively different from group behaviour and not simply the lower order phenomenon out of which group behaviour is constructed.

7. I am here treating both the norms and the values and beliefs upon which they are based as cognitive phenomena per se, so that the distinction between norms on the one hand and beliefs and values on the other, though important for other types of analysis, is not germane here.

Network analysis and social theory
Some remarks

GEERT A. BANCK

I. The use of the word 'network' in social science has until quite recently been no more than a common language word, indicating that social relations were a complicated matter indeed. At the moment however, many an anthropologist is perhaps already longing for the good old times – never to return – in which everything was so easygoing and this word, of all words, just a word. Since Barnes (1954) gave a more special meaning to it, interest gradually arose in the use of the metaphor and at the moment one can speak of an ever swelling stream of information on what is now called the *concept* of social network.

At the same time one cannot say that there is much consensus about what a social network is. Clearly, we are in the explorative but important phase of classification, in which each author classifies social networks according to his own needs. That this is often done in the form of a sort of dichotomy and/or with the help of formal graph theory as an analogy, shows the as yet immature, though certainly not fruitless stage, in which network analysis is at the moment.

What stands out, however, is the basic notion that networks have to do with (social) individuals, rather than with groups. Linked with this focus of attention are the following three notions about social networks. a) Firstly, ego has social relations with other individuals, who in their turn have social relations with others, these being linked directly with ego or not, and so on. b) This formal statement is closely tied up with the perhaps too strongly emphasized presupposition that a network means: 'the interlocking of relationships whereby the interactions implicit in one determine those occurring in others' (Nadel, 1957: 16). In other words, ego is entangled in a network of social relations, the structure of which influences the behaviour of ego. c) Finally, opposed to the second notion, the individual is supposed to be able to manipulate to a certain measure his social network for his own ends.

The consequences of this emphasis on the individual, albeit a *social* individual, is of the utmost theoretical importance, and it is necessary:

'fundamentally to revise our theoretical framework' (Boissevain, 1968: 544). This is a task indeed, and I certainly do not claim to fulfil it. In this short paper I only wish to emphasize the importance of defining the concepts used. As the level of abstraction often changes with the introduction of a new kind of analysis, the definitions of the general sociological concepts involved have to change too or we have to construct new concepts.

Clearly, the shift in emphasis from group to individual means such a change in level of abstraction. And we must expect that what is analytically beautiful and elegant at the group level may be clumsy and refractory at the level where social individuals are under scrutiny.

First I shall deal with some problems specifically linked with this change in level of abstraction. Thereafter I shall discuss some questions concerning the level of abstraction within network analysis itself. Finally, as many of the statements about "network" involve propositions about role-playing' (Reader, 1964: 22), I try, tentatively, to introduce some rethinking in role theory.

II. Crucial to this part of the paper is Boissevain's remark about the indoctrination of anthropologists in the corporate group concept: 'The view of an observable, static society composed of enduring relations and groups of different orders is part of the stock in trade of every anthropologist' (1968: 542). So, even if one perceives that network analysis, as regards the level of abstraction, is different from structural analysis, there is a tendency to stick to old definitions and concepts, in this case the corporate group concept. This group-centred thinking is for instance visible in Bott's '*constructed reference group*' (1957: 167) and, though he is aware of it, the dialectical process of indoctrination versus new research demands is apparent in Boissevain's classification of groups and non-groups.

More important as a source of confusion is this half-way situation between group level and network level for the arguments put forward in theoretical discussions. Let me take as an example Boissevain's suggestion for the use of a continuum.

At one pole of the continuum there is the interacting individual, at the other the (corporate) group. Between these poles intermediate social forms (such as quasi-groups) are ranged. After having expressed that '. . . the forms with which I am concerned at present are those which are intermediate between the individual and the corporate group', he concludes with the statement: 'Once they become pure groups I cease to be interested' (1968: 544).

I think that this statement is not so much true or untrue but rather superfluous. For at the level of abstraction at which we are interpreting empirical data *as if* they do fit into social networks, one simply cannot use the concept group, defined as corporate group, for the propositions underlying network analysis, such as for instance ego manipulating his social network for his own end, are in complete opposition to the high level abstraction of ego, seen as a member of a corporate group, sharing with other members rights and obligations from the enduring group structure. Once the network analysis is chosen (a strategic choice concerned with the question of getting the best possible explanation of the empirical findings) one has to stick to the propositions and level of abstraction implied. One cannot voluntarily cease to be interested in pure groups; one must, I would rather say, do so *by definition.*

Though it is perhaps methodologically possible to construct a sort of alternation model, in which group and network analysis alternate, the confusion might be greater than the relevance and in any case one has to keep the two approaches conceptually distinct.

The danger of theoretical confusion can be demonstrated in Boissevain's own argument. He is right, albeit I think, for the wrong reason, in ceasing to be interested in pure groups when analysing intermediate social forms. But the undue choice of the corporate group as one pole of the continuum, though it is apparently only a logical and analytical construct, is apt to suggest that social process may be only generated by a historical sequence from the interacting individual, via quasi-group, to corporate group, as Boissevain's examples, especially the Maltese, do in fact suggest.

I think, however, that the 'process of creation' (p. 544) is of much greater importance within what is, on another level of abstraction, called the 'corporate group'. Renovation and change of these groupings, even their disappearance, through pressure from within or without, via personal networks and factions, manipulations and coalitions, is of utmost importance for the study of social process and change. To stick to the 'corporate group' concept is dangerous not only because it is not possible to analyze these processes with the concept but also because these processes may then be easily overlooked.

Therefore, when we are analysing social reality with the help of the 'network' concept, I prefer to avoid the concept of corporate group and with that the use of the continuum. Yet the continuum is perhaps still useful, as it gives us a 'visual' projection of the levels of abstraction (and explanation) we are able to choose among for attaining the best possible explanation of the empirical data.

But by simply refuting the concept of corporate group we have not solved the problem. We still have to face a very difficult question of definition, for which I do not have a solution at this moment (partly, I think, because I too am entangled in the dialectics of the group – non-group dichotomy).

Clearly, at the empirical level there are groupings which have boundaries and members (and non-members). The group concept must therefore be maintained, I think, but membership must not be *a priori* defined in terms of rights and obligations derived from the group nor may we on *a priori* grounds accept that the members share common interests and goals. On the other hand, when analysing for instance a personal network, the actions of ego may be for a part related and circumscribed by his group memberships. How we can bring these two ends together, I do not see at the moment.

III. When talking about social networks, another question can be raised about the level of abstraction. For when analysing social networks, are we always doing this at the same level of abstraction? I think that the answer has to be no. But let me try to set out the argument.

The central clue to this problem is the opposition between the second and third statement, mentioned on page 37, namely a) the influence of the structure of the social network on the individual's actions, and b) ego's manipulation of his social network for his own ends. There is an apparent opposition between the two statements, which however might be reduced to a difference in level of abstraction. Of course, the gap between the two levels is considerably more narrow than the gap between network level in general and group level. Yet still there is a difference in view and basically another system of bracketing away some specific allusions to the Toms, Dicks, and Harries.

Two mainstreams of network research are closely linked with respectively each of these two statements. What may be labelled family studies are mainly linked with the first statement and political studies (in the broadest sense of the word) with the second.

All the network research in Bott's line is related to the influence of the structure of the network on individual action. In fact this approach is more or less an offshoot of the Durkheimian quest for solidarity and consensus. Though the starting point is no longer the *G*roup or *S*ociety, but the network of social relations, one can for instance easily translate the influence of a close-knit network of a married couple into a remark about a relatively sharp social control which reinforces solidarity or consensus.

Conversely political studies are more concerned with individuals manipulating their social networks for their own ends (i.e. the broker). Certainly here too, the question of consensus and solidarity is of importance, but more indirectly so. Through emphasis on the process of bargaining more stress is laid on the possibility of manipulating or evading mechanisms of social control altogether.

I think that we have to keep the two approaches separate, for each has its own premisses and is linked to its own general body of theory.[1] I may sum up the difference by quoting two sayings used by Davis for another, though related, purpose (1962: 449). Family studies have much to do with the saying 'Birds of a feather flock together', whereas political studies have much in common with the saying 'Politics make strange bedfellows'. The first stands for interaction theory, the second for exchange theory.

Network analysis, in the sense Bott uses it, is more or less an extension of interaction theory, which says that the frequency of interaction is directly related to the degree of liking: 'Thus, the greater the interaction between two persons, the greater, in general, the sentiments of affection they feel for one another' (Homans, 1951: 43). The only difference I see is that the interactions between the individuals, with whom ego is interacting, are also taken into account (Bott, 1957: 59, note 1).

Political studies, on the contrary, refer to processes of bargaining, and are therefore closely linked with exchange theory and game theory.

So again, here too, we have to be aware of the fact that going from one level to the other, the definition of the concepts may have to change. For instance, Bott may define *role* as 'behaviour that is *expected* of any individual occupying a particular social position' (1957: 3) and that may be sufficient as regards her analysis. On the level of manipulating individuals it may not be a proper tool for explanation of the social phenomena under scrutiny.

In the following paragraph I will deal tentatively with some aspects of role theory, which are important for network analysis. Thereby I am explicitly referring to the level of network-manipulating individuals.

IV. There are many diverging definitions of the concept role, but 'there is one nearly universal common denomination, namely, that the concept pertains to the behaviours of particular persons' (Biddle and Thomas, 1966: 29). The concept, as it was expanded in the Lintonian tradition in structural-functional analysis gave perhaps 'the most important "meeting" point between individual behavior and societal functions' (Eisenstadt, 1965: 30; *cf. also* Dahrendorf, 1965).

Dahrendorf's *homo sociologicus* concept is a good example of this structural approach (1965: esp. 43-44). Within his system the individual behaves *as if* totally fulfilling the role expectations belonging to his social position. Roles are allocated to the individual by Society and Society is able, through the use of negative and positive sanctions to enforce conformation of the individuals to these role expectations.

Again I maintain that such a definition of the role concept may be a very good one, but it is only so if it is to fit in a highly formal analysis with some social entity like a group, category or Society at large as the starting point of the analysis (Dahrendorf himself states this too in a postscriptum to his original essay; 1965: 128-131). But in the same way as we had to change the definition of the concept group, when analysing empirical data at social network level, we have to be aware of the fact that the definition of the concept role may have to change too. For at the level of the manipulating individual it is a great disadvantage to use the Lintonian definition for such 'definitions commit us to considering only those roles that are collectively recognised' (Biddle and Thomas, 1966: 29). (Social scientists are apt to refer to theatre as an analogue, when speaking about roles. If then the structural role concept may be compared with the prescriptions of classical theatre, the role concept at network level ought to be compared with modern 'free theatre' role improvisation and manipulation of the audience by the actors.)

Obviously, we need another look at the concept, but in network analysis this problem is still unexplored. However in more general sociological discussions it is understood that 'the concept of role should not be taken as "given" as a pattern of behavior . . . which is given and fixed in the institutional structure of society and to which the individual must adjust himself through the process of socialization and through interaction with other people' (Eisenstadt, 1965: 31).

At the network level we should not wonder so much about role expectations *a priori*. The emphasis must be first of all on the fact that the individual has to play many roles: he is a *role-bearer* or *role-performer*, manipulating via his roles his network of social relationships. It was Southall who stressed that 'relationships are the crucial aspect of role from a sociological point of view' (1959: 19).

By initiating one new role ego may establish several new relationships (or by ending a role he may free himself of several old ones). Moreover playing a role is not always relationally fixed to specific individuals: ego is sometimes able to choose or change the other individual making up the other end of the role dyad involved, and in doing so he is able to manipulate the relationship within a certain range for his own ends, for one individual may be more rewarding as the other end of a particular role dyad for ego than another. By manipulating existing role relations or initiating via a new role new ones, ego is able to establish social links, which may promise him (in reality or as mere wishful thinking) 'command over another's actions or command over existing benefits or resources' (Nadel, 1957: 115).

This is a rather optimistic view of the manipulative power of the role-bearer, for certainly alongside incentives for his choices, constraints are constantly modifying and limiting these very choices. Certainly questions of social control and consensus are here again involved. They are, however, translated in terms of exchange and game theory: the role-bearer's range of manipulation is an outcome of the strength of his bargaining power in transactional *processes* (*cf.* Barth, 1966: 1 ff.).

Though this line of thought is only roughly sketched, it may be a starting point for a discussion about a concept of the utmost importance for network analysis, as it brings the individual within the realm of sociology.

ACKNOWLEDGEMENTS

I wish to thank Prof. Jeremy Boissevain, Prof. J. Clyde Mitchell and Prof. Robert Stebbins for their critical comments on the original version of the paper.

NOTES

1. In a personal comment Prof. Stebbins rightly remarks that the two notions of social network, though being '. . . at somewhat different levels of abstraction, . . . are related, in that they occur at two different places in the sequence of events. That is to say, our view of our own network guides, in part, our subsequent manipulations of various interpersonal relationships within our network for our own ends'.

Some applications of the notion of density to network analysis

RUDO NIEMEIJER

1. INTRODUCTION

Recent studies of networks have given rise to a host of concepts for gathering the information available in a specific description of a network in terms of one or more structural variables (see for example Barnes, Boissevain, Bott, Kapferer, Mitchell and others). Since data on a single network contain much specific information on the persons studied, it is only natural that one should try to grasp the significance of these data by means of variables which lend themselves easily to study and comparison. This is even more necessary if the network studied becomes fairly large.

Two problems pertain to the use of such variables. The first is whether the data necessary for the calculation of these measures can in fact be obtained. While both the network concept and other concepts related to it can easily be used as metaphors, research workers have experienced great difficulties in applying them practically as tools. Several writers mention the difficulties encountered simply because of the number of persons composing part of a network (Mitchell, 1969: 11; Cubitt elsewhere in this volume). The two first-order zones studied by Boissevain demonstrate this problem forcefully (Boissevain elsewhere in this volume). In some, but not all, cases the sampling approach worked out in this paper may be of some help. By resorting to this sampling method at least some of the promising hypotheses developed hitherto could be tested. It may be expected too that a more systematic study not based on mere impressions will give a lead to a more developed theoretical framework.

The second problem is the sociological significance of the concepts developed so far. Although the concepts dealt with in this paper were stimulated partly by sociological questions, their exact definitions stem from a mathematical background. The notion of loose-knit and close-knit networks as put forward by Bott was more precisely defined by Barnes (1968), who gave us a more mathematically rigid definition. While there is nothing wrong with this, it is important to remember that the more rigid the definition of a concept the narrower its range of meanings. One should therefore ask whether the more specific characteristics of such a formulation still cover everything in the original. One could also turn this problem around. By analysing carefully the characteristics of such rigid concepts one can try to delineate their possible sociological meanings. This is attempted in this paper.

The concept of density provides the focal point of this paper. Its meaning and use are explored partly by attempting to describe and analyse the related concepts of *degree*, *cluster* and *boundary*. The sociological significance of these concepts is in itself a reflection of the importance of the notion of density. For the more technical parts of the discussion the reader is referred to the Appendix at various stages of the argument. In this way the general reader may skip the more mathematical part of the analysis.

2. THE CONCEPT OF DENSITY

Barnes defines density as the proportion of the theoretically possible direct links actually in existence (1969: 63). This definition can be expressed as a function of the number of actualized relations and the number of persons involved:

Formula 1

$$D = \frac{100 \times Na}{\frac{1}{2}N \times (N - 1)} \%$$

D = density
Na = number of actual relations
N = number of persons involved
$\frac{1}{2}N \times (N - 1)$ = number of theoretically possible relations

Figure 1 demonstrates the operation of this definition. Persons A, B and C could have three relations between them: A-B, A-C and B-C. This number equals to $^1/_2 \times 3 \times (3 - 1)$. In fact only two relations exist. The density of this network therefore will be 66,7 %.

Figure 1

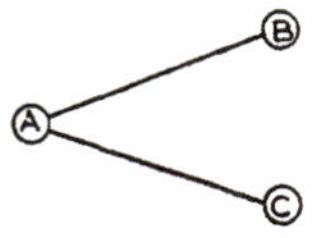

D = 66.7 %
d = 1.33

Figure 2

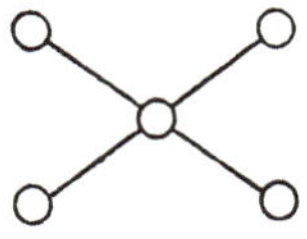

D = 40 %
d = 1.6

Figure 3

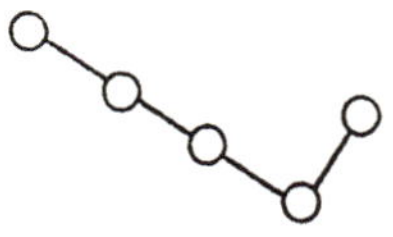

D = 40 %
d = 1.6

Both Mitchell (1969: 18) and Barnes (1969: 63) show that this variable of networks only partly reflects network structure. Networks with entirely different structures may have the same density. In fact the spreading of a rumor can be hypothesized to be much faster in networks like the one in figure 2 than in networks resembling figure 3. But none the less one would generally expect a connection between the density of a network and the amount of time it takes for a rumor to penetrate to all persons in the networks concerned.

The density of a network incorporates only part of the original information contained in a description of a network. Another characteristic complicating the interpretation of measures of density is the relation existing between the density of a network and the sheer number of persons involved. As may be seen from the definition the number of actual relations is divided by almost half of the square of the number of persons. Consequently two networks with the same density may differ very much because of the difference in the number of members: in the larger of the two, people have more relations with one another than in the smaller one. The two first-order zones studied by Boissevain (elsewhere in this volume) illustrate this fact. The slight difference between the respective density figures obscures the existing difference in interrelatedness between both first-order zones.

One may in fact rewrite the definition of density as a function of two factors, *degree*[1] and *size*. The *size* of a network is the number of persons included in the network. The *degree* of a network is the mean number of relations network members have with other network members:

Formula 2

$$d = \frac{2 \times Na}{N}$$

d = degree of a network
Na = number of actual relations
N = size or number of persons included

The degree of a network tells us to what extent the persons are on average connected to the network in question. If the degree of a network equals three, one knows that the members have an average of three relations with other network members.

If two networks have the same degree, their densities can be shown to relate as follows (see Appendix section 1):

Formula 3

$$D_A = \frac{D_B}{1 + p}$$

D_A = density of network A
D_B = density of network B

$$p = \frac{M - N}{N - 1}$$

M = size of network A
N = size of network B

This becomes clear when one realizes that the definition of density may be rewritten by substituting $\frac{2 \times Na}{N}$ by d:

Formula 4

$$D = \frac{100 \times Na}{\frac{1}{2}N \times (N - 1)} = \frac{100 \times d}{(N - 1)}$$

Expressed in words: the density of a network varies directly with degree and inversely with size. If a network is large and has the same density as another but smaller network, then the degree will be greater. Table A illustrates this conclusion.

Table A

Network:	A	B	C	D	
Density of network	100	90	9.1	9.1	(per cent)
Degree of network	9	9	9	90.8	(relations)
Size of network	10	11	100	1000	(persons)

The following lists of possible interpretations could lead to a further clarification of the concepts of degree and density.

degree = the average number of relations members have with other members
= the average number of ways in which members are linked in the network

density = the percentage of theoretically possible links actualized
= the percentage of the maximal possible degree of a network actualized
= the probability of a member chosen at random having a relation with another member of the network similarly chosen at random

This last interpretation becomes clear when it is remembered that density is defined as the percentage of possible relations actualized. Thus if one picks combinations of persons out of all possible combinations at random the density gives the percentage of cases that can be expected to be linked. This characteristic leads directly to a means of estimating the density of a network through sampling. By taking a random sample from all possible combinations of members one finds a certain number of actual relations. On the basis of this number one can estimate the density of the network involved (see Appendix section 2 for a detailed discussion of the sampling distribution of density and an estimator function).

While degree and density are here defined only as attributes of networks, one may also define them in relation to a person and the network in which he is enmeshed. The *degree of a person* is the number of relations he has within the network, i.e. the size of his number of his 'first order star' (*cf.* Barnes, 1969: 58). The *density of a person* is the percentage of all relations he could have theoretically within the network that are in fact actualized.[2] The same list of interpretations may be applied here. The degree of a person is the number of ways in which he is linked to his network, while his density may be seen as the probability that he has a relation with a member of his network chosen at random.

These different interpretations need to be related to more sociologically meaningful interpretations. The first point to note is the way the data on the original network are reduced in order to calculate the value of these measures. The measure of density defined by Barnes implies that all relations are divided into two classes: actual versus non-actual. This reduces its sociological value to some extent. Relations are often defined in a way leaving scope for other more appropriate means of classification and measurement. In calculating the degree of a network or a person, this problem does not arise. Although the degree of a network may be calculated on the basis of a binary classification of relations, ordinal or stronger scales may also be applied.[3]

In using a binary classification of relations, one should remember that the classification may rest on any attribute or combination of attributes of the relations concerned. This may be 'knowing or not knowing each other' or 'having or not having some complex weighted amount of interactional frequency and intimacy or intensity'. The specific meaning of these variables depends on the classification used.

The usefulness of these concepts should be considered in relation to sociological theory in general. Both concepts may of course be used as objective variables. This is exactly what was done by Bott (1957) when she related density (connectedness) with conjugal role segregation. A like hypothesis would be to suggest that it is more difficult to organize a dense pattern of relations in a large group of people than in a small group, and that therefore a candidate for office in a situation as described by Mayer (1966: 106-113) is faced with a definite choice problem. He should either play safe by canvassing among a small population using many multipronged and lateral connections or spread his attention over a larger part of the electorate thereby risking greater gains or losses. To some extent this problem resembles that of management encountered by political leaders when their team becomes large (*cf.* Bailey, 1969: 80-84). It is a direct function of the degree necessary to maintain dense networks.

But one might want to use these measures as subjective variables too. One wonders whether people apprehend their networks in a way which correlates with those measures. Although the persons in a network have more or less the same, if not more, information about the networks around them than the sociologist they too would have to make some abstractions. This question has as yet received scant attention. Action theories such as Blau's exchange theory (1964) or Barth's contract theory (1966) certainly imply that this should be considered.

3. RANDOM MESH

The interpretation of density as the probability of a relation between two persons selected at random in the network draws our attention to an important technique of network analysis. The relatedness of two persons is not the result of a complete random process but of systematic factors such as kinship, work, education, politics and others. Seen in this light these factors produce deviations from 'random mesh', i.e. *a network structure only influenced by random processes.* One characteristic of random mesh would be that it is evenly spread over the entire network. It could of course so happen that some parts of the network are more dense than others, but if these differences are large one would suspect that some systematic factor is operating.

If a network is divided into two or more segments on the basis of some criterion, it is possible to calculate not only the density of the network itself but also the densities of the different segments. Table B gives an example of the figures that may be obtained in this way.

Table B

Whole network	Size	=	30
	Na	=	140
	D	=	30 %
Only segment I	Size	=	20
	Na	=	95
	D	=	50 %
Only segment II	Size	=	10
	Na	=	25
	D	=	56 %
On boundary	Cl	=	20
	B	=	10 %

B = density on boundary (see definition below)
Cl = number of actual relations crossing the boundary

The number of relations that cross the boundary[4] is an indicator of the relation between the two segments. Its social significance may be great. If there are only a few cross-linking relations and if it is also important for persons to reach into the other segment, one may expect the operation of brokers. One could also hypothesize that leaders will find it more difficult to organize supporters in other segments than their own when confronted with an important boundary.

An indicator of the relative strength of a boundary may be defined as the density of actual relations on the boundary.

Formulas 5 and 6

$$B = \frac{100 \times Cl^{12}}{N_1 \times N_2}$$

$$Bc = 100 \frac{\sum_{i} \sum_{j} Cl^{ij}}{\sum_{i} \sum_{j} N_i \times N_j} \quad i < j$$

B = density on boundary
Cl^{12} = number of crossing relations between segment 1 and 2
N_1 = size of segment 1
N_2 = size of segment 2
Bc = combined density of the boundaries between the segments i, j, . . . n.

The combined density gives an indicator of the divisive influence (not causal) of a certain variable. Both B and B_c may be interpreted in the same way as ordinary density scores. Both stand for the probability that some pair of persons across the boundary selected at random are linked.

As pointed out before, one expects the density to be equal in all parts of a network if only nonsystematic factors influence the distribution of relationships. Further elaboration of this point leads to the formulation of a statistical test of the significance of differences between densities or the existence of boundaries. A detailed description of this test is found in the Appendix (section 3).

The outcome of such tests may be used in diverse ways. If, for example, a network of first and second grade cognates is split up into two segments on the basis of location on opposite sides of a river, then the significance (statistically) of the boundary between the segments leads us to two different types of conclusions. The first of these could be:

> Location causes, or correlates with some other factor that causes, a certain distribution of relations of kinship.

The second conclusion might lead us to the following hypothesis:

> If a leader of a faction should base his recruitment on kinship alone, the probability is great that he would have to consider the river a barrier delimiting his faction to his own side of the river (at least relatively). If it is of importance that a faction would have large support on both sides, then a person with good links across the river will be invaluable.

These two conclusions may be typified respectively as (a) an inference of the cause and (b) confidence about the existence of a boundary.

4. ESTIMATION OF DENSITY

In testing hypotheses about network variables, the data necessary for the evaluation of these variables constitute one of the main obstacles. To my mind the use of sampling procedures offers a solution. This is of course not always possible. Fairly often there seems to be no way of defining a population of a network because of the radiating character of networks. Much will depend on the question posed since the empirical content given to the concept of network is directly related to the process studied and the kind of variables included. But, even when it is possible to resort to sampling it is not always advisable.

The first consideration is one of cost. Sampling and estimation yield precise figures but take a lot of time and energy. Do we really need such precise figures? This is in effect a question about the state of theory. One should not collect exact data which cannot be related to exact conclusions. Are the same conclusions possible on the basis of data requiring less time and energy? One might suggest that very often the fieldworker is able to jot down sufficiently competent statements about density and crosslinkage. But on the other hand far too often this competence may be misleading. One should decide whether the risk one incurs by using less quantitative methods is small enough. If this is not the case sampling will be inevitable. The evaluation of these risks constitutes an important field of study. At present decisions of this kind will have to be based on subjective judgements of risks and costs.

A second consideration is related to the question of reliability and validity. Have the data been collected in such manner that the precise figures calculated are justified? Repeated measurement may result in contradictory figures. This lack of reliability may be judged in the same manner as was pointed out above about the use of other techniques. Whether to invest more time and energy in order to reach a higher reliability depends on the possibility of accepting false hypotheses for right ones and vice versa. The validity depends on the criteria used to differentiate between actual and non-existent relations. Do these criteria represent what they were meant for? Is the binary classification justified for the problem studied? Again a decision whether to be satisfied with a certain procedure is largely dependent on the strength of the correlation between factor and structure. For example, if a boundary is strong, one will detect it both with a highly valid instrument and with a less valid instrument. In that case there is no reason to refrain from using a less valid but also less time consuming instrument. Thus while density can only be calculated when using binary classifications of relations, the values obtained will still be of help when studying networks. Even when a binary classification into actual and non-actual links would sound ridiculous, the density figures calculated give a raw measure of interconnectedness that can be used to test important hypotheses.

5. CLUSTERS

Another concept directly related to the concept of density is the concept of cluster. Barnes defines a *cluster* as 'a set of persons whose links with one another are comparatively dense, without necessarily constituting a clique in this strict sense' (Barnes 1969: 64).

When speaking of a clique he means a set of persons with a density of

100 per cent. A cluster would therefore be something like it but not necessarily as dense.

Barnes suggests an operationalization with the aid of two arbitrary thresholds. Only a set of more than five persons with a density of at least eighty per cent would constitute a cluster. He points out that one might choose different threshold values. The exact value would have to be determined on the basis of experience. But I maintain that not only arbitarry thresholds but any threshold method leads to contradictions if based on density.[5]

These contradictions result from the relation pointed out before between density, size and degree. I will try to demonstrate this, by examining an example used by Barnes (1969: 65).

Figure 4

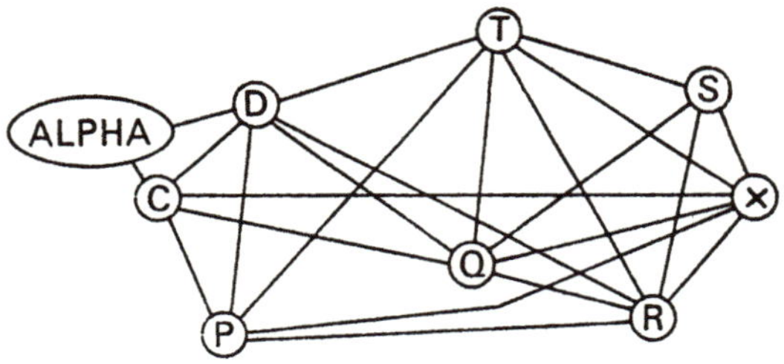

Barnes demonstrates that in the situation as illustrated in figure 4 persons C, D, P, Q, S, R and X form a cluster of seven members with a density of 81 per cent. If Alpha is added to the cluster the density falls below the cluster criterion (67 per cent). If instead of Alpha, T is added to the cluster the density remains above the critical 80 per cent and becomes 82 per cent. Barnes therefore concludes that Alpha is not a member while T is (Barnes, 1969: 64-66).

According to this method, Alpha with only two relations with members of the set does not belong to the cluster. How many relations with them would have been sufficient? Calculation leads to the conclusion that he needed six relations with cluster members in order to be considered a cluster member himself. For with only five relations with other persons, the density would have fallen below the threshold of 80 per cent. But most of the 'established' members have less than six links with their fellow members. Even after T has also been added C has only four relations with others. It appears that this method puts an extra barrier to newcomers that the 'established' did not pass. A different starting point would lead to different conclusions: if a person Beta has four links with the cluster then the order will determine whether he or C should be considered as members.

This disappointing result is a consequence of the relation between density and size. As was shown before the densities of two sets of persons may differ not because of the number of relations members have with other members but because of the difference in size. To keep the density at a certain level one should add to a cluster persons with an increasing number of relations with its members.

While accepting Barnes' definition of a cluster as 'a comparatively dense' set of persons, one still needs another criterion to distinguish between clusters and non-clusters. Such a criterion cannot be found in a comparison between cluster density and network density. A close look at figure 5 would immediately bring this to light. Set B certainly is identifiable as a separate entity although the total network has a higher density. The reason for this conclusion lies in an unexpectedly low number of relations crossing the cluster boundary. This points to another criterion:

A cluster has a low number of external relations in relation to its internal relations.

Figure 5

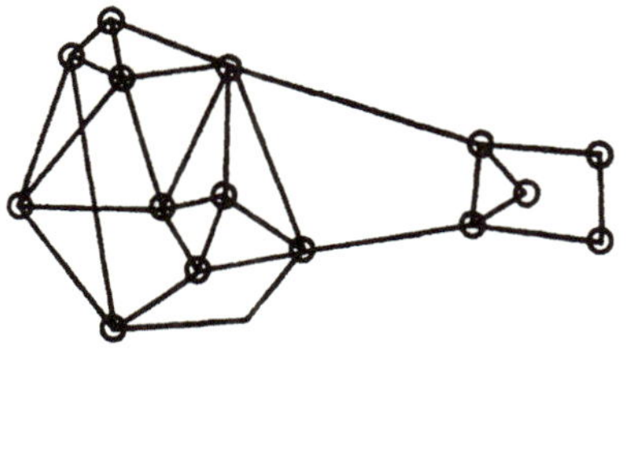

The method of Bock and Husain (1950) capitalizes on this notion.[6] Their adaptation of Holzinger's β-coefficient includes both the internal and the external relations. Originally Holzinger's β-coefficient was intended for the clustering of correlated tests. Bock and Husain interpreted this coefficient in a way which also made it useful for clustering in networks. They came up with the following definition, which, quite clearly, is related to the concept of density.

Formula 7

$$B_{(u)} = \frac{200\,(n - p)\,S}{(p - 1)\,T} = \frac{D}{B} \times 100$$

$B_{(u)}$ = ß — coefficient of cluster
S = sum of relations in cluster
T = sum of relations on boundary
n = network size
p = cluster size
D = density of cluster
B = density on boundary

The general idea behind the procedure suggested by Bock and Husain is that, one by one, those persons should be joined to a cluster that have the highest number of relations (or the highest intensity of relations measured in an internal scale) with the cluster. Each time one should calculate $B_{(u)}$. When there is a sharp drop of $B_{(u)}$ one should end the procedure and continue to generate a new cluster. For a more detailed description of their method the reader is referred to the original publication.[7]

While it is clear that the method of Bock and Husain produces clusters with a comparatively high density, the criteria by which a person is considered a member of a cluster still remain arbitrary (see Appendix, section 5). Bock and Husain remark that a careful study should be made of the significance of a sharp drop of $B_{(u)}$: there is no criterion to decide whether a drop is sharp or not. This leaves the problem of deciding clearly whether a person is a member of a cluster still unsolved.

A solution to this problem may be found starting with a definition of the criteria for membership. Such a definition should take into account that a cluster has a relatively high density. The variable of *personal degree* is easily turned into an instrument with the required characteristics. Using this concept we arrive at the following definitions of clusters and cluster membership:

> A person is a member of a cluster when his personal degree with cluster members is higher than his degree with non-members.
>
> A cluster is a set of persons that have a higher personal degree with other set members than with non-members.

Obviously such definitions would fulfill the necessary conditions. With all persons having more relations within their sets, the number of relations that cross boundaries will be minimized. This is in accordance with the notion of clusters as illustrated in figure 5. A detailed procedure of cluster analyses based on this definition of membership is given in the Appendix (section 6).

One advantage of this approach over the other methods mentioned before is that the analysis may be done on both interval- and ordinal-scaled relations. It therefore becomes possible to make cluster analysis sensitive to differences in strength of relationships.

Cluster analysis may be of use under different circumstances. By applying a cluster analysis one delineates segments surrounded by boundaries. One gets insight into the factors correlating with the boundaries between different clusters by observing the characteristics that the persons within clusters have in common. Not only the characteristics of the persons but also the characteristics of the relations themselves may be of importance here. If the clusters concerned were based on the analysis of certain aspects of relations, it would be of interest to know what other aspects coincide with these.

Clusters may, for example, be the result of some divisive political process, large or small. The fact that economic relations reveal certain clusters may be the result of some, possibly even very old, political issues.

If it is necessary to perform a detailed analysis of the position of a specific person or number of persons in a network, cluster analysis may be of great help. In such a case it functions as a way by which relations contained in a network can be ordered in a manner that makes an analysis easier. The position of the persons in a network in relation to boundaries and clusters becomes more visible.

If one had prior hypotheses about such placement, cluster analysis might be used as a test of these hypotheses. But it seems difficult to develop rigid tests for hypotheses evaluated in this way. Cluster analysis as a tool of network analysis derives its importance from the way it reduces complex data on networks. One should use it as an aid to analysis or as a raw evaluation of predictions. Whether clusters are important subjective variables needs to be investigated. It would be of great interest to see if clusters correlate in some way with concepts used by members of a network when contemplating action or evaluating alternatives. The study of these subjective concepts is an important field for network theorists.

APPENDIX

Section 1

1.1 $D = 100 \times Na \,/\, \frac{1}{2}N\,(N - 1)$

1.2 $d = 2\,Na \,/\, N$

substitution of 1.2 into 1.1 gives

1.3 $D = 100 \times d / (N - 1)$

then if D_A is the density of network A with size M and D_B is the density of network B with size N while both have the same degree d:

$$1.4 \quad \frac{D_A}{D_B} = \frac{N - 1}{M - 1}$$

by dividing (M – 1) through (N – 1) one arrives at *formula 3.*

Section 2

The sampling distribution of D may be obtained by looking at the sampling distribution of Na, for D is a function of Na and sample size.

Two cases may be distinguished. If the population involved is very small one should sample without replacement. The sampling distribution of Na will then be the hypergeometrical.

$$2.1 \quad f(Na) = \binom{a}{Na} \binom{p - a}{n - Na} / \binom{p}{n}$$

Na = number of actual relations in sample
a = number of actual relations in population
p = total number of possible relations in population
n = total number of possible relations in sample

In this case a maximum likelihood estimator on the basis of one sample would be

$$2.2 \qquad \frac{p+1}{n} - 1 < a < Na \frac{p+1}{n}$$

(a is an integer)

Proof

The likelihood function of a [L (a)] in the case of only one sample is equal to f(Na). This function will have a maximum when L(a–1) <L(a) and L(a+1) <L(a). Solution of these two inequalities leads to formula 2.2.

When the population involved is very large or when one samples with replacement the following distribution may be used:

$$2.3 \quad f(Na) = \binom{\frac{a}{p}}{Na} (\frac{a}{p})^{Na} (1 - \frac{a}{p})^{n - Na}$$

In this case a has the following estimator function:

$$2.4 \quad a = p \frac{Na}{n}$$

Sampling procedure

To estimate the density of a given population of persons one should select random combinations of persons, discarding all cases in which a person is combined with himself. When sampling from a small population without replacement or when sampling from a large population one should also discard combinations that were selected previously.

The resulting sample of relations will be divided into actual and non-actual on the basis of observations.

Section 3

Under several circumstances one might want to test whether a certain boundary is significant, i.e. whether the number of relations crossing the boundary is significantly low. Two different tests may be used for this problem: Fisher's Exact Method and the chi-square test. It depends on the nature of the data which test should be used. If either sample or total population of relations are thirty-six or smaller one may use Fisher's Exact Method; otherwise the Fisher's Exact Method is less convenient because no tables are available. If the conditions for use of the chi-square test are met, this last test will provide a more efficient solution.

One may test a boundary for both the original population or for a sample from this population. If the test is done on a sample then this sample should be taken *with replacement.* Only when the original population is very large compared to the sample is such replacement unnecessary.

As an example the data given in Table B will be tested. The total size of the network of Table B is 30. The total population of relations therefore amounts to 435 of which 200 relations cross the boundary. Because of this the chi-square will be used. The following tables summarize the calculation.

	Table 3.1		*Table 3.2*	
	OBSERVED		EXPECTED	
within segments	120	115	75,6	159,4
between segments	20	180	64,4	135,6
	actual	non-actual	actual	non-actual

df = 1
Chi-square = 83,60
$p < 0.001$

From these tables one may conclude that the relations between the two segments in fact are below expectancy. The two segments may be called compartments for this reason.

To use Fisher's exact method a table like Table 3.1 should be prepared. For a detailed account of this statistical test the reader is referred to Bradley (1968) or any other text on non-parametric statistics.

Section 4

In sections 2 and 3 it was assumed that it was possible to take a sample from the theoretically existing relations of a network. For several reasons the research worker may decide that this is impracticable or inefficient. Under certain conditions it is possible, however, to test the significance of boundaries also on a sample of the network members. The following circumstances should be present:

a. The sample should be taken with replacement if it is large in comparison to the population;
b. The expected density of actual relations should be very low;
c. The number of persons in each segment should be known beforehand.

In this case the significance of a boundary between the two segments may be tested by the following procedure:

Step 1: From each individual in the sample one obtains the number of persons with whom he has an actual relation in his own segment and in the other segment.

Step 2: If N is the total size of the network and P and Q are the number of persons in segments A and B respectively then the obtained scores are corrected in order to produce the table below:

	*Within own segment**	*With other segment*
Persons from segment A	$\frac{\frac{1}{2}N}{P-1} \times X_i$	$\frac{\frac{1}{2}N}{Q} \times Y_i$
Persons from segment B	$\frac{\frac{1}{2}N}{Q-1} \times X_i$	$\frac{\frac{1}{2}N}{P} \times Y_i$

Step 3: On this table the Wilcoxon Matched Pairs Signed-Ranks Test may be performed (Siegel, 1956: 75-83).

* X_i and Y_i denote the scores obtained for individual during step 1.

If the exact size of the segments was not known beforehand, but one expects them to be about equal in size, the Sign test (Siegel, 1956: 68-75) may be used. This test should be performed directly on the raw data. Before performing the Sign test it should be verified whether the assumption of equally large segments is justified. If P denotes an estimation of the number of persons in the larger of the two segments then:

4.1 $$\frac{Q}{P} > \frac{1}{P} + \frac{x}{x \times 1}$$ (x is the largest number of relations any of the sampled persons has in one segment)

The inequality above should also be valid at the higher end of the confidence interval for P. One should be careful when selecting confidence levels for this confidence interval and for the Sign Test itself.

If for some reason the number of actual relations a person maintains in the network is limited to some fixed quantity – a person may have only one patron – neither the Wilcoxon nor the Sign test will be allowed.

Section 5

The ratio

5.1 $$R = \frac{B_{(u)}*}{B_{(u)}**}$$

$B_{(u)}*$ = ß – coefficient of a set
$B_{(u)}**$ = ß – coefficient of the same set when joining a person to it.

may be calculated in order to show the circumstances that lead to a drop in $B_{(u)}$, i.e. to a ratio R that is larger than 1. When denoting the number of relations between the person who was joined to the set and other persons in the set by e and his relations to persons outside the set by f, it may be shown that R has the following value:

5.2 $$R = \left(1 + \frac{1}{p-1}\right) \left(1 + \frac{1}{n-p-1}\right) \left(1 - \frac{e}{S+e}\right) \left(1 + \frac{f-e}{T}\right)$$

In most cases R will be smaller than one when f is smaller than e, i.e. when the person joined to the cluster has more relations to the cluster than to others outside it. But when the person joined to the cluster has only one relation in the whole network it depends on characteristics of the already existing set whether R will become more than one and a drop of $B_{(u)}$ occurs.

It can be shown that when $e < \frac{S}{p - T}$, i.e. when the person joined to the set has the same personal degree to the set as other set members or less, then a drop of $B_{(u)}$ will occur if $f - e$ is not at least larger then $T/(n - p)$. From this it may be seen that characteristics of the already existing set influence the criteria for membership.

Section 6

A given description of a network of size n may be represented by a n-order matrix *A*. The values of a_{ij} represent some measure of relationship between persons i and j. All a_{ii} entries are zero. The following method of cluster analysis may be used when the entries in *A* are neither binary (0,1) or in an interval scale. When instead all measures are ordinal in character *step 2* should be different.

Step 1: Define a hypothetical boundary partitioning A into four almost equal quadrants. This boundary has a value k when it lies between cell k and cell $k+1$.

Step 2: Calculate a difference vector DIF:

6.1 $\text{DIF}_i = x_i - y_i \; (i < k)$ $\qquad$ $\text{DIF}_i = y_i - x_i \; (i > k)$

$$x_i = \sum_{j=1}^{k} a_{ij} \qquad\qquad y_i = \sum_{j=k+1}^{n} a_{ij}$$

Step 3: Interchange rows and columns of two persons p and q, each from a different segment, whose entries in DIF show the largest negative value of their segment. If DIF_p or DIF_q equal to a_{pq} *another combination* not satisfying this condition should be chosen.

If there are negative entries in one segment only, then go to *step 4*.

If there are no negative entries then go to *step 5*. Return to *step 2*.

Step 4: If negative entries exist in one segment only, one should change rows and columns in such way that the person with the largest negative entry becomes part of the opposite segment. This means that the boundary should be changed into either k—1 or k+1. Return to *step 2*.

Step 5: If no negative entries remain, the process is finished. The same type of analysis may be done on each of the clusters generated. If the boundary was changed during the process and subsequently all in the network belong to one segment then obviously no clusters exist.

The following example may illustrate the procedure:

	1	2	3	4	5	6	DIF
1	0	1	0	1	1	0	− 1
2	1	0	1	0	0	1	+ 1
3	0	1	0	0	0	1	0
4	1	0	0	0	1	0	0
5	1	0	0	1	0	0	0
6	0	1	1	0	0	0	− 2

	6	2	3	4	5	1	DIF
6	0	1	1	0	0	0	+ 2
2	1	0	1	0	0	1	+ 1
3	1	1	0	0	0	0	+ 2
4	0	0	0	0	1	1	+ 2
5	0	0	0	1	0	1	+ 2
1	0	1	0	1	1	0	+ 1

If measurement is ordinal with the *same scale* applying throughout the whole matrix (and not only to the relations of each person) *step 2* may be revised in order to incorporate the information contained in the ordinal measurement. The following tables illustrate the procedure followed:

	(a)		(b)		(c)		(d)	
Rank:	1	2	1	2	1	2	1	2
Number of relations in own set	2	3	2	2	2		1	
Number of relations in other set	3	1	3		1			
score					+2			+3

Table (a) above represents the original scores of a person. This person had 3 relations with scale value 2 to other persons of his own set against only one relation of this type to persons outside his set. First this last relation is cancelled against one of the others in this category. The result is shown in table b. Next to this the remaining two relations of rank two are cancelled against two relations of rank one. In this way the process is continued until no entries remain. During this process of cancelling one counts the number of cases in which a relation of a higher rank was cancelled against one of lower rank. The resulting score (in this example 3) is then treated as a normal DIF score. If a relation of a higher rank from the relations outside the set was cancelled against a relation of lower rank of the persons own set, the score has to be diminished by one.

When using this method the critical condition for chosing another combination in *step 3* does not apply. Instead of this one should keep track of the rows and columns interchanged one cycle before. If the same combination should be interchanged but now in the reverse direction, another 'second best' combination should be selected.

NOTES

1. This term is in accordance with the name graph theorists give to a similar notion (Harary, 1969: 14).

2. The density of a person is then the degree of that person divided by network size and multiplied by one hundred.

3. If the scale used is ordinal then the degree gives us an idea of the mean sum of ranks. The procedure of cluster analysis presented later in this paper may be with ranks too. The result will be meaningful under the circumstances specified in the appendix. One should adhere strictly to the procedure described there.

4. The term *boundary* is used in a different sense than that proposed by Barnes (1969: 67). He defines a boundary as a network region with no links of importance crossing. Here boundary is used in a relative sense: if two sets of persons have an unexpectedly low number of links between them there exists a boundary between these sets. Likewise the definition of *segment* differs from *compartment* as proposed by Thoden van Velzen elsewhere in this volume. While a segment would be any category of persons of a certain network differentiated on some basis, a compartment would be a segment with *statistically significant boundaries.*

5. For yet another reason the definition is in need of some refinement. The way it now reads would seem to suggest the existence of clusters within clusters. To put it extremely: within a set of seven persons with a density of 100 per cent there would be 21 clusters. This problem could be circumvented by stating that a cluster is the maximum number of persons possible with a density that is still above the threshold.

6. Beum and Brundage (1950) have suggested an alternative method of identifying clusters. In fact their method does not prove very useful, especially when all relations are considered symmetrical (as in the case of a binary classification). Beum and Brundage themselves note that the process of identification is slow and not always successful. As a matter of fact, if one changes their own example from asymmetrical into symmetrical relations, an unsuccessful case would result. All other examples tried gave the same result. While the process indicated that one should terminate the procedure, improvement of the result was still possible, sometimes to an even large extent.

7. A note of warning should be sounded here. Firstly, it appears that their calculations contain a minor error. Secondly their method should not be used on ordinal data. In order to use this method one's data should be either in an interval scale or in a binary scale. The suitability of the sociometric data used by Bock and Husain is subject to question for this reason.

Part 2

Networks compared

Network density among urban families

TESSA CUBITT

The aim of this paper is to examine some of Bott's (1957) suggestions in the light of a recent research project and to suggest further general characteristics of social networks. By her use of the concept of network, Bott has given a method of looking at the informal contacts of people. At the time of her research, the network was a new tool for analysing social situations involving non-groups, an aspect of social relationships which had not been previously emphasized.

One of the difficulties of the concept of the social network is that it is a wide term covering a complexity of social relationships. As a result, though characteristics of an individual's network have been assessed, it seems unlikely that these characteristics because they cover such a collection of social relationships will apply uniformly to all parts of the network. It may be possible to generalise about the overall nature of the network, but this is not in fact of great use since general network characteristics may be distorting the picture and covering up significant but rather different characteristics in sections of the network. The nature of the different segments of one network may vary greatly within the network.

If we look at the main feature of Bott's network – the extent of connectedness – we can see how this might be the case. At this point it is necessary to clarify the terminology used. Bott talks in terms of close- and loose-knit networks which she calls connectedness. Barnes (1969), however, has recently distinguished more clearly the terms connectedness, connectivity and density. He points out that confusion has arisen because the term connectedness has been used to cover a variety of meanings, all similar and yet, when more closely scrutinised, different. The term has been used to refer to relationships which are both directed, that is, where the direction of the flow of interaction is specified, and undirected, where no distinction in the direction of the flow of interaction is made. The term has been used to refer to the structure of linkages irrespective of the directedness of the relationships, that is, whether they are reciprocal or not. But high connectedness usually carries with it the implication that behaviour immediately involves a large proportion of those concerned. Therefore if the relationships are non-reciprocal then the notion of reachability is also intimately involved. Hence the same term may refer to two quite different concepts, one being the reachability of one point from another and thus the number of other points communication must flow through, while the other refers to the number of links between a collection of points all directly linked to ego. Barnes suggests that this latter idea, which Bott calls connectedness, should more accurately be called density. 'In our terms, Bott means density rather than connectedness and she is referring to the density of the first-order zone of the root constituted by condensing the husband and wife by treating them as a single point in the undirected graph' (1969: 225). Since Barnes' terms are more specific and reflect these finer distinctions, I shall use his terms in the rest of this paper. Therefore, when referring to the number of links between a set of points each directly in contact with ego, I shall talk of density and therefore what Bott called connectedness. The close- and loose-knit nature of the network will therefore be referred to as high and low density. 'The qualitative contrast she (Bott) makes between "close-knit" and "loose-knit" must then be understood as a contrast between high and low density' (1969: 225).

The significance of the high/low densities in urban British society may be questioned by pointing out that only one of Bott's families had a really high density network and not only did the majority tend towards the low density end of the continuum, but since they consisted mostly of the more mobile middle-class families, they represent the type of family which is on the increase. If researchers are then much more likely to find low density networks, is the term in fact useful? As Lancaster has pointed out 'a more accurate picture of a loose-knit network might be suggested by a metaphor implying a radial pattern rather than reticulation' (Lancaster, 1961: 326). This seems pertinent since the main point of using the metaphor of the network is that it implies a mesh of linkages. Where the mesh is close-knit, the mesh can clearly be seen, but where the density of the network is low, the mesh is of little significance and the metaphor does not seem to be appropriate.

However, I think the metaphor can still be of great use if we look more closely at the network rather than trying to see the whole in one shade of density. Epstein (1961) was one of the first to point out that a network may not be connected in its totality but highly connected in parts. This suggests that a network may consist of high density 'knots' loosely linked or perhaps not linked at all, except through ego, with other high density areas. If this *is* the case, how are we to characterise this netwotk; is it of high, low or intermediate density? This seems a weak point in the general description of a network and I would suggest that the picture described above is typical of most people's networks. We must therefore take network analysis further and ask why the high density 'knots' occur, where they occur and why some parts should be of greater density than others.

Boissevain (1968) has partly solved this problem by saying that one of the factors which influences the structural characteristics of the network is the relative importance of certain activity fields, and he says that the degree of connectedness can also vary within different segments of a network. Boissevain goes on to discuss how other network characteristics such as the ratio of ego's intimate to effective links may vary according to activity fields and segments. It therefore seems that it is these areas which are responsible for high density areas and we must look more closely at the terms. Boissevain does not define them, but in an earlier article Jay (1964) described an activity field in the following way – the activity field 'of any individual or group consists of all the units with which that individual or group maintains a certain type of relationship. The boundaries of such a field are meaningful only with reference to the individual or group under consideration. The units of a field may be individuals, families, communities or other social aggregates, but the field as such does not "constitute a group" ' (1964: 138).

One of the difficulties of using the term activity field seems to be that the notions of role and field became confused. An activity field is a social field but defined by a particular relationship. Boissevain gives an example of the way activity fields vary in connectedness by comparing kinship links and economic links. But what exactly are economic links – are they links with work associates or would a loan to a kinsman be an economic link or a kinship link? It seems that while the work situation and kinship are two fields, an economic link is a relationship and implies a certain role. Also is kinship really an activity field; it is a social field, but does not the notion of activity field rather distort the type of linkage here? The point that arises here is that ego will have a different relationship with the various members of a social field, but that the relationships of all the members of one field with ego are taken to be equivalent for analytical purposes. Boissevain does not define segment and he uses the two terms fairly generally.

What seems to be the important point when looking at clusters of contacts within the network is the type of link, seeing this more in the light of field theory than role relationships. It seems more likely that there will be greater density where the members of the network have the same type of link with ego than a similar role relationship. Thus ego may have the role of confidant with a neighbour and an old school friend, but the two are not likely to know each other through sharing this role. In the same way ego has an economic relationship with his butcher and his bank manager, but the two are not likely to be connected through this. On the other hand, two neighbours, two old schoolfriends, two members of the same golf club are more likely to know each other through sharing this similar 'field' type link.

I would therefore suggest that we look at different sectors of the network to find out where the high density areas occur. By sector here, I mean part of the network in which ego has an analytically equivalent relationship with all members of it. It may be that by talking about sectors instead of segments here I am being pedantic. The only reason for the use of the term sector instead of segment is that geometrically the segment is a section of the outer part of a circle and not related to the central point, whereas a sector is related to the central point and as we are discussing ego-centred networks, the latter seems more relevant.

It is then the sectors of the network where density may be high while the density of the total network for most people is fairly low. It is true that some of the traditional community studies revealed low density networks, but I think this may also be explained in terms of sectors in two ways:

1. The ego-centred network of most people in Bethnal Green for example tends to be limited to very few sectors and then primarily to kinship. Kinship by its nature tends to be a more close-knit sector. In Boissevain's words, 'where kinship links are more numerous as compared with economic ones for example, there is likely to be greater connectedness' (1968: 547). Klein's analysis (1965) of the extent of the neighbourliness in Bethnal Green is relevant here. She points out that the extensive neighbourliness there was due to the fact that most of the neighbours were kin. It is because most people interact with kin and their network is comprised mostly of kin that there is a lot of activity and people know each other.

2. Also in these traditional working class areas, there tends to be an overlap of the different sectors of the network. Thus these various sectors converge on the same people. In Bethnal Green (Young and Willmott, 1959) kin, neighbours, work associates are all the same people. It is as if the different sectors were superimposed producing a network of high density.

As these families become more mobile and as they move into new working environments, their networks take on the characteristics of the middle-class network, the sectors become separate and the density of the network decreases. Here there are more sectors and less interaction between members of different sectors. As Susser and Watson have said of the middle class, 'They work with one set, play golf with another, entertain another and live beside yet another' (1962: 142).

The literature on traditional working class areas then has shown how limited and overlapping sectors have in the past brought about high density networks. However, recent studies have shown, though not specifically in these terms, that most networks overall tend to be loosely knit but with some high density areas. Bott's (op. cit.) own material reveals the general low density of the majority of the networks. Attempts to examine her thesis more closely are also interesting in this light. Two of these studies showed that Bott's thesis was applicable only in lower-class groups, but is not really relevant for middle-class couples. Udry and Hall in their study of parents of students found some tendency for husbands who were most involved in a high density network to have a medium conjugal role segregation pattern but they conclude in general 'Bott's original hypothesis is applicable only to lower class couples' (1965: 395). Nelson (1966), too, using a sample of 131 working class wives supports Bott's thesis. It can be suggested that the reason why her thesis is applicable only in lower class groups is that for middle class groups the notion of general density for a total network becomes meaningless. Most middle-class couples have the type of network mentioned earlier, where the range between the highest and the lowest densities is very small and most of the networks are of fairly low density.

Aldous and Strauss say that their findings, as such, disprove Bott, but that really they have failed to give the theory adequate testing because most of the sample's networks were near to the low density end of the pole. But their comments here are interesting: 'We believe, however, that our sample is likely to prove fairly representative as to the kinds of social networks existing in industrial societies. The person in a close-knit network is fairly uncommon we suspect, as compared with persons in loose-knit networks' (1965/66: 580). It is interesting to see that the range of densities of the different networks in this study is fairly small. There really was not very much difference in the density of the networks of all the wives. The distinction between high and low density is not very useful for this middle-class sample.

Turner (1967) though he did not set out to examine Bott's hypothesis, was able to use the data from his Leadgill research to examine her ideas. He found that the variable which was related closely to network density was geographic mobility. This seems very logical and was, of course, suggested by Bott. People who live in one place all their lives are far more likely to have high density networks than those who travel around and know people in different parts of the country. It is extremely unlikely that their friends in one part of Britain would know those in another. This is also compatible with the previous remarks about class. The middle-class are more likely to be mobile and therefore to have the low density networks associated with this mobility. One of Turner's main conclusions is that the Bott hypothesis has not yet been properly tested, though he does not elucidate this more fully.

One of the reasons why the two previous studies, which set out to examine Bott's ideas, did not do this properly is that they did not examine network density properly. In two cases, informants were asked to name either the 8 or the 4 people they saw most frequently. The density of those most frequently seen was then calculated. When Bott talks of networks, however, she surely means more than the four or eight friends of the wife. By taking the few people seen most frequently, the researchers have intended one of two things:

1. This is what is meant by a couple's social network;
2. The density of this small network is a good indicator of the total density of the network.

It cannot be supposed that a couple in an urban environment have a network of 4 or 8 people and clearly this is not what Bott described. If, however, these few are supposed to represent the total network it would seem to me a very dubious indicator.

The validity of this was tested by comparing the density of extended networks of couples in Edinburgh with the density of the ten most frequently seen people, which may be called *the effective network*. Each husband and wife was asked individually who were the five people each saw most often – making a total of ten people for each couple if all the people they named were quite different. The extent to which these ten people knew each other was then estimated and the density among them compared with that of the density of the extended network, which is defined on page 11. In the cases of both the effective networks and the extended networks the couples were divided in terciles of high, medium and low density. It can be seen that there is little correlation between these two groups and high density of the most frequently seen network does not necessarily mean high density of the extended network.

Table 1

		No. of couples with stated density of extended network			
		Low	Medium	High	Total
No. of couples	Low	4	6	2	12
with stated	Medium	4	2	6	12
density of	High	*4*	*4*	*3*	*11*
effective networks	Total	*12*	*12*	*11*	*35*

The Goodman-Kruskal gamma for these table is .057 indicating that there is no real relationship between the density of the effective and extended networks.

Christopher Turner has tried to cover a more general and wider network, but even so the largest network in his study only contains twelve households. It must be remembered, however, that his research was carried out in a rural area and it is clear that variations in urban and rural networks occur. My own research shows how the density of the social networks of 35 Edinburgh couples tends to be generally low with high density sectors.

The project was intended to investigate various characteristics of networks, but only the data on density will be discussed here. As a depth study was necessary to get all the information that is involved in networks, only 38 couples were studied. So as to investigate possible class differences half of those chosen were middle-class and half working class. As this was not a stratification study and as one objective indicator of social class position was necessary, the Registrar General's classification was used. Thus the middle-class couples are from the professional and managerial groups I and II and the working class couples from III, IV and V. Since the position of clerical workers in group III is so debatable, these were excluded and the bulk of the working class sample are skilled and semi-skilled manual workers. Couples were also selected for the research from different stages of the developmental cycle of the family so as to estimate the influence of the stage of the cycle of the family on social networks.

The data were collected by a combination of methods. Initially when the couples were contacted, they were asked to take part in a series of interviews. In addition to the interviews, I got to know most of the families well enough to 'pop in' uninvited. Participant observation on these occasions proved quite rewarding. In one of the interviews, informants were asked to recall the various activities, who they had seen and what they had done during the previous month. They were also asked to keep a structured diary for a week. This consisted of a form for each day of the week, which was divided into different periods of the day, and informants were asked to complete these. Diaries can provide an accurate record of all meetings with people and details of the type of meeting and are therefore a very useful source of information. The difficulty here is that there is a limit to the length of time an informant will keep a diary and though they provide a good record, if they only cover a week's activities, many members of the extended network will not be included. The combination of participant observation, interviews and diaries covers a set of techniques ranging from general to accurate and broad to narrow coverage. In this way I got information on the broad outline of the social network and also more accurate detailed information on the more frequent contacts. The networks, here, like Bott's, are first-order zone of the root since they only deal with ego's contacts and not those known to the contact, but unknown to ego.

One of the problems in measuring network density is which level of social contact to take to include in the network. First of all it is necessary to define a social contact to decide precisely who is included in the social network and therefore make network characteristics comparable. The researcher may either limit the network in his own terms or ask the informant who are his friends, neighbours, etc. If he takes the first path he will find it difficult to find a suitable criterion. One suggestion is that all who enter ego's home should be included in the network. This, however, reveals the middle-class bias of the interviewer for while it may be a good indicator of a relationship in middle-class circles, there are many working-class informants in Edinburgh whose companions they see most frequently and who constitute an important part of the network, but never enter their homes. This sort of arbitrary limitation of the network can lead to superficial results. The alternative is to ask people about categories of relationships – friends, neighbours, etc. The difficulty here is that people's conceptions of these terms differ so much. One or two of the older men in my research set insisted that they had no friends at all, while a trade union secretary considered all the members of his union friends. A deeper analysis showed that some of those who said they had no 'friends' had a more intimate relationship with some members of their network than the union secretary did with other members of his union. Similarly some informants considered as neighbours only their two immediate neighbours while others referred to those living in a whole district of Edinburgh as neighbours.

Thus in deciding what a social contact is, an attempt was made to include two dimensions of a relationship – frequency of contact and emotional content. A social contact is therefore defined as anyone with whom ego has social contact once a month or with whom ego has an effective relationship, that is either with a kinsman or someone considered a friend. Social contacts defined in this way made up the extended network.

These two aspects of a contact were also used to define a network member by Christopher Turner, though he took fortnightly contact instead of monthly. He says 'Members of a focal individual's network were defined as persons (1) to whom the focal individual was bound by positive affectional ties (i.e. kinsfolk and friends) and (2) with whom the focal individual had regular social contact, (in this instance regular is defined as at least once per fortnight on average throughout the year)' (1967: 123).

Each social relationship included is therefore reciprocal since ego and the social contact both know each other and there is no measure of the direction of the flow of communication. The network graphs of these data, therefore, are undirected.

With regard to density all the informants were asked about each member of the network and which other members he or she knew. This clearly is not the perfect way to get data on density, but it is almost the only possible way for a researcher with limited time and resources and anything more than a very small number to deal with. Bott of course used this method and also Aldous and Strauss when assessing density. Ideally each member of the network should be contacted and asked if he knows the other members, but with networks ranging from 18 to 53 members, this would just be an impossible task.

These data were recorded in matrix form and network density calculated. Both the density of the extended network and that of the individual sectors were worked out. Table 2 shows the extended network densities for the couples in the research set. Network density was calculated in the form of a percentage, as expressed in table 2. All the links between the non-focal members of ego's network (i.e. all the network members excluding ego) were added and this figure was then expressed as a fraction of the total number of possible links between all members of the network. The resulting scores tend to be low.

I used as a criterion for extent of density the one that Christopher Turner used. He says 'A loose-knit network is characterized by the existence of interconnecting linkages between less than one third of the non-focal households in a particular network. The equivalent proportions of interconnecting linkages for a medium-knit network is between one-third two-thirds, and for a close-knit network more than two-thirds' (1967: 123). A similar concept of network density is used by Aldous and Strauss. They say, 'Though the criterion of connectedness was not a stringent one – the women only had to "know" each other – the average score was just 2.3. Such a score indicated that on the average each of the eight closest associates named by the respondents knew only about two of the other women listed. Despite the low network closure scores, . . .' (1965-66: 578). The women in Aldous and Strauss' sample therefore knew on average just under a third of the other women in the network and Aldous and Strauss considered this a low density network.

If we take the highest density network of the Oxington informants, that of the Dees, we see it has a score of 22.5. The non-focal links in the net-

Table 2. Network Density

Middle Class	No. of non-focal network members	Density	Working Class	No. of non-focal network members	Density
Wilson	47	18.37	Lawson	41	19.6
Currie	24	14.68	Dee	24	22.5
McGregor	32	18.6	Kane	46	20.9
Row	38	20.75	Carnegie	36	15.22
Nelson	42	14.75	Wood	40	20.2
Hicks	53	10.4	Dunlop	27	14,75
			Canning	33	20.4
Coates	36	18.5	Steel	36	17.75
Jackson	51	21.8	Brown	33	11.0
Rogers	32	19.58	Turner	43	13.2
McMillan	34	9.25	Gardner	32	16.1
Marshall	34	18.6	Warren	30	21.1
Scott	37	16.45	Hobson	36	20.6
Wilkins	40	14.6	Sanderson	45	17.4
White	29	20.5	Jenkins	40	12.8
Rankin	32	9.5	Blake	35	19.5
Mitchell	51	8.55	Cowen	38	13.1
Spencer	18	15.0	Menzies	21	21.8

Average network densities		*Standard deviation*	
Middle class	– 15.87	Middle class	– 4.19
Working class	– 17.62	Working class	– 3.49

Range of density		
Middle class	– 8.55	– 21.8
Working class	– 11.0	– 22.5
General	– 8.55	– 22.5

work were added and divided by the number of network members. Thus, the average network member knew 5.16 other network members. Since the network consisted of twenty-four people, this represents less than a third. Thus the network with the highest density among the Oxington informants fell into the category of low density networks. One problem with calculating measures of network density is that the potential number of interconnecting linkages increases at a much faster rate than the number of people in the network. The number of network members is therefore an important factor to take into consideration. The networks I am considering are rather larger than those discussed by Christopher Turner, Aldous and Strauss and Udry

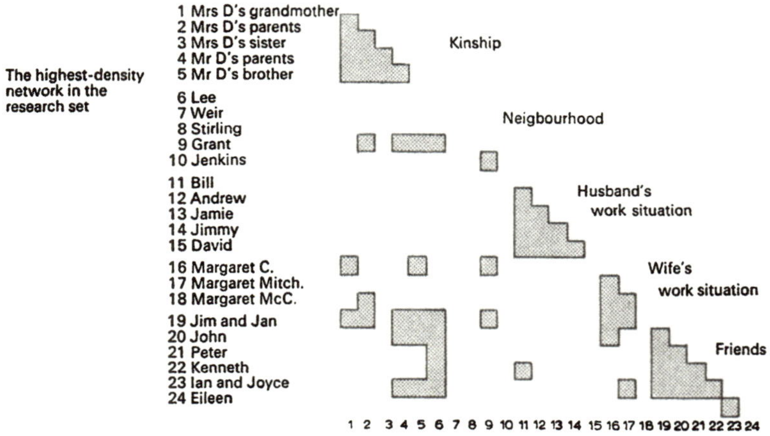
The highest-density network in the research set
1 Mrs D's grandmother
2 Mrs D's parents
3 Mrs D's sister
4 Mr D's parents
5 Mr D's brother
6 Lee
7 Weir
8 Stirling
9 Grant
10 Jenkins
11 Bill
12 Andrew
13 Jamie
14 Jimmy
15 David
16 Margaret C.
17 Margaret Mitch.
18 Margaret McC.
19 Jim and Jan
20 John
21 Peter
22 Kenneth
23 Ian and Joyce
24 Eileen
Kinship
Neigbourhood
Husband's work situation
Wife's work situation
Friends
1 2 3 4 5 6 7 8 9 10 11 12 13 14 15 16 17 18 19 20 21 22 23 24

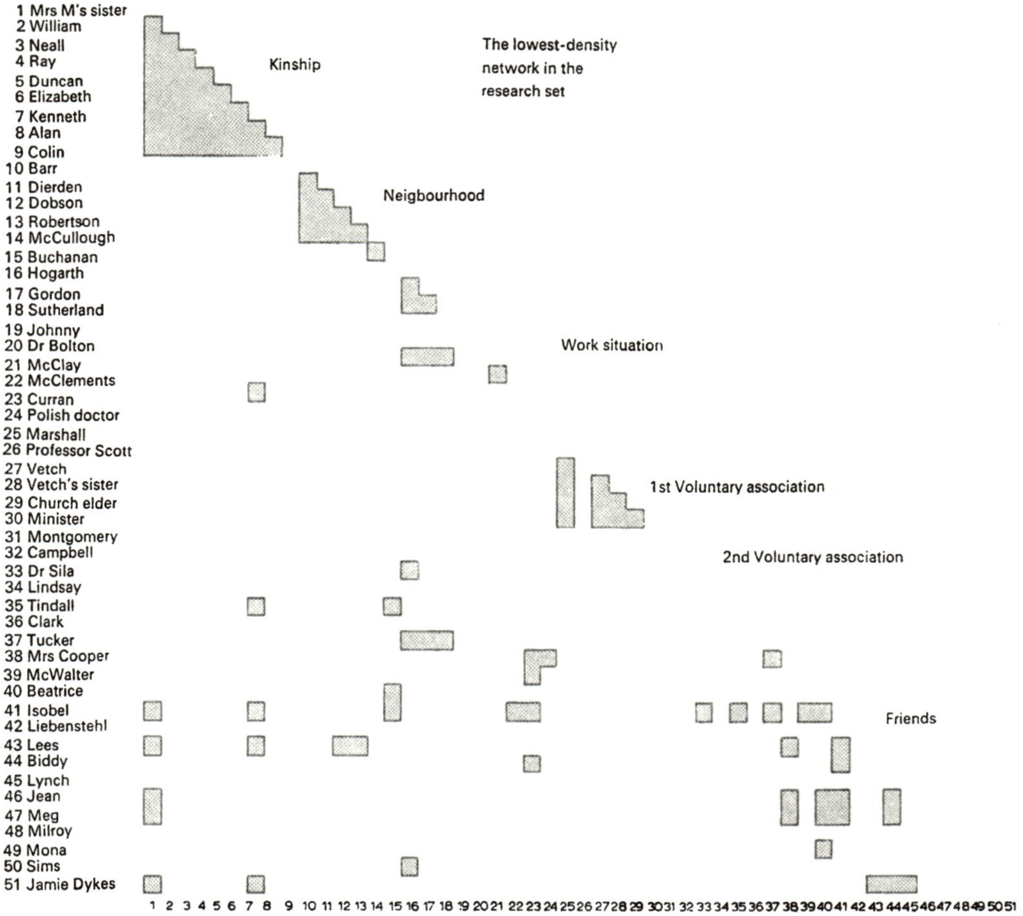
The lowest-density network in the research set
1 Mrs M's sister
2 William
3 Neall
4 Ray
5 Duncan
6 Elizabeth
7 Kenneth
8 Alan
9 Colin
10 Barr
11 Dierden
12 Dobson
13 Robertson
14 McCullough
15 Buchanan
16 Hogarth
17 Gordon
18 Sutherland
19 Johnny
20 Dr Bolton
21 McClay
22 McClements
23 Curran
24 Polish doctor
25 Marshall
26 Professor Scott
27 Vetch
28 Vetch's sister
29 Church elder
30 Minister
31 Montgomery
32 Campbell
33 Dr Sila
34 Lindsay
35 Tindall
36 Clark
37 Tucker
38 Mrs Cooper
39 McWalter
40 Beatrice
41 Isobel
42 Liebenstehl
43 Lees
44 Biddy
45 Lynch
46 Jean
47 Meg
48 Milroy
49 Mona
50 Sims
51 Jamie Dykes
Kinship
Neigbourhood
Work situation
1st Voluntary association
2nd Voluntary association
Friends
1 2 3 4 5 6 7 8 9 10 11 12 13 14 15 16 17 18 19 20 21 22 23 24 25 26 27 28 29 30 31 32 33 34 35 36 37 38 39 40 41 42 43 44 45 46 47 48 49 50 51

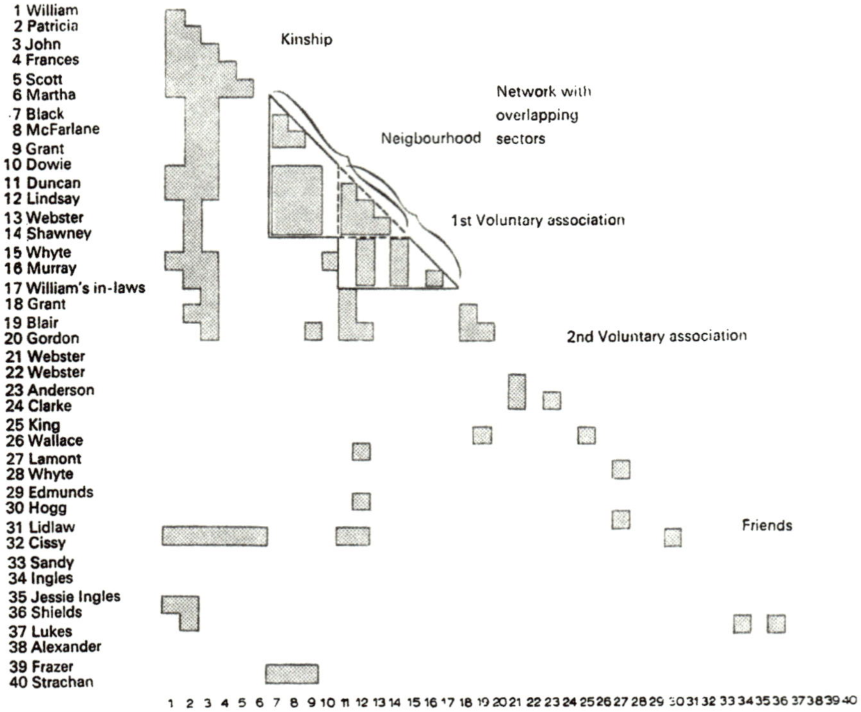
1 William
2 Patricia
3 John
4 Frances
5 Scott
6 Martha
7 Black
8 McFarlane
9 Grant
10 Dowie
11 Duncan
12 Lindsay
13 Webster
14 Shawney
15 Whyte
16 Murray
17 William's in-laws
18 Grant
19 Blair
20 Gordon
21 Webster
22 Webster
23 Anderson
24 Clarke
25 King
26 Wallace
27 Lamont
28 Whyte
29 Edmunds
30 Hogg
31 Lidlaw
32 Cissy
33 Sandy
34 Ingles
35 Jessie Ingles
36 Shields
37 Lukes
38 Alexander
39 Frazer
40 Strachan
Kinship
Network with overlapping sectors
Neigbourhood
1st Voluntary association
2nd Voluntary association
Friends
1 2 3 4 5 6 7 8 9 10 11 12 13 14 15 16 17 18 19 20 21 22 23 24 25 26 27 28 29 30 31 32 33 34 35 36 37 38 39 40

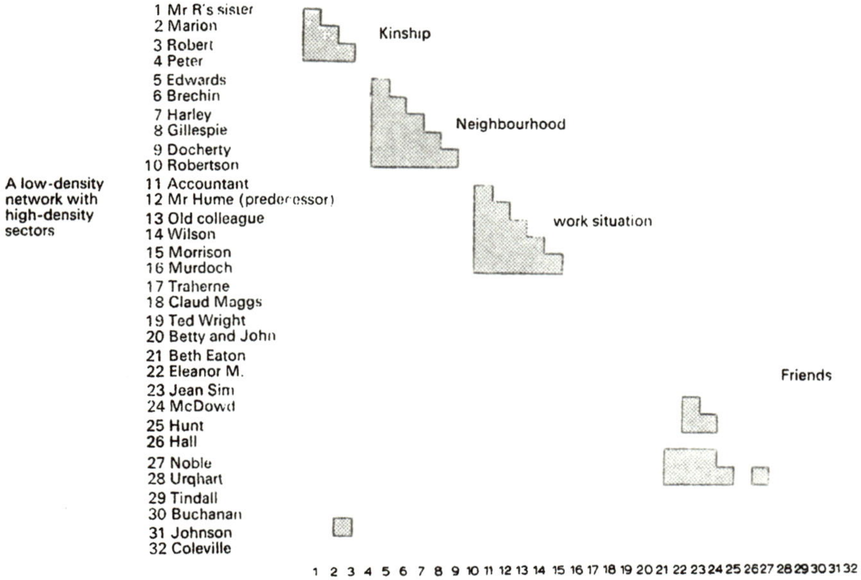
A low-density network with high-density sectors
1 Mr R's sister
2 Marion
3 Robert
4 Peter
5 Edwards
6 Brechin
7 Harley
8 Gillespie
9 Docherty
10 Robertson
11 Accountant
12 Mr Hume (predecessor)
13 Old colleague
14 Wilson
15 Morrison
16 Murdoch
17 Traherne
18 Claud Maggs
19 Ted Wright
20 Betty and John
21 Beth Eaton
22 Eleanor M.
23 Jean Sim
24 McDowd
25 Hunt
26 Hall
27 Noble
28 Urqhart
29 Tindall
30 Buchanan
31 Johnson
32 Coleville
Kinship
Neighbourhood
work situation
Friends
1 2 3 4 5 6 7 8 9 10 11 12 13 14 15 16 17 18 19 20 21 22 23 24 25 26 27 28 29 30 31 32

and Hall and therefore there will be a greater tendency for the number of existing linkages to form a smaller proportion of the total possible number in my networks than in theirs. The point must also be made that when a network has a couple as the central point, it is more likely to be of low density than a network focused on an individual, since the former represents two networks, one anchored on the husband and one on the wife. However, we still find that using the criterion of high/low density mentioned above, these networks fall well into the category of low density. Irrespective of stages in the developmental cycle, and of social class, the density of all the extended networks can be considered low.

The range of densities is only from 8.55 to 22.5 despite the different types of families involved. The average rate of density for all the families is only 16.74.

To investigate the earlier suggestions about social class differences, the density of the two social groupings in this project can be compared. Density of the middle-class couples varied from 8.55 to 21.8 and that of the working class couples from 11.0 to 22.5. The average density for the middle-class was 15.87, while it was 17.62 for the working class. The standard deviation for the middle-class group is 4.19 and that for the working class group in 3.49. Thus for both groups the deviation from the mean is quite large and since there is a difference of only 1.75 between the two averages, it seems that there is very little difference between the two distributions. In these cases the working class networks did tend to be slightly denser but the difference was not big enough to suggest distinct class differences.

Despite the low density nature of the extended networks, some of the sectors were very dense. Table 3 setting out the densities for the different

Table 3. Average sector densities

	Middle class	Working class	General average	*Average no. of non-focal sector members*
Kinship	100.0	98.3	99.15	7.08
Neighbourhood	76.6	66.8	71.7	7.94
Work (husband)	80.7	90.2	85.45	6.2
Work (wife)	100.0	100.0	100.0	5.4
Voluntary associations	79.9	83.6	81.75	4.84
Friends	17.1	14.9	16.0	7.14

sectors shows a much higher rate than the extended networks. In fact, if we take the average density for each other, we find they were as high as 71.7 for the neighbourhood, 85.4 for the husband's work situation, 100 for the wife's work situation, 81.75 for the voluntary associations. It must be remembered that these sectors refer to all those who had a similar link with ego. Thus the density of the neighbourhood is the density of the network of all the neighbours whom ego knew, not the whole neighbourhood, the density of which would probably be less. The figures for sector density were high showing definite high density areas and they contrast strongly with those of the extended network.

The importance of the number of network members in calculating density must be mentioned again here. The number of network members in each sector is clearly smaller than the number in the extended network. Therefore one would expect the density of sectors to be higher than that of the extended network, on the basis of the different numbers involved. Nevertheless the difference between the densities of sectors and that of the extended network is larger than would be expected purely on the basis of the different numbers of network members. The low density of the sector of friends demonstrates that low densities in sectors can quite well occur. This is the only sector that has a low density, which is interesting because it is rather an arbitrary category. Those included in the sector were friends who were not recruited from any of the other sectors. Therefore despite allowing for the difficulties involved in density calculation the data do show that it is in the sectors that high density occurs.

Of course there is considerable variation between sectors of different couples and some of course have some sectors which are less dense. The differences in density vary between couples and between sectors.

The density for kinship is extremely high because only families of origin of husband and wife and their own families of procreation were considered. The reasons for this were that:

1. Firstly the research project showed a very distinct difference between contact with the members of the family of origin and contact with other kin. With the former contact was frequent and regular, whilst among others numerous kin contact was far more sporadic.

2. The data on kinship included every living relative and would therefore have been rather unwieldy to deal with in addition to all the other members of the network.

3. The density of kin is rather less interesting than that of other sectors, since one can assume a fairly high level of connectedness through the kin-

ship tie. It is not the fact that they know each other so much as the type of relationship between them that is of interest.

Variations in density of the different sectors does not seem to follow any general pattern and appears largely individualistic. It seems likely that it is the specific characteristics of a certain neighbourhood, for example, which influence its density.

Matrices demonstrate these characteristics of the network visually. If members of each sector are plotted alongside each other, high density areas will appear along the diagonal showing the presence of high density sectors. If overlapping sectors are placed next to each other then the density resulting from these can clearly be seen. The diagrams 1, 2, 3 and 4 demonstrate the density of all the non-focal members of the extended network. The central conjugal pair and their links with network members are therefore not represented.

Having seen then a rather different picture of density from that painted by Bott, we can again ask its value and relevance. We have now seen the answer to the where and the why of the high density areas – they exist in certain sectors of the network – principally those of kinship, neighbourhood, work situation (both husband's and wife's) and voluntary associations – because it is there that ego has similar links with the members of his network.

The interest in density lies in the fact that high density networks may provide norm enforcing groups. From this data then, it would appear that it is one or maybe one or two of these cliques or clusters in each network which may form a norm enforcing group.

From the discussion on this research project, it is clear that there are various difficulties in attempting to compare the densities of large networks. Firstly the data suggested that the social networks of urban couples tend to be of low density and that the high density network would be a rare case. Thus the contrast of high and low density would not be applicable in most cases. Secondly, the difficulties involved in the calculation of density make comparisons of networks of varying sizes difficult. As pointed out, the greater the difference between the sizes of the networks, the more distorted the calculation of density becomes. Because of these dangers in treating density as a general category, I suggest that it would be more useful to look at the density of individual sectors.

This paper has attempted to outline some general characteristics of social networks of married couples in urban Britain. The main conclusions were firstly that in the area of research under discussion, both the middle class and the working class married couples had low density networks. Secondly, these networks had high density areas focussed on certain sectors such as kinship, neighbourhood, the work situation and voluntary associations.

Bott suggested that couples had close-, medium- or loose-knit networks and that there was a relationship between this connectedness and the conjugal role relationship. I am suggesting that the whole network density is not as significant as this, since most networks have low density, but that what is significant is which sectors provide the high density areas. It is therefore the high density sector in which ego interacts most or which is most important to ego, rather than the whole extended network, that will be responsible for norm enforcement.

Social network and conjugal role in urban Zambia: Towards a reformulation of the Bott hypothesis[1]

BRUCE KAPFERER

1. INTRODUCTION: THEORY, CONCEPTS AND ASSUMPTIONS

The success or failure of a new concept rests ultimately on its theoretical utility in the sense that through its application hypotheses can be developed and tested. Furthermore, the speed of the acceptance or rejection of a new concept is dependent on the extent to which it directs attention towards examining and explaining processes and behaviour which have hitherto not been successfully investigated through the application of other concepts currently at our disposal. Recently some anthropologists and sociologists have claimed that the concept of social network permits us to examine not only the processes of individual interactional behaviour but also problems connected with social change. These aspects of social process have not, it is claimed, been adequately handled in the terms of the mainstream sociological theoretical frameworks of normative consensus models and structural-functionalism.[2] Boissevain's article (1968) is representative of this point of view.

The high expectations which have been advanced concerning the utility of the concept 'social network' have largely not been realised even allowing for the recent introduction of the concept into sociological and anthropological usage. In fact it is of considerable significance that the most interesting application and development of the concept to date was in the work of Elizabeth Bott who used it in her study of familial relationships. Moreover, Bott was working in the tradition of the anthropological and sociological orientations of normative consensus and structural-functionalism. Much of the literature using network analysis following the intial impetus given to it by Bott has either without due consideration applied Bott-like hypotheses or used the concept as an excuse to present in great detail field-work material. Moreover few interesting hypotheses or statements containing useful sociological insight have emerged which were dependent on the application of a network analysis.

For example, many of the fascinating insights Epstein (1961) gives into African urban life in the course of tracing the social contacts of his research informant were not in fact derived from his use of a network analysis. Social network used by Epstein in this article was more a technique for the ordering of fairly complex field material. Gutkind's (1968) argument in a recent article on unemployed men in Lagos and Nairobi in no way depends on the concept of network but rather on the more timeworn notions of 'community' and 'association'.

I consider that two main factors account for the present failure of network analysis to realise the high expectations of it, particularly from the aspect of developing testable hypotheses. Firstly, too much emphasis has been placed on the task of classification and definition without due attention to the basic theoretical assumptions which should guide this work. I suspect that this has arisen because of the tendency to view social network analysis as a theory in itself rather than a concept or set of rules by which we seek 'to organise human perceptions' (Meehan, 1968: 35). A concept is one step beyond a description in the sense that it suggests a specified set of rules for organising human experience. A description, though it is an organisation of perceptions, specifies no clear and preferably unambiguous set of rules whereby these perceptions can be organised. A concept is not a natural entity. It provides a means by which we 'identify the entities we think about, classify entities into related sets, relate entities into time and space, define attributes, and perform all of the other functions implied in the term organization of experience' (*ibid*). The most important aspect of a concept is that the 'rules of organisation' contained in it are derived from a theory. In my terms a theory consists of basic assumptions together with a set of derived propositions which are interlinked and capable of being tested. It is the theory which explains the events we observe while concepts occupy the critical position of relating the theory to the events and the events to the theory. Concepts of themselves do not explain behaviour whereas a theory does. However, a theory is incapable of explaining behaviour except through the medium of a set of concepts.

The concept of network for my purposes refers to a set of points (individuals) defined in relation to an initial point of focus (ego) and linked by lines (relationships) either directly or indirectly to this initial point of focus. These are the minimal set of organisational rules for the concept of network. More rules or additional concepts or sub-concepts may be required for a network analysis. Thus when used in network analysis I view *density* as a sub-concept. It depends on the central concept of network and refers to the extent the points linked to the point of focus are linked by lines to each other.

Network and network density when applied to sociological data do not explain anything in themselves. An explanation is provided by a theory and unless theoretical assumptions and propositions underlying network analysis are specified more clearly and in the case of propositions, tested, then I contend that network analysis is not likely to advance very far.

The second point can be made briefly and is related to the first. There are a number of assumptions and propositions underlying Bott's analysis which still lie at the root of much concept formation and research. Although a number of sociologists have subjected some of Bott's hypotheses deriving from her network analysis to empirical test, the central assumptions and propositions have in the main remained unchallenged. It is conceivable that the very nature of these assumptions and propositions may impede the further development of network analysis.

A cursory examination of some of the assumptions contained in Bott's analysis should illustrate some of the points I have made and will serve to indicate the course I intend to take in this paper. Three general comments can be made in Bott's analysis which will guide my discussion prior to a consideration of some of the results obtained from my own fieldwork in Zambia using network analysis. First although in anthropology and sociology there is a wide acceptance of the basis on which Bott rests her assumptions there is some justification for being wary of accepting them unreservedly. Secondly, some of Bott's major assumptions appear to be arranged in a causal order and this causal ordering is open to question. Thirdly, although Bott is aware of other structural aspects of a network she has, I will argue, placed too much emphasis on the aspect of connectedness or density.[3] This emphasis may disguise other structural aspects of networks which might better explain the kinds of behaviour she observes.[4]

These three points in addition to some of the earlier ones I have made, particularly the important role which should be given to theory in network analysis, can be illustrated if network connectedness or density is examined. Bott states that the density or closure of a familial network affects the role relationships of the partners to a marriage (Bott, 1964: 60). Those with close-knit or densely interconnected networks have a segregated role relationship; those with loose-knit or open unconnected network a joint relationship. In her argument density or connectedness is only an explanation for the pattern she discovers when certain of her theoretical assumptions are considered. A weakness in Bott's exposition is that these are not clearly and systematically presented or argued but nevertheless they are there. It also supports an earlier statement in this paper that Bott's consideration of network connectedness or density has been guided by certain of these theoretical assumptions. Let me briefly list some of them. Firstly, one of her assumptions is that where a number of individuals interact with one another then there will be high degree of normative consensus. A second assumption follows on from this: Where there is a high degree of normative consensus there will be more pressures operating on the individuals inolved to conform to various standards of behaviour.

This leads to the third assumption and is related specifically to the role relationship between the spouses. Where the spouses belong to such a set of

Diagram 1a

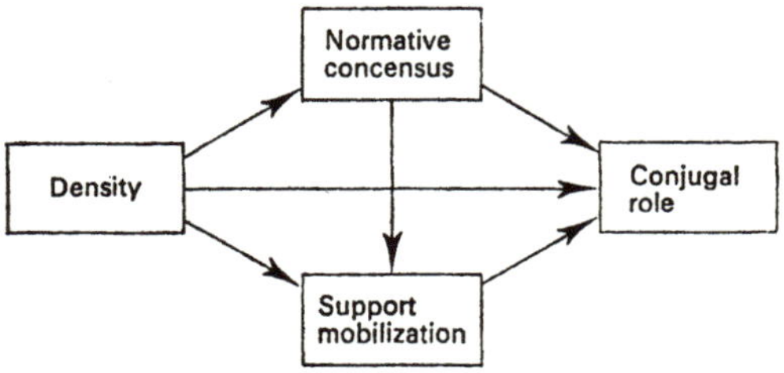

relationships then they are less dependent on each other for they can depend on the individuals in their set of relationships who are supposedly normatively constrained to help them. Each of these assumptions or propositions can be causally related to the others (see Diagram 1a). Thus if the network is closed, and there is a high degree of normative consensus, which in the terms of Bott's theoretical orientation logically follows from a network's closure, then the network has a high mobilising potential, which in turn weakens the spouses' dependency on each other and leads to a segregated role relationship.

I suggest that there are a number of theoretical difficulties contained in these assumptions, that is, provided my crude statement of these assumptions is accepted. Although I have referred to them as assumptions, the assumptions in Bott's analysis are in fact propositions capable of being tested. Indeed, both the proposition that there tends to be a normative consensus among those who regularly interact with one another and the proposition that those who interact in a connected set of relationships are likely to be subject to pressures leading them to fulfil their obligations to one another appear to have met with a considerable degree of validation. This is particularly so in the spheres of industrial, group dynamics and communication research. But take the first proposition again. We know from anthropological and sociological research that given certain conditions such as an unequal distribution of resources or differentiation in the allocation of status and power that a marked lack of consensus over norms can be produced in situations where the social relationships are relatively close-knit. Moreover, if we have a lack of normative consensus in a close-knit set of relationships, this close-knit set of relationships may facilitate the development of even greater differences over norms. For example, Robert Merton has argued with reference to the role-set that if a high connection in relationships between the role others in the role-set should develop, then the status occupant who occupies the focal point of the role-set may be subject to an increased conflict in expectations as to his role behaviour. Obviously if we are to accept that normative consensus is likely to arise in a close-knit set of relationships the condition under which this is likely to occur must be specified more clearly.

The other assumption I have mentioned also has some difficulties attached to it. Although it might generally be accepted that normative pressures demanding fulfilment of obligations will tend to be greater in a close-knit set of relationships this may not always be true and may vary according to the type of close-knit relationships we are considering.

Although many anthropologists and sociologists would suspect the applicability of research results in experimental laboratory conditions to 'real life' situations I think it would be in error to ignore them completely.[5] Experimental findings indicate that different structures lend themselves in varying degrees to the communication of information. Guetzkow, (Collins and Guetzkow, 1964: 63-65), for example, conducted an experiment on three groups of five individuals. Each of the five individuals had five out of six standard pieces of information and by communication with each other they were able to determine and to convey to the experimenter which piece they held in common. The experimenter was able to control the channels of communication used, and he was able to assess the speed by which the problem was solved for three types of communication net shown in Diagram 2. The importance of the result of this experiment for the argument presented here

Diagram 2

is that the task was most rapidly solved by the Wheel communication net, followed by the All-channel net and the Circle.[6] In the terms of a social network analysis these communication nets are representative of varying degrees of density. The all-channel net can be considered of highest density followed by the Circle and Wheel. Suppose, for the sake of the present argument, the problem had not been one of information identification but one of exerting normative pressure on the individuals in the nets or perhaps mobilising their support to joint action. It is conceivable that the most loose-knit structure represented by the Wheel, in accordance with the experimental findings briefly described, may allow for the exertion of more effective normative pressure or support mobilisation. The general point which should be stressed is that effective normative pressure or support mobilisation, for instance, may not be solely related to the number of communication paths or relationships linking a particular set of individuals. Guetzkow explains the more rapid problem-solving capability of the Wheel because of the key position of one individual for the processing and transmission of information. Thus it might be the particular structure of the network and the position of individuals within it which is related to certain processes of behaviour in addition to the density of the relationships linking a number of individuals together.[7]

So far I have indicated that at the very least we need to approach the assumptions in Bott's network analysis with some degree of caution. I will now examine briefly the implicit causal ordering she gives to these assumptions. A consideration of this causal ordering raises some important problems connected with theory. Bott implies that a close-knit set of relationships gives rise to normative consensus and that both these factors together promote a pressure towards a fulfilment of social obligations for the individuals involved in the dense set of relationships (see Diagram 1a). Because of this effect marriage partners can depend on the individuals in their networks and are thus less dependent on each other. Bott appears to argue that it is the

Diagram 1b

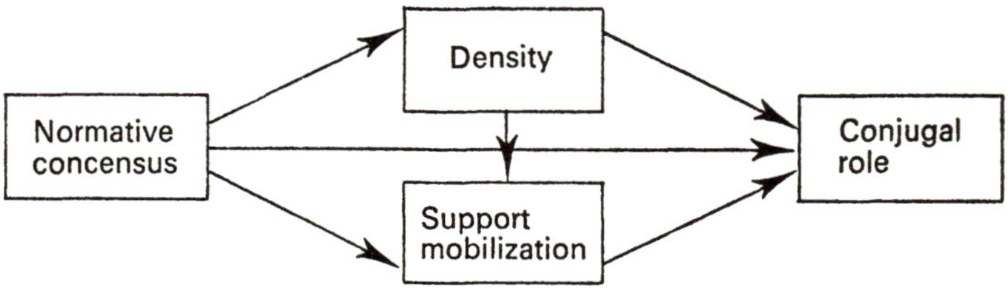

occurrence of an overlap in *activity situations* which gives rise to a close-knit set of relationships in the first place. (Bott 1964: 102-108). Thus individuals who come together in a number of different activity situations such as at work, in the neighbourhood and at the pub, are likely to belong to a dense set of relationships. It is possible that the causal sequence which Bott outlines could be readjusted, dependent on the particular theoretical orientation used. If a normative consensus orientation guides the analysis the causal sequence implicit in Bott could be re-ordered in the following way. That a number of individuals share a common set of beliefs and customs may facilitate the development of a dense set of relationships. Diagram 1b shows the re-ordering in the set of causal sequences which would result from this approach.[8]

Bott's implicit causal model begins by stressing the opportunities for and the pattern of interaction and then shifts to an emphasis on the importance of norms in explaining the type of behavioural pattern she observes. Although I do not wish to deny the importance of norms in the explanation of behaviour, it will be part of a later argument that Bott's analysis would have been more successful if she had focused more explicitly and consistently on the patterns of interaction and the various types of interactional structure represented in the networks.

I now come to the third and final point of this introductory discussion. Earlier I made the claim that Bott's over-emphasis on the factor of density in networks disguises other important structural aspects. For example, an important point in Bott's analysis deals with mobilisation. She argues that dense networks have a higher mobilising potential than loose-knit networks. Apropos my earlier argument in relation to experimental data I will argue that the mobilisation of support is dependent on such features as the form the interaction takes between individuals in a network (e.g. content and directional flow of this content) and the span of the network (i.e. the number of individuals included in the network). I will discuss these and possibly other structural aspects of networks which it may be important to consider in relation to some fieldwork examples.

The remainder of the argument in this paper will be presented with reference to an example drawn from my fieldwork. This example concerns an examination of the role behaviour of two married couples who live in the African mine housing area of the Kabwe (Broken Hill) lead and zinc mine in Zambia. Through this example I hope to demonstrate and expand on some of the points I have already discussed. Thus I will attempt to show the importance of considering other structural aspects of networks. But, perhaps, more central to the following description and analysis of fieldwork material will be the importance of theory for both the development of concepts in network analysis and providing the explanatory framework in terms of which social behaviour is to be understood. Throughout the ensuing analysis network and related concepts provide the means by which abstract theoretical principles can be used to explain concrete events.

The sociological theory which guides most of the subsequent analysis is that usually referred to as exchange theory. In its present form it is in an early stage of development and there are a number of separate though related exchange theories. One of the most recent and, I consider, the best development of exchange theory is that presented by Peter Blau in his book *Exchange and Power in Social Life.*[9] Blau's exchange theory is a synthesis of a number of theoretical trends in the social sciences. Thus it combines assumptions and propositions drawn from neo-classical economic theory, the stimulus-response school of behavioural psychology, game theory and symbolic interactionism. Basically the theory assumes rational choice but in Blau's view it is a rational choice[10] taken on the basis of limited information and restricted perception. In addition it is a theoretical perspective which assumes that individuals act in terms of their own self-interest. But this self-interest is not of a simple ego-centred variety. It is crucial towards an understanding of Blau's theoretical perspective that individuals are social beings and that they cannot satisfy their own self-interest without to some extent satisfying the self-interest of others. However, the central advance which Blau makes is his emphasis not only on the factors which influence the choices individuals make in the process of social action, which is where most of the recent exchange theories leave off, but also on the emergent properties of social action which feed back into the process influencing further choices and actions. These emergent properties are not found in individuals but arise from the process of individual interaction. Finally, Blau's theoretical orientation sees norms and values as being generated in the course of interaction and often influencing this interaction. But norms and values are not seen as the necessary precondition in terms of which interaction must take place. Criticising Gouldner's view of the norm of reciprocity as a starter for interaction Blau states, '... the fundamental starting mechanism of patterned social intercourse is found in the existential conditions of exchange, not in the norm of reciprocity. It is a necessary condition of exchange that individuals, in the interest of continuing to receive needed services, discharge their obligations for having received them in the past .... Not all social constraints are normative constraints, and those imposed by the nature of social exchange are not, at least, originally' (1964: 92-93).[11]

The limitations set by the length of this paper prevent me from expanding on other various important aspects of Blau's exchange theory. Other assumptions and propositions contained in exchange theory and which are essential to my argument should become evident as the analysis proceeds.

2. THE SOCIAL NETWORK AND THE CONJUGAL ROLE RELATIONSHIP: THE EXAMPLE OF TWO URBAN AFRICAN FAMILIES[12]

Bott's hypothesis which states that the degree of network connectedness or density is related to the form of conjugal role relationship between a husband and wife provides the basic problem in terms of which the following field data are analysed. A discussion of two cases drawn from my field data provides an opportunity to (a) refine and develop the methodology of network analysis (in a direction, however, often implicit in Bott's original work) and (b) to suggest a possible reformulation of the initial hypothesis.

The two couples whose networks form the basis of this analysis were selected for two reasons. Firstly, in broad terms their role relationships were not those which would be expected from Bott's hypothesis. Secondly, the overall social and cultural characteristics of the two couples were sufficiently alike to reduce the effect of variables other than the social network in explaining the role relationships. However, it should be emphasised here that it is not argued that other social and cultural variables are ruled out as will become clearer later in the discussion.

In her analysis Bott does not examine the social networks of the husbands and wives separately but treats the husband and wife as a single unit in terms of which the family network is defined. To emphasise my point that Bott's hypothesis does not fit my own I will, initially, attempt a replication of her mode of analysis to my material. Diagrams 3 and 4 show in matrix form the networks of Kabamba and his wife Steli and of Mweo and his wife Teresa.[13] The two family networks (i.e. the combined networks of husband and wife in each married pair) of the Kabamba family and the Mweo family are roughly comparable in size and density.[14] The size of the Kabamba family network is slightly smaller than that of the Mweo family, consisting of 36 individuals compared with 43. But the density of the Kabamba family network (34.2) is higher than the Mweo family network (20.2). The lower density of the Mweo family network can be partly explained by its greater size, though as should become clear later other factors may account for this difference in density between the two networks. Field material collected on other families in Kabwe (Broken Hill) would suggest that in general the Kabamba family network is relatively close-knit whereas the Mweo family network tends towards being loose-knit. But such a statement is dependent on more accurately processed material on other families in this town. In any case I suggest that the issue is of little concern to the argument as it stands at present. Whether the Kabamba family network is close-knit and the Mweo family network loose-knit, or both networks intermediate or both loose-knit, to use Bott's terminology, they do not predict the role relationship between the respective psuses.

I have assessed the respective role relationships between the spouses in the two families on the basis of interview information, daily diaries recording the activities of the two couples over three months and data gathered during periods of intermittent direct observation during eighteen months of fieldwork. Bott defines a role relationship 'as those aspects of a relationship that consist of reciprocal role expectations of each person concerning the other . . . In effect the term role-relationship means the reciprocal role expectations that were thought by husband and wife to be typical in their social circle' (Bott, 1964: 3). In fact throughout her analysis Bott continually shifts between the use of the term relationship in the sense just defined and the sense of a description of what the marital partners actually do. Because of this confusion in Bott's own analysis I have decided to assess the role relationships between the spouses both in terms of their expectations as collected through interviews and in terms of their actual behaviour as directly observed. In the two families I have taken for the purpose of this discussion, at least, there seems to be little difference between the expectations of the marital partners and their actual observed behaviour.

Mweo and his wife Teresa have what Bott might have regarded as a segregated role relationship. Both expect the other to participate in different and separate activities. Mweo controls the family budget and is expected to do so by his wife. Teresa does all the cooking, household cleaning and the maintenance of the vegetable gardens surrounding the house and on the outskirts of the township and is expected to do so by Mweo. Their activities are markedly segregated. Mweo normally eats separately from his wife. When Mweo's friends visit him at his home Teresa immediately retires into another room. Teresa and Mweo seldom join each other in other activities such as going together to watch a soccer game, attend a trade union meeting[15] or drink with each other at the Beer Hall. However, both of them do enjoy these activities separately. Despite a general agreement in their expectations of each other as to household activities, there is some divergence in their expectations as to extra-household activities. Thus Mweo feels strongly that Teresa should remain throughout the day around the house minding the children and engaging in various household tasks. He strongly disapproves, save for the occasional excursion to the gardens or the market place, of Teresa's moving round the township visiting friends and relations or going to the Beer Hall.

Kabamba's relationship with Steli is in marked contrast to that of Mweo and his wife. Bott might have regarded Kabamba's relationship with Steli as a complementary verging on a joint conjugal role relationship. Each expects of the other some assistance in household tasks. Steli does all the cooking but Kabamba chops the firewood and lights the brazier for her – a task which Mweo never does for Teresa even when the latter has been ill. Kabamba gives Steli eight pounds out of his wages at the beginning of every month so that she can organise the family budgeting and buy the necessary food. Mweo only lets money out of his hands in small amounts throughout the month and only on Teresa's demand. Steli and Kabamba eat together and participate jointly in many activities such as going together to the Beer Hall, soccer matches, trade union and political party meetings. Steli is regularly assisted by Kbamba in the maintenance of their gardens surrounding the house and on the outskirts of the township.

If, as I have suggested, the density of the family networks bears little relation to the conjugal role relationships between the spouses, it is possible that the role relationships could be explained by the different social backgrounds and position in the general urban environment of the individuals concerned. An explanation solely in these terms is not satisfactory as the following brief consideration of such factors should indicate.

Both Mweo and Teresa belong to matrilineal tribes (Kabende and Ushi respectively) which originate in the Luapala Province of Zambia, and which share the same language and many other cultural features. There is approximately eight years difference in their ages (Mweo is 36 and Teresa is 28) both being born and brought up in the rural area. Teresa has been in town for 14 years, most of her urban experience being in Kabwe, while Mweo has lived in town for a similar period (13 years), again mainly in Kabwe. Mweo and Teresa met each other through a mutual friend at the Beer Hall in 1959 and were married in the same year. They now have three children aged between 1 and 5 years who live with them. Teresa is a Roman Catholic though not an active church-goer; her husband, however is an important official in a small sectarian church known as the Sacred Heart of Jesus Church or *Bana Mutima.*[16] Both have little education, Mweo has four years schooling while Teresa has two. For most of my fieldwork Mweo had an unskilled job in the zinc refining department of the Kabwe lead and zinc mine, but towards the end of fieldwork received promotion to a skilled job in the same department.

By way of comparison Kabamba and Steli are of the same tribe, Lala, which is a matrilineal group originating in the Central Province not far from Kabwe. The Lala are culturally and linguistically very similar to the Kabende and Ushi to which Mweo and Teresa respectively belong. Like Mweo and Teresa there is only eight years separating the ages of Kabamba and Steli.

Kabamba is 35 and Steli 27. Both the latter were born in a rural area but Kabamba has spent 13 years in town, mostly in Kabwe, compared with Steli's 9 years in the same town. Unlike Mweo and Teresa, Kabamba and Steli were married at their rural home but they have been married for a similar length of time, 8 years as against Mweo's and Teresa's 6 years of marriage. They have four children living with them aged between 8 and 3 years. Kabamba until recently was an active member of the Jehovah's Witness sect but he has since left it. Steli is a nominal Roman Catholic. Both Kabamba and Steli went to school for two years. Like Mweo, Kabamba works in an unskilled occupation in the zinc processing department of the mine but unlike the former he was not promoted to more skilled work.

Mweo's family and Kabamba's family reside close to each other in the same neighbourhood area of the mine township.

Despite some differences in the backgrounds of the two sets of spouses under discussion there are marked similarities. It is only when the structure of their networks is examined in greater detail that more noticeable differences become apparent.

3. DESCRIPTION OF DIAGRAMMATIC REPRESENTATION OF NETWORKS

Before I proceed with this closer examination it is necessary to explain briefly what Diagrams 3 and 4 on page 98 represent. Recorded on the top left of the diagonal on each diagram are the individuals with whom the husband comes into direct interactional contact and the interactional relationships which link each of these individuals. The same is recorded for the wife on the bottom left of the diagonal below the centre horizontal axis. Grouped down the diagonal are the major clusters which form out of the interactional relationships present between each of the individuals who has a direct interactional relationship with either the husband or wife. The clusters are based on the social context which most often defines the interaction both in respect to the individuals concerned, with each other and to the particular husband and wife. Thus the work clique on Diagram 3 includes all those whose most frequent context for interaction is the work place. Of course there is some overlap, many interacting with each other in other contexts as well. Individuals 1 and 2 on Diagram 3 also interact regularly with Kabamba as neighbours. It is evident to the reader that the category kin is not a social context. Nevertheless a similar principle is involved for here it is kinship which most often defines the interaction, as it is work or neighbourhood in the other major categories selected. The entries in the cells away from the diagonal (they are not bounded by heavy lines as are the others) indicate the interactional relationships which cross-link the individuals who belong to separate contextual cliques. The entries enclosed in the rectangular box away from the diagonal at the bottom of the matrix represent the cross-links between the separate networks of husband and wife. Along the vertical and horizontal axes which quarter the matrix are numbers which indicate the type of direct relationships, if any, which each spouse has into the other's network and the type of direct relationships which they have to their own network members. On the left half of the horizontal axis are the wife's links to the members of her husband's network, and on the right half the husband's to the wife's network. The top half of the vertical axis records the direct interactional relationships of the husband with his network members and the bottom half, the wife's. An entry in a cell of 1 indicates an interactional relationship the content of which is normally sociational. An entry of 2 indicates an interactional relationship which at the very least has some instrumentality of content and which is usually multiplex or many-stranded. By sociational content I refer to interaction which is purely sociable or convivial. Conversation, the sharing of gossip and the enjoyment of drink together are, for example, instances of sociational content. But the lending of money, assistance at times of personal crisis, help at work are examples of instrumental content. As might be expected, interactional relationships in which instrumental content is represented also possess elements of sociational content, and thus can be regarded as many-stranded. The extent to which an interactional relationship tends to be sociational in content or instrumental in content and multiplex is taken to be an index of *investment*. The more sociational in content a relationship is, it is assumed, the lower the investment, whereas the more it tends to be an instrumentality of content and multiplexity the higher the investment. Obviously, in certain instances, I have had to be somewhat arbitrary in my judgment as to whether I should score a particular relationship as 1 or 2, but, in my view, the scores give a reasonably accurate picture. 2 indicates where the interactional relationship is between members of the same household (e.g. husband and wife). One final point should be stressed before I continue with the analysis. No claim is made to the effect that all the individuals with whom the two couples come into contact are recorded on the matrices. All that can be stated is that as far as possible I have included on the matrices those individuals who were observed to come into regular contact with the couples concerned. That is, they met each other at least three times in the week and spent a relatively long time in each other's company. I have not included those individuals with whom contact was fleeting. Such contacts which all the couples had are often categorized in the language of the town as 'Hello! Hello!' friends. It is possible that some of these are crucial to the analysis but in general I had no information which indicated this. But perhaps more important than this, though of a more technical nature, their inclusion on the matrices would have made the diagrams unwieldy and difficult to analyse for present purposes.

4. STRUCTURAL FEATURES OF NETWORKS

If I am to analyse the networks of the two couples I have selected then there must be some refinement in the method of analysis. I argued in the introductory part to this paper that an over-concentration on density or connectedness may obscure other important structural aspects of a network which may demand attention. Although Bott recognises the need to look at the separate networks of husband and wife, throughout most of her analysis she does not. She treats the family as a unit for the purpose of network analysis – in much the same way as I have done up till now. Mitchell has recently argued that the focal point of a network should be at the lowest level of abstraction as possible, that is the individual (Mitchell, 1969). It is essential for a network to be defined in terms of such a low level of abstraction if certain refinements are to be made. In the remainder of this analysis the family unit of husband and wife ceases to be the focal point of a network, the focal point of each social network being the individual spouse.

Once a social network is defined in relation to a specific ego a number of structural aspects can be identified. There are five, for example, relevant to this analysis and which assist in drawing attention to important differences in the four networks now being described. These are:

a) *Density*

This has already been defined but can be briefly stated again as the number of actual relationships between the individuals in ego's network, excluding ego's own direct relationships to these individuals, over the number of possible relationships.

b) *Span*

Here span refers to the number of individuals with whom ego has a relationship. No precise measure of span for the type of network discussed here can be derived. This could only be achieved if the number of individuals with whom ego could have a relationship is known.[17] In the context of this argument span is relative. An individual has a high or low span to his network relative to another individual's network.

c) *Zone*

Some anthropologists, taking their lead from Bott, have distinguished between the *intimate*, *effective* and *extended* areas of social networks. I define the *intimate* zone of a network as including those individuals whose direct relationships with ego tend to be instrumental in content and many-stranded. On Diagrams 3 and 4 all those whose relationships to ego are scored by a 2 are members of ego's intimate network. The *effective zone* of a network consists of those individuals who are linked to ego by an ineractional relationship which is more sociational in content. Those who in my view come into ego's effective network are scored by a 1 on the relevant diagram. The *extended* zone of a network refers to that set of individuals whom ego personally knows but with whom he has not established any regular interactional relationship. Thus Kabamba knows a number of the husbands of the women in his wife's network but seldom comes into any contact with them.[18]

d) *Degree of clustering*

This aspect of a network refers to the extent to which there is a tendency for the individuals in a network to be clustered into independent cliques.

e) *Degree of cross linkage*

Cross-linkage is closely related to the *Degree of Clustering*. Within an egocentric network the degree of cross-linkage refers to the number of interactional relationships out of the total possible linking the members of the separate clusters within a network. As in this analysis I consider it important to assess the degree to which separate egocentric networks overlap. I distinguish between two types of cross-linkage, a) Star and b) Zone. Star cross-linkage refers to the extent husband and wife are directly linked to the same individuals in each other's networks. Zone cross-linkage refers to the extent the individuals in the network of one spouse are linked to the individuals in the network of the other spouse.[19]

The four networks being analysed can be described in terms of these five aspects of network structure. Kabamba's network has a higher density (60.9) than that of Mweo (29.1) but the network densities of their wives is almost the same (Steli's network density is 48.6 while Teresa's is 49.1). In accordance with the dimension of span additional differences become apparent.

Diagram 3. Kabamba and Steli

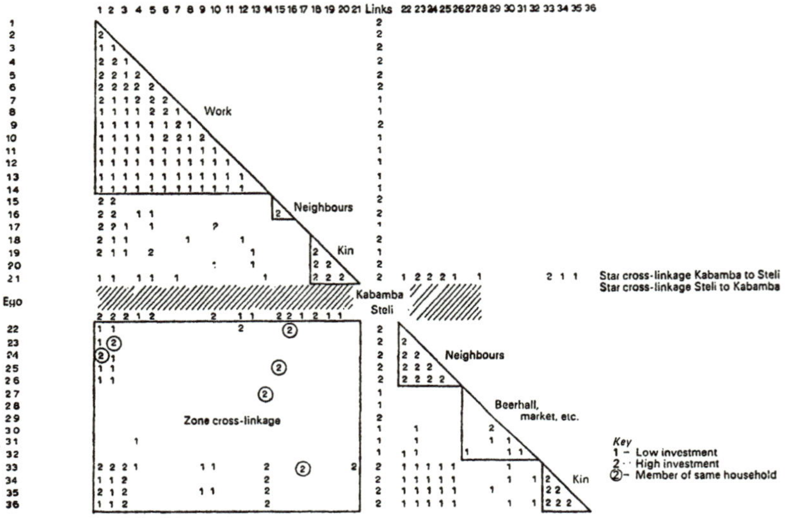

Diagram 4. Mweo and Teresa

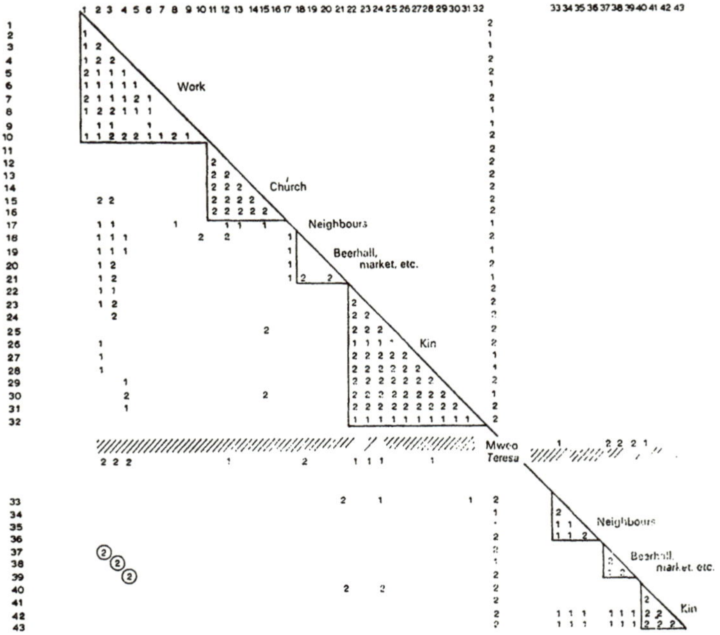

Thus Kabamba's network is more restricted in span than Mweo's, while Steli's network is more extended in span than Teresa's. However, it is noticeable on Diagrams 3 and 4 that both the women in comparison with the men have networks which are restricted in span. In general, men in town by virtue of the fact that they are engaged in wage employment, whereas women most often are not, are given a greater opportunity to enter into regularised interactional relationships. Evidence for this is clearly shown on the respective matrices. Differences between the four networks can also be discerned in terms of the degree of clustering. Each network is seen to be divided into relatively discrete clusters, based mainly on the social context in which the interaction most frequently occurs, with limited interconnection between them.[20] The networks of Steli, Teresa and Kabamba have the discreteness of the clustering in their networks considerably modified by a relatively high degree of interconnection, which, it should be noted, occurs predominantly in the intimate zones of their networks. Although there is some interconnection in Mweo's network, as in the others, mainly in the intimate zone, this is far less noticeable, which is in accord with the greater discreteness of the clusters in his network.

As a final point of description attention should be drawn to the degree of cross-linkage between the networks of the respective husbands and wives. The higher degree of cross-linkage between Kabamba's and Steli's networks when compared against Mweo's and Teresa's is evident. Kabamba and Steli (Star cross-linkage 12.0) have more direct interactional relationships which are frequently instrumental in content, to the same individuals, than do Mweo and Teresa (Star cross-linkage 2.3). Furthermore, in contrast to Mweo and Teresa (Zone cross-linkage 32.6), who have comparably few cross-links between their separate networks, there is a relatively large number of relationships linking the members of Kabamba's network to Steli's (Zone cross-linkage 63.8) and *vice versa*. This cross-linkage between Kabamba and Steli's networks occurs principally among the members of the intimate zones of their respective networks.

So far I have used such network structural aspects as density, span and cross-linkage to describe some of the important points of difference and similarity between the four networks. But how these are related into an explanatory framework with regard to the conjugal role relationships of the two couples is dependent on some basic theoretical assumptions and propositions. Social exchange 'refers to voluntary actions of individuals that are motivated by the return they are expected to bring and typically do in fact bring from others' (Blau, 1964: 9). But individuals exchange in conditions of risk and uncertainty. That is they cannot be certain that the gifts, services, support at times of crisis, social approval, etc. which they bestow on others will be returned, though not necessarily in kind, at some future date. Consequently they run the risk of a loss. For example, the time and energy alone which is expended in the support of another at a time of crisis would constitute a loss if this other did not show some indication that he would discharge the obligations he incurred at some later stage (p. 101). Individuals seek to minimise the uncertainties and risks they encounter in social life by generating trust in their relationships. Trust in a relationship is likely to increase the more the partners to it discharge their obligations to each other. Commensurate with this increase in trust is the added preparedness of the partners to the relationship to advance various benefits on credit. The effect of this increase in trust is to stabilise the relationships over time (p. 99).[21] The exchange processes which generate trust in relationships also constitute investments. Investment refers to the amount of time and other resources individuals are prepared to expend in a social relationship in order to induce various social rewards. To the extent that the time, effort and expenditure of other resources in a relationship means that other investment opportunities elsewhere are foregone, such an investment constitutes a commitment. In varying degrees all investments in social relationships imply commitment (*ibid*).

A central point which emerges from this discussion is that an individual stands to incur considerable social cost if another should withdraw from a relationship to which an individual has committed himself. For as I have suggested above, if for nothing else, he has incurred a cost by failing to invest time and resources in a more socially rewarding relationship. If this is accepted then it can be assumed that individuals will direct considerable energy towards protecting and safeguarding their investments. Data I collected among African workers involved in a dispute at work in the Kabwe mine plant seems to provide some validation of this. The workers concerned appeared to direct their behaviour in a way which resulted in the least cost to their investments (Kapferer, 1969).

A problem then arises concerning the circumstances under which an individual may choose to withdraw from certain of his commitments such as refusing either to perform various services or to advance credit with respect to specific benefits. I have already stated that a failure to honour trust and discharge past obligations may result in the discontinuance of a relationship. But the argument has so far been presented mainly through reference to a single relationship. It is a basic assumption that the processes in one relationship (its maintenance or discontinuance) may be dependent on processes in other relationships.

Two related propositions derived from this discussion can now be stated. Firstly, failure of one individual to discharge the obligations in his relationship to another will put the former's other relationships at risk, provided all the individuals concerned participate in a common set of relationships. Clearly if an individual betrays trust in one relationship the other individuals commonly connected to the two parties involved may expect an increased risk of failing to receive a return on their investment in their relationships with the individual concerned. A corollary to this proposition is that the effect of a betrayal of trust in one relationship will be reduced if this relationship is relatively isolated from the others.

This first proposition and its corollary can be illustrated with reference to the network data collected for the two married couples. The analytical concepts of density, degree of clustering and cross-linkage can be used to ascertain the extent to which the individuals in a particular ego's network belong to a common set of relationships. As described earlier the individuals contained in the networks of Kabamba, Steli and Teresa have a relatively high density to their networks and have a tendency to cluster reduced by considerable cross-linkage. Thus in accordance with the first proposition I would predict that a failure to discharge their obligations in one of their relationships would reduce the amount of trust accorded them in many of their other relationships. Mweo, however, has a relatively low density network, with inadequate cross-linkage to offset the tendency towards clustering. In comparison with the other networks a failure to discharge obligations would have proportionately less effect on his other relationships.

The second proposition has some connection with the first. Individuals in order to safeguard their investments in as many relationships as possible will concentrate their time and effort in protecting key relationships. A key relationship is defined as that in which ego has considerable investment and in which the partner to the relationship is at the centre of a number of relationships to other individuals to whom ego is directly linked.

These two propositions need further testing possibly both in normal anthropological field situations and experimental settings. However, subject to this, if they can be accepted for present purposes they suggest a way in which Bott's original hypothesis could be reformulated and the conjugal role relationships between Kabamba and Steli and Mweo and Teresa explained. My restatement of the original Bott hypothesis depends on a distinction being made between 1) the internal structure of the respective networks of the spouses, and 2) the nature of the relation between the networks of the spouses. I emphasise, however, that the factors I outline for predicting the role relationship between marriage partners will only be significant when both those relating to the internal structure of the networks and the relation between the networks are examined.

In accordance with the above distinction I propose that joint or complementary role relationships are most likely to be found where a) there is a high density in the separate networks of husband and wife; b) there is a low degree of clusterability within each of the separate networks; c) there is a high degree of star cross-linkage between networks, in the sense that both husband and wife are directly linked by social relationships to the same individuals; and d) there is a high degree of zone cross-linkage between the networks, in the sense that the individuals located in the various zones of the respective networks are directly linked by social relationships to each other. Factors a) and b) refer to the internal structure of the separate networks of the husband and wife; factors c) and d) refer to the relations between the respective networks. In the consideration of factors c) and d) in particular, it is stressed that the likelihood of joint or complementary conjugal role relationships being present is increased where the cross-linkage involves relationships which constitute high investments, where the cross-linkage occurs predominantly between the intimate zones of the husband and wife networks and where these relationships involve individuals who are *key* to the set of relationships of the respective spouses. Conversely, segregation in the conjugal role relationship, for example, is most likely to occur where the separate networks of the husbands and wives have a high degree of clusterability and consist of few or no relationships cross-linking the separate networks.

In the presentation of this reformulation of the original Bott hypothesis I emphasise that all the factors I have outlined must be considered. However, I do not maintain that each of the factors be given equal weight. In Bott's hypothesis the prime factor is density and moreover a density based on the set of relationships of the husband and wife taken together. In my reformulation the factor of density, but, it is stressed, a density based on the relationships of husband and wife taken separately, is reduced in importance. Indeed density may be subordinate to other factors such as the extent to which the husband and wife are directly linked to the same individuals in their respective networks and the degree of cross-linkage between the individuals in the separate networks. Early in this paper I stated that Bott's concentration on density and her specific application of it could disguise other structural features of the set of relationships of husband and wife which may bear a greater relation to their type of conjugal role relationship. In my terms an association of a high network density with a joint or complementary role relationship would only occur where there is a tendency for the other factors outlined above also to be present.

Further clarification of the above reformulated hypothesis can be made with reference to the role relationships of the two couples and the structure of their relationships as viewed from the perspective of a network analysis. Kabamba and Steli have a complimentary verging on joint role relationship. Relative to Mweo and Teresa, for example, Kabamba and Steli have a high degree of cross-linkage between their networks. Their networks overlap in the sense that many of the same individuals are members of both their networks and in the sense that individuals to whom each spouse is directly linked have direct relationships to individuals in the other spouse's network. Some of the closest friends of Kabamba are husbands of women who have established a very close relationship with Steli. The general point is that the degree of overlap and cross-linkage between Kabamba's and Steli's networks is indicative of the fact that they participate in a common set of relationships. This is all the more significant as the set of relationships in which they commonly participate by and large constitutes the *intimate* zones of their respective networks. To a large extent each spouse is dependent on the other for the maintenance of trust in his social relationships and the continuance of these relationships. Moreover, because of the high density and low degree of segmentation in their separate networks they have an increased dependence on each other. It is the aspect of joint responsibility for their set of social relationships which explains the character of Kabamba and Steli's role relationships. Kabamba's close relationship with 1 on Diagram 3 is strengthened by Steli's close relationship with 24 who is the wife of 1. Alternatively, the failure by Steli to discharge an obligation to 24 could weaken Kabamba's relationship with 1. By participating jointly in activities outside the household at the beer hall, political and trade union meetings and at soccer matches, for example, each increasingly commits the other to many of the relationships held in common. It is these outside activity situations which provide frequent opportunity for individuals who belong to a common set of relationships to meet and interact.

In addition shared activities within the household increase the degree of commitment in the husband and wife transactional relationships which will have a feedback effect of their set of relationships. The house often provides the context in which an individual will interact with others in his network. In such a situation one spouse may be expected to participate in action which contributes to the relationship between the other spouse and the visitor. When friends come to visit Kabamba his wife is expected to provide food and assist in the customary serving of beer. Steli's failure or refusal to fulfil Kabamba's expectations of her could not only embarrass him in the eyes of his friends but also have a damaging effect on his relationship with the individual(s) concerned. A husband, for instance, by investing in his relationship with his wife may ensure her performance of such duties as a means by which she can discharge her obligations to him. It is important to note that the pressure towards the investment by a husband and wife in each other through a joint role relationship may be increased as a result of the high density, high cross-linkage and consequent low clustering in their separate networks. The ramifications of a single failure to meet an obligation would be more widespread and possibly damaging because of the many channels for the communication of information in such a structure. Obviously, the pressure towards a joint role relationship will increase in direct proportion to the number of opportunities available for the marriage partners to affect each other's relationships.

Mweo and Teresa provide a contrast to Kabamba and Steli. In terms of the preceding discussion their segregated role behaviour is consistent with the tendency for Mweo and Teresa to be involved in separate sets of social relationships. Because of the relative low degree of cross-linkage between their networks the extent to which they are dependent on each other to safeguard the investments in their relationships is reduced.

It may well be that my reformulation of the Bott hypothesis is unsatisfactory. However, apart from my own limited information presented here, it appears to receive some support not only in the evidence Bott herself reports but also in recent research which has indicated that Bott's hypothesis is not of general validity. Although Bott's material it too meagre to test my revised hypothesis on her data, her description of the Newbolt family network appears to lend some support. The Newbolts have a segregated role relationship and although there is some indication that their separate networks are close-knit, the only points of cross-linkage appear to be between their kin (Bott, 1964: 65-73, 118-58). Turner's research on the networks in the Pennines suggests that the revised hypothesis as presented here may be applicable to his material. In relation to his study of 115 married couples, and in an attempt to account for the failure of his material to support Bott's hypothesis, Turner at one stage in his argument states, 'The social network of a married couple can be conceptually split into the social networks of the husband and wife respectively. Inspection of the . . . data suggests that the degree to which the two fail to overlap is an important variable. Amongst the thirty-two couples in which the husband's friends constituted a close-knit *male* network, and the wife's friends a close-knit *female* network, there was a high degree of conjugal role segregation . . . When the networks of husband and wife show considerable overlap, no distinctive pattern of conjugal role relationship is associated with them' (Turner, 1967: 125).

In the analysis of the networks of the two married couples I have examined various theoretical principles which might account for the association of a certain type of network structure with specific forms of conjugal role relationship. As far as possible I have attempted to avoid explanation of behaviour in terms of the particular local circumstances in which the behaviour was observed. Clearly a more complete explanation of the behaviour I have observed would have to take into greater account such aspects as the history of the social relationships of the spouses, their values and attitudes and various other personal social characteristics. For example, the fact that Mweo and Teresa met and married in town may be crucial for explaining the different way their networks relate to each other as compared with the way Kabamba's network relates to Steli's. Mweo and Teresa had both been in town for a period of years prior to their meeting, thus they had already established separate sets of relationships which they then brought to their marriage. Kabamba and Steli, however, married in a rural area and when they came to Kabwe neither had many social relationships. Therefore, in the urban setting they built up their relationships together. An initial isolation from others in the urban situation probably forced a greater dependence on one another in the first place and this was maintained by the way this led them gradually to establish their urban set of social relationships.

Factors such as these are of undoubtful significance but direct attention away from a major point which I wish to stress. I have been principally concerned with why particular structures identified through network analysis are associated with certain types of conjugal role behaviour. I have tried to do this through the application of abstract theoretical principles for it is considered that only through such a procedure will generalizations of wide validity be established while avoiding the danger of explaining social behaviour by reference to the unique aspects of the situation concerned. Once the utility of certain abstract theoretical principles is established for the understanding and explanation of behaviour, the way particular situational factors such as social mobility, the presence of a stable population, different customs and values mediate and restrict the operation of various principles can be determined. In this paper I have examined the networks of individuals who have a similar cultural background and experience and looked for variations in their marital relationships through a network analysis based on exchange theoretical assumptions. It is possible that my reformulation of Bott's hypothesis may not hold in other cultural contexts but it has not been so much my intention to make statements of wide empirical validity as it has been to suggest the utility of combining a particular analytical technique with an exchange theoretical approach in the study of family behaviour.

5. CONCLUSION

Network analysis does not constitute a theoretical scheme in itself and if sociological explanations are to be achieved through network analysis then such analysis must be conducted in conjunction with a theory. While I accept that many theoretical assumptions do underly many analyses using the concept of network these have been implicit rather than explicit. It is central to the argument I have presented that unless these assumptions are made more explicit then not only will the concept of network be reduced in its effectiveness for sociological explanation but also the development of network analysis as a methodological technique will be restricted.

In the early part of this paper I showed that some of the assumptions implicit in Bott's pioneering analysis when made more explicit were open to challenge of a theoretical nature. Firstly, I argued that the bases of some of her assumptions were open to challenge if we searched elsewhere in anthropological and sociological theory. Thus Bott suggests that a higher degree of normative consensus is likely to emerge in close-knit rather than loose-knit relationships. But the degree of normative consensus and the degree of connectedness or density of social relationships need not be related in this way. Indeed a process of a set of individuals becoming increasingly more interconnected through developing social relationships may create the conditions whereby a marked lack of consensus over norms could be made more apparent. Secondly, I stated that Bott does not consistently argue her case. I noted that in her analysis there is a shift from a stress on the patterns of interaction to the emphasis on the importance of norms in explaining forms of conjugal behaviour.

It was argued that the implicit causal ordering given by Bott to her assumptions was dependent on whether the theoretical perspective was interactionist or normative. I attempted to show that the causal ordering given by Bott to her assumptions and derivative propositions could be altered according to the specific theoretical perspective taken. The third argument presented against Bott was directed towards what I consider to be her over-emphasis on the factor of connectedness or density of a network. The criticism of this emphasis was in part derived from the earlier discussion of other problems contained in Bott's analysis. The main point made was that her emphasis on connectedness or density disguised other structural features of networks which it could be important to isolate in order to achieve a more satisfactory explanation.

To demonstrate the points made in the introductory analysis I examined the conjugal role relationships of two African couples. Their conjugal role behaviour could not be predicted if a similar mode of network analysis to Bott's was adopted. This led me to take a different analytical approach, largely directed from the perspective of Blau's theory of social exchange. Particular concepts fundamental to this theoretical framework such as those of *investment*, *commitment* and *trust* directed me to isolate specific structural features of social networks.

An assumption basic to the analysis is that individuals attempt to protect those relationships in which they have heavily invested. Furthermore, it is assumed that investments and relationships of trust are exposed to greater risk if they are part of a highly interconnected set of relationships. An important principle by which individuals evaluate their participation in relationships with others is on the basis of their observation of these others performance in other relationships. I propose that the ability to observe the performance of others and the effect of this on an individual's set of social relationships is likely to be greater where the relationships are closely interconnected. The factors of density and clusterability were aimed at determining the extent of the interconnection between the individuals included in the respective networks discussed. At the same time an effort was made to assess the degree of investment represented in the interactional relationships included within each of the networks.

Following an examination of the internal structure of the four networks selected for analysis I then considered the nature of the relation between each of the two couple's networks. Where individuals belong to a common set of social relationships failure to discharge their obligations in one relationship may endanger their ability to sustain their transactions in other relationships. In particular I considered that the husband-wife relationship could be critical for the maintenance of the separate spouse's social relationships. However, I hypothesised that such a relationship would only be critical in this way when the spouses have highly interconnected networks (high density and low clusterability) and there is a high degree of cross-linkage (star and zone) between their separate networks. In addition, in a reformulation of the original Bott hypothesis, I proposed that joint conjugal role relationships are most likely to develop in conditions where the separate networks are highly interconnected and represent a high degree of cross-linkage. Given these conditions the ability of a husband and wife to affect the social relationships of the partner would be considerably increased. I suggested that in order to safeguard these relationships a spouse (in the cases shown more particularly husbands, as they had more to lose indicated by the larger span of their networks) may increase the number of activities in the household he performs jointly with his partner in a bid to increase or maintain commitment to the relationship. Through increased commitment the husband may win the support of his wife in safeguarding his set of social relationships.

Clearly the above assumptions and propositions must be subjected to closer examination both empirically and on a more abstract theoretical level. Other problems require more detailed consideration. For example, what are the factors rooted in specific cultural and social contexts which lead to the development of certain types of network structure? However, the general contribution I hope to have made in this paper is that if network is to be developed as an analytical tool and as a method whereby sociological explanation is achieved then it must be used in conjunction with a theory and not viewed as a theory in itself.

NOTES

1. This paper owes much to regular and rewarding discussion with Professor J. C. Mitchell who is primarily responsible for introducing me to the uses and abuses of network analysis. I also wish to thank Professor Jeremy Boissevain, Dr. Kingsley Garbett, W. Sharrock and Don Handelman. An earlier version of this paper was given to the May Staff Seminar held in the Department of Anthropology and Sociology, University of Manchester.

2. It is important to make a distinction between these two approaches as stressed, for example, in a recent paper by Harsanyi (1969). Although in much sociological writing they are part and parcel of the one theoretical orientation, recent theoretical discussion has increasingly evidenced a discarding of normative consensus orientations though clinging, I contend, to structural-functionalism. This is significant because recent methodological advances from within the perspective of structural-functionalism have emphasised greater focus on individual action within general social processes. The development by Gluckman of 'situational analysis' and the extension of this methodological approach by Mitchell, Turner and van Velzen is an example.

3. As Mitchell points out (1969: 17-18) a distinction should be made between density and connectedness. I have used them interchangeably to avoid confusion with Bott.

4. It should be pointed out that I am only concerned with the more sociological assumptions contained in Bott. As Barbara Harrell-Bond (1969) has demonstrated in a recent article Bott also makes reference to a number of assumptions and variables of a psychological nature.

5. I accept that in many, perhaps most, cases experimental findings may not be applicable to real-life situations. Nevertheless, I have some sympathy with Homans who states 'the laws of human behaviour are not repealed when a man leaves the field and enters the laboratory. Naturally the same laws working in different circumstances lead to different results, but not, once the circumstances are taken into account, to inconsistent results. Experimental studies and field studies each can do some things the other cannot do.' (1961: 16).

6. I have only referred to Guetzkow's experiment to illustrate a general point. It should be noted that repeats of this experiment have not always yielded the same result. There is some indication that the differences in the results are dependent on the complexity of the problem being solved. Also there are some criticisms which can be made against the method employed by the experimenters concerned. See Burgess (1969: 128-130).

7. The experiment reported by Guetzkow would seem to suggest that an over-abundance of communication paths might create 'informational confusion' and reduce the efficiency of communication.

8. Mitchell makes some very similar observations (1969: 2-4).

9. A number of recent writers have made what I view as a considerable error by appearing to regard Blau's theory as a simple extension of the earlier statement by Homans (1961). See Ekeh (1969: 42) and Kunkel and Garrick (1969: 136). To a great extent, as Blau (1964: 6) himself implies, it is a corrective to the kind of psychological reductionism characteristic of Homan's analysis.

10. It is of some importance to emphasise that Blau is not confined to the use of the concept of rationality in its strict and limited economic sense. He recognizes that there are many different kinds of rationality – a point incidentally also emphasised by Homans (1961: 79-82) and Garfinkel (1967: 262-283) – and to a considerable extent his theoretical orientation is designed to establish the conditions under which individuals will organize their rationality in one way rather than another. For example, Blau sets out the conditions under which individuals will pursue their own self-interest rather than the joint interests of the group to which they belong.

11. A more comprehensive treatment of exchange theory in relation to data is to be found in Kapferer (1971).

12. The fieldwork for this example was carried out over a period of eighteen months between March 1964 and March 1966 while I was a recipient of a Commonwealth Scholarship. General background information on Kabwe can be found in an account of a social survey conducted by me in 1964. This survey, however, only deals with the municipal African population. A classic study of both the mining and commercial African housing areas was carried out by Wilson (1940) and is still of great relevance today.

13. The information presented here is based primarily on my own participant observation. However, where necessary, I have also used various interview techniques.

14. Measures for density were calculated in accordance with a formula originally developed by Kephart (1950). $\left(Na/N\frac{(N\text{-}1)\ 100}{2}\right)$ Na = number of actual links.

15. Women in the mine areas often take an active interest in trade union activities and frequently attend trade union meetings.

16. This is a breakaway sect from the Roman Catholic Church.

17. In another paper (see Kapferer, 1969) I use a slightly different definition of *span*. There it is defined as the number of relationships out of the total number of actual relationships in the situation which ego captured through his direct links to individuals. I was able to develop this definition of *span* because of the bounded nature of the situation in which I was working.

18. The basis in terms of which I define *intimate* and *effective* zones of a network is essentially similar in principle to that recently stated by Boissevain (1968:

546-547). However, unlike Boissevain, I consider that it is more useful to restrict the term *extended* zone to those whom ego knows but with whom he has not developed a regularized interactional relationship. To include in the *extended* zone those whom ego does not personally know but could get to know, as Boissevain suggests, puts almost limitless bounds on the network and may promote methodological problems. Barnes (1969) also uses the term zone but does not distinguish between its various areas; in Barnes' usage I am concerned principally with the first-order zone but have recognized distinctions within it.

19. Precise measures for cross-linkage can be used. Thus star cross-linkage is calculated by dividing the relationships each spouse has in common with the other by the total number of relationships of each spouse combined. Zone cross-linkage is measured simply by excluding each of the spouse's relationships to their network members and the relationships between the network members *within* each separate network and expressing the number of actual cross-links between the two networks as a percentage of the possible number of cross-links. I use these measures later in the paper.

20. It is conceivable that the composition of these clusters down the diagonals would undergo some re-ordering if, for instance, the method proposed by Beum and Brundage (1950) for clustering had been used.

21. Reference should be made to all of Chapter 4 in Blau (1964).

Two types of partial networks in Burundi

A. TROUWBORST

Burundi has two institutions forming the basis of two types of networks, which I shall analyse as ego-centred partial networks in this paper.[1] By partial network I understand that part of an individual's network which consists of social relations with a like content.[2] On the basis of a comparative analysis of both types of networks, I hope to arrive at a few conclusions about the structural importance of the differences between them. I will make this comparison in terms of, amongst others, the quality, the aims and the resources involved, the criteria of directedness, density and multiplexity, the numbers and composition of the people involved, and the ways in which both networks can be interpreted from the viewpoint of the concept of action-sets. An important difference between both networks will appear to be that one of them in distinction to the other is based on a local group of relatives and neighbours, constituting what might be called the local core of the network. I finally will enter into some of the problems of the analysis of the interconnections that may exist between different partial networks.

1. TWO TYPES OF NETWORKS

The two types of networks I have referred to are based respectively on the exchange of beer and food and on gifts consisting of cows and land. The first type is best characterized by the term *ukuterera*, which means 'to give food and beer during ceremonial occasions'.[3] Each married male in Burundi finds himself enmeshed in the centre of a network of people from whom he receives beer or to whom he gives beer at ceremonial or festive occasions. These people are known as *abatererezi* by the Rundi, a term I shall render as 'beer friends'. In principle this network embraces all one's relatives, neighbours and friends.

The second type of network is founded on the institution of clientship, known in the Rundi language as *ubugabire*.[4]

The gift of a cow establishes a lasting relationship between the person who gives the cow, the patron, and the person who receives the gift, the client. The patron is supposed to extend his help and protection to his client, while the latter is expected to lend assistance in the form of labour, beer, food and a part of the cow's offspring to the former.

In principle, there is no end to the agreement. A man can be both patron and client at the same time, although understandably in relation to different persons. Likewise a man can also have various patrons and clients. Thus also in respect of clientship relations one could state that they form a network with one individual at the centre.

2. SOME DIFFERENCES

The differences between both types of networks can be considered as follows.

a) The first difference concerns the *quality* and the *directedness* of the relations between people in both institutions. Within the context of the beer exchange the partners are considered as equals, even if they have an unequal status in other contexts. This may be so because like objects are exchanged: beer against beer. No extra privileges or prestige accrue to any of the partners on the basis of having given goods of a superior quality. In clientship agreements, the man who has given the cow is superior to the receiver because he has given something of higher value. Mostly the client is poorer than his patron and his request for a cow as a gift is indicative of his subordinate position. The concern about immediate material and other benefits is very noticeable in client relationships. The patron is enabled to enhance his prestige and extend his influence, while the client comes into the possession of a highly prized article which otherwise might not have been possible. Despite this element of reciprocity in the relations between patrons and clients, a certain amount of competition, mutual distrust and opposed interests is always discernible in them. In the case of beer exchanges, the chief aim is said to be the establishment and confirmation of pleasant social relations that take place in a sphere of relaxation. While it is true that the possession of many beer friends signifies wealth and influence, yet at the same time individual exchanges of beer cannot be used directly to further interests to the detriment of other people. One could thus state of clientship relations that they have a vertical character in contrast to beer relations which are horizontally oriented. Client relationships form a bridge between the higher and lower strata in the society. They also have an asymmetrical character in that goods of a different nature are exchanged by each of the partners, in contrast to relations where beer is given in exchange for beer. The diagram of a star as used by Barnes (1969: 113) gives insufficient expression to these features.

b) Another difference between both networks is that while all Rundi are to some extent party to exchanges of beer, only a portion of the population contract clientship agreements. The *number* of people taken up in a network of beer friends is considerably higher than those in a clientship network. Since the Rundi regard all relatives living in the neighbourhood and all neighbours as beer friends, it is understandable that the network of beer friends reveals a high degree of *density*, at least in so far as the core of the network is concerned. In contrast, clientship networks have a low density.

c) When a man organizes a feast, it could happen that he sees most or all of his beer friends. This seldom happens in the case of clients and patrons, who very often live far away from one another and whose relationships reveal a private character. More than beer friendships, client relationships contain many elements of secrecy and intrigue.

d) From the viewpoint of *multiplexity* one can make one or two remarks about the differences between both networks. It appears to me in agreement with all existing formulae and definitions elsewhere when one states that multiplex relations are those relations consisting of different strands.

It is not clear however what these different strands are. Kapferer (1969: 213) defines multiplexity in terms of exchange contents (N.B. something else than Mitchell's 'content' or 'normative content') of a relation where each exchange represents a separate strand.

Mitchell also links the concept of multiplexity with content. Although he does not formulate it in this way, his view implies that he wants to use the concept for situations in which different partial networks overlap (Mitchell: 1969). That might entail as Mitchell seems to suggest that a partial network, by definition, has a uniplex character. I am of the opinion that, if one wants to do justice to the many elements encased in a social relationship, it would be more prudent not to label beforehand the relationship within a partial network single-stranded. Naturally this means that whenever the relationships of partial networks overlap, one always meets a situation of multiplexity.

From the above it will be apparent that beer networks are always enmeshed in multiplex situations. This is already evident from the fact that the exchange of beer is a confirmation and expression of another relationship. In the core of the network, the neighbourhood, there are even signs of a high degree of multiplexity. The members of the neighbourhood meet each other under a variety of circumstances, e.g. economic, political, juridical, religious and social. On the other hand, relations with beer friends outside the neighbourhood are far less multiplex. This does not detract from the fact that relationships with close relatives living far from each other may also consist of a great many different strands. If relatives are not too far away from one another they will continue to meet each other in very many situations.

The clientship network is much less multiplex. There is often no question of partial networks overlapping. While it may certainly happen that relatives and neighbours are involved in clientship relations, clientship agreements are often entered into for the sake of creating wholly new relations. In the old Burundi it frequently happened that a man went out to offer himself as a client elsewhere.

One wonders whether the patron-client relationship can be denoted as single-stranded. I am inclined to answer negatively. Such a relationship covers a variety of situations and has therefore a very complicated nature. The patron is at the same time protector, the judicial adviser, the beer friend, the 'father' and formerly the military chief of his client.

e) To a certain extent one could say of both the beer and the clientship networks that they form bounded networks, A person is a patron, or a beer friend, or nothing at all. Yet it is not so simple as *prima facie* evidence seems to suggest. At present especially, a clientship relation can gradually wither away, making it difficult to state with all certainty that a person is still a client. The same applies to beer exchanges. Here, too, relationships can fall by the wayside or come to an end, and in such cases it is not easy to determine when this actually took place.

3. THE LOCAL CORE OF A NETWORK

Many of the differences as discussed in the previous section are related to the fact that the network based on beer exchanges in contrast to the clientship networks is invariably based on a local group of relatives, very often constituted as a local lineage, and neighbours. I shall call this group the local core of the network. Although such a group does not have a very formal character, it is very important in the daily life of the Rundi. To a certain extent one might even say that a core constitutes a point of anchorage for a network together with other cores of the same structure.[5] The neighbourhood as a whole assists in the organization of big feasts given by its members. It may also happen that the members of neighbourhood as a group may receive one single drinking tube (by means of which the beer is drunk from the jars) when they visit a feast elsewhere.

To the individual this means that he is restricted in his freedom of choosing beer friends since in principle all members in his local group automatically belong to his network. Be this as it may, and here the use of seeing neighbourhoods as points in a network ends, a man is at the same time free to choose beer friends outside the neighbourhood. In actual fact, the number of beer friends one person has can differ considerably from that of another. A rich man would generally have more beer friends than a poor man.

To clarify my use of the term core, I may note that its meaning does not tally fully with what Boissevain calls an intimate personal network (Boissevain, 1968: 547). According to this author this zone of a network is composed of 'those persons, whether relatives or friends, with whom ego is on closest terms'. One will note that this definition leaves undecided the question of the way of recruitment of the persons who belong to the intimate network. On the other hand, when I speak of the core of a beer network I mean to include all persons who *automatically* belong to it on the ground of their being relatives or friends who live nearby. Another characteristic which the definition of the intimate network leaves undecided is the fact that the core, as I see it, is composed of people whose own networks largely overlap each other precisely as regards their cores. Furthermore, in my definition of a core those relatives not living in or near the locality of ego do not belong to the core of ego, whereas they belong to the intimate personal network according to Boissevain's views.

There is no local core in the clientship network. It is also futile to speak of an intimate personal network in respect of these networks. As already noted, the clientship network has a very small degree of density. It could happen that the various patrons of a person do not know each other, let alone the clients. Very often the various clients and patrons of one person are unacquainted with each other.

4. HORIZONTAL VERSUS VERTICAL RELATIONSHIPS IN NETWORKS

Another set of differences between the two networks is related to the vertical, asymmetrical character of clientship relations and the horizontal symmetrical character of relationships in beer exchanges. As was said before partners in the context of *ukuterera* are considered to be equals and to exchange goods and services of equal value. I think that this explains why in beer networks only the first-order star of relations (see Barnes, 1969: 58) is of importance. An agreement within the framework of *ukuterera* is never concluded with the view to further possible wider relations and is not used as an instrument of social mobility.

Clientship relations on the other hand derive their importance in part from the fact that they may form a bridge with third parties. I purposely express myself somewhat cautiously in the last sentence. It is certainly not true to suppose that all clientship agreements provide the means for laying indirect contacts or are concluded with the view to such contacts.

The chief aim of many clientship agreements is the direct contact between those involved and the ensuing material benefits. Moreover in traditional Burundi it was always possible for the simple man to have direct access to high dignitaries. Well known was the sight of subjects sitting in front of the court of the kings and the chiefs awaiting their turn to put in their pleas for certain favours.

This does not detract from the fact that clientship networks are concerned with very rare and special resources and may be beneficial in making contacts which could lead to others later on. This was important to both patron and client alike. The factions which in the past played a substantial role in the political struggle for power in Burundi were to a large extent dependent on the support they received through the clientship agreements at all levels (on the national level these factions were the Abatare and the Abezi, i.e. members of the two branches of the royal family and their supporters).

From the above the importance of the vertical element, the bridge between the higher and lower strata in society, is again clearly borne out in clientship networks. In the beer exchange network, however, the accent is more on the horizontal relations between equals concerning domestic matters. The relations accompanying beer exchange do not lend themselves so easily to manipulation. A gift of beer as an individual incident is not so weighty that one is entitled to, for example, political support. At the most one could say that a person with many beer friends has more influence, possesses more information and has greater access to places than someone who has relatively few beer friends. But this is due to the latter's position in society, rather than to his place in the beer network.

5. NETWORKS AND ACTION-SETS

It is useful also to trace the differences between the clientship networks and beer exchange networks from the point of view of action-sets. One might say of both networks that they form bases for the recruitment of action-sets.

Elsewhere I have indicated that political factions are recruited to a large extent from clientship networks. For any political purpose a man may appeal to his clients who in their turn may call for the help of their clients. The set of people mobilised in this way for the attainment of a particular political goal may be said to constitute an action-set (Barnes, 1969: 70).

Beer networks are also important for the creation of action-sets albeit action-sets of a significantly different character than those mentioned above. It appears to me that one could speak of an action-set whenever a person calls upon his beer friends to help him with the organization of a feast. One should bear in mind that a person seldom asks all his beer friends at any one time for help. Small scale feasts require but a few, mostly members from the local core of the network.

The aim of these action-sets which time and again differ in composition and size, is mostly to confirm symbolically a social event: birth, marriage, burial, the initiation of an arbiter (Trouwborst, 1970); but it could also be an economic activity, e.g. the building of a house in which case beer friends also will render assistance. Here it appears again that only first-order contacts are relevant. Any second-order contact who would contribute beer for the occasion would per definition become a beer friend and form part of the first-order star of the organiser of the feast. An action-set of this kind might be called following Mayer (1966: 109) a simple action-set in contrast to the complex action-set based on clientship relations.

As Barnes (1969/70) has remarked '. . . the concept of "action-set" needs careful handling', which means that further distinctions will have to be understood 'if it is to have precise meaning and yet be widely applicable'. One such a distinction can be made with regard to what Mayer calls 'bases for linkage' of the action-sets (1966: 108). Applying his terminology to the action-sets based on beer exchange and clientship relations, one might say that the 'inward base' in the first case consists of the collection of beer, in the second case of the mobilisation of political support. One might state further that the outward bases in both cases are of various natures: kinship, neighbourhood, services rendered, etc. This however would be a simplification of a very complicated matter.

In the case of beer exchange the purpose of an action-set (its 'inward base') corresponds to the content of the partial network. This implies that *all* the participants in an action-set are recruited from one single partial network, which owed its existence to the purpose the action-set serves. The situation is different in the case of an action-set based on clientship relationships. The inward base may clearly be political support, but not all supporters of a political leader are necessarily his clients. A chief for instance was aided by his subjects most of whom were not his personal clients. Clientship agreements were only one of the means used to obtain political support. This brings me to state a further general remark on the difference between both partial networks. Beer exchange networks served one main purpose: the exchange of beer to confirm and symbolise existing relationships and social events (*cf*. Trouwborst, 1970); the clientship networks did not confirm existing relationships but were based on agreements often with the purpose of establishing entirely new relationships. Moreover, clientship agreements did not serve one single purpose as expressed by the gift of a cow. This shows, by the way, that the concept of 'content' in connection with partial networks is not so clear as might seem. My material suggests that one could distinguish at least between

a) partial networks that link other existing partial networks, as is the case with the beer exchange network.
b) partial networks that may make use of links of existing partial networks but do not have as their function to connect these.

6. THE INTERCONNECTIONS BETWEEN PARTIAL NETWORKS

As Mitchell has noted (1969: 22) the problem of the 'identification of distinct contents in a network link' is not an easy one and depends partly 'upon the analytic purpose of the observer'. This implies that partial networks being defined in terms of contents are also not easy to identify. Partial networks are abstractions from real life where the different strands of a relationship are intertwined in an intricate way to such an extent that one often has to be in doubt whether a certain element of behaviour belongs to one or another institution on which a partial network is based. The isolation of institutions like those of the beer exchanges and clientship agreements as has been done in this paper is therefore necessarily somewhat arbitrary and artificial. As it is the very purpose of the network approach to examine the coincidence of different normative frameworks in a single relationship (*cf*. Mitchell, 1969: 49), the analysis of distinct partial networks cannot be complete without an effort to indicate the extent to which these networks can be isolated and the ways in which they are interconnected. These problems can be demonstrated very well by the examples of partial networks discussed in this paper.

To start with the beer exchanges, it is difficult to separate these from food exchanges on the one hand and from other kinds of beer exchanges on the other hand.[6] Food exchanges are mainly the domain of women but they take place at the same occasions as the beer exchanges. When a man contributes beer, his wive may give food at the same time. The main difference between both kinds of exchanges is that only close relatives and friends exchange food, whereas beer is exchanged in a much wider circle of relatives and friends. Furthermore, beer exchanges are not restricted to the context of *ukuterera*. At every social event and in every social relationship of some importance beer is exchanged, very often with the same people who are one's beer friends. Of special interest here is the fact that a patron and his client may be or become each other's beer friends but also exchange beer at other than ceremonial occasions. It is a common duty for a client to present beer to his patron. In fact, one of the reasons for a patron to enter into a clientship relation may be the gifts of beer from his client which enhance the splendour of his feasts. A still more complicated situation exists in those situations where, as may happen, a patron and a client are relatives or neighbours of each other.

I may finally add that people render each other all kinds of services, for instance in the construction of huts or the herding of cattle, which may be conceived of as being given on the basis of kinship, neighbourliness, patronage, as well as of beer friendship.

We meet the same kind of problems in the case of the clientship network. First of all, though it may be argued that the institution of clientship is confined to gifts of cattle, many other kinds of gifts and exchanges in the form of goats, hoes, lands and other valuable goods and even functions and titles may be designated by the same terms or are governed by the same rules (*cf.* Trouwborst, 1961 and 1962). Besides there exist quite a number of other sorts of cattle agreements which are not always so easy to distinguish from clientship agreements, not even to the Rundi themselves. I have assisted at court sessions during which this issue arose, the judges having to decide whether a certain agreement concerned a gift under a clientship agreement or not. I must also point out that marriage agreements especially those involving gifts of cows had much in common with clientship agreements (*cf.* Trouwborst, 1961). Besides, it is not uncommon for a patron to pay for the expenses – the bridewealth included – that his client has to incur for a marriage.

Up to this point the problems of the coincidence of the strands of a relationship sound rather familiar; they have also been amply discussed from the point of view of role theory (see for instance Nadel, 1962: 63 *ff*). As the role concept however 'remains essentially dyadic' (Mitchell, 1969: 46) it is necessary to move on and see what the implications of multi-strandedness are for the relations between *sets* of people connected in networks, in other words, how different partial networks affect each other.

Having in mind the difficulties involved in the identification of individual partial networks, I think that a starting point then could be not so much the distinct partial networks themselves as the total strategy an individual adopts when he tries to secure his place in social life. He disposes of a certain amount of time and resources that he can within certain limits use in different combinations of alternative ways. These alternative ways may be offered to him by the institutions associated with different partial networks. This point of view implies that a useful way to look at the interconnection of partial networks is to see these as different ways of investing the sum of resources a man disposes of. In terms of the networks discussed this means that we examine the different uses of beer and other resources as afforded by the institutions of *ukuterera* and *ubugabire*. Many decisions are involved, too many to be enumerated, but all are interconnected, as the investment of a resource in one partial network implies the decision to forego the possibility of investing it in another partial network. Such a decision has to be made also in reference to earlier decisions and eventually to decisions to be made later. Furthermore, a man has to decide whether a given resource will be invested in an already existing relationship (for instance when a man gives a cow to a relative) or in a completely new relationship, as in the case of a gift to a stranger.

Though I did not investigate this decision making process in the field, my data of existing networks may give some insights. As I hope to demonstrate there is some kind of balance in the investment of resources as between beer networks and cattle clientship networks as well as between the different categories of people belonging to one network.

In the first place there is a connection between the number of persons both kinds of networks are composed of: a man who has many beer friends also has many clients and/or patrons. This connection can be explained by the fact that a man who possesses much cattle will be able to attract many clients who till his fields and give him beer, which allows him to look for many beer friends. Inversely, though this is more difficult, a man who disposes of much beer will be able to obtain cattle which opens the way to enter into other new relationships.

The reader will understand that in actual fact the interrelations are much more complicated, if only because there are many other different ways to invest beer and cattle. Generally speaking, however, one can say that a rich man has many beer friends as well as patrons and clients.[7] It is a matter for further investigation to establish to what extent this generalisation holds true.

As regards the composition of the people belonging to an individual's network, I have to point out that there is a host of possibilities of combinations of different categories. I will enumerate a few of the most important:

beer friend – neighbour
beer friend – relative
beer friend – relative – neighbour
beer friend – neighbour – patron
beer friend – relative – patron
beer friend – client – political subject

It is now my supposition (which I did not test in the field) that a man, intentionally or not, keeps a balance of different categories of people with whom he is connected in different ways. I found, for instance, that a man generally distributes his cattle over different categories of persons: relatives and non-relatives, influential as well as unimportant people, people far away and from nearby. This is quite understandable for the following reasons. Especially in the case of the cattle clientship agreements, the terms under which these were concluded differed considerably. They were not very onerous for relatives, they did not include menial labour for rich influential clients and so on. That could mean that it would be disadvantageous for a man to give the cattle only to relatives or to people who gave him nothing but political help. He might be in need also of the labour of unimportant people, who had to work under strict rules. A client living in a distant place might be useful to a patron in those cases where the latter needed summer pastures in a low-lying district.

As for clients, these also have to take into consideration several factors. A man who lives on land granted to him by a chief who has also given him some cows is tied to his patron in a way that he cannot be tied to other patrons. In the same way, a commoner who has to work for cows granted to him is limited in the number of patrons to whom he can render his services.

There seem to be less strict limitations in the choice of partners in the beer exchanges. This may be because the investment in any single relationship has much less value than in a clientship agreement. Moreover, it is a characteristic of the clientship agreements that they showed considerable variations as regards the terms under which they were concluded. In beer exchanges there was much less latitude in this respect. However, as I have already pointed out, it can be said in a general way that the number of people in a network depends on the wealth of the man in the centre: a poor man has very few beer friends, a rich man has many.

Full support for my views would require a detailed analysis of a considerable number of different networks which space does not allow here, but I hope to have made clear the fruitfulness of the approach suggested. I think that it is a further advantage of the approach that it is perfectly suitable to be applied in situations of social change, I have described the institutions of beer exchange and cattle clientship in very general terms which have remained valid, despite the many changes these institutions have undergone since the time of the German occupation at the end of the last century.

The changes involved not only implied an alteration in the formal rules of the institutions, but also the introduction of many new forms of transactions giving rise to new partial networks. I do not think that a complete enumeration of all these innovations would make much sense. It seems more rewarding to show how in recent times changes in the overall system of the distribution of resources in Burundi affected the structure and composition of networks. To give an example: old informants told me that formerly beer exchanges took place on a much more limited scale than today. I suggest that this phenomenon may be explained as follows. Owing to the fact that the king, the chief and the subchiefs, who nowadays (in 1958) have fixed salaries and are reduced in number, no longer depend on taxes in kind, large quantities of beer have become available for exchanges in the domestic sphere. This is all the more important because the decline of the traditional political institutions implied a sharp reduction also in the number of functions defining to a large extent the status of people. Nowadays the alternative way of defining the status of people (see Trouwborst, 1970) by the exchanges of beer during ceremonials has become more elaborated. As regards cattle clientship agreements, these are no longer very important on high political levels, where they have been replaced by bureaucratic relations. However, these new bureaucratic relations have apparently adopted many features of the old clientship system (*cf.* Lemarchand, 1970: 373). Changes then in networks can be traced to the reallocation of resources.

7. CONCLUSIONS

As I did not use the concept of network in the field, it has been impossible for me to substantiate all my generalisations and hypotheses. I hope, however, to have demonstrated the usefulness of some analytical distinctions and of a way to establish connections between different partial networks. My main conclusion is that the analysis of distinct partial networks is of limited value and interest if the interconnections between them are not shown. I have become convinced on the other hand that an undifferentiated treatment of personal networks without doing justice to the differences of the partial networks it is composed of does not bring us very far.

As an exercise, the analysis of my data from the point of view of networks, though they were collected in an institutional and dyadic framework, has drawn my attention to hitherto unsuspected connections between social relationships.

NOTES

1. The material for this article was collected during my visit to Burundi in 1958 which was made possible by a subsidy given to me by the Netherlands Organization for Pure Scientific Research (Z.W.O.). While consultant to Unesco in 1968, I was given a further opportunity to conduct a supplementary research. I would like to stress that I did not work with the concept of network in the field.

2. For the meaning of the concept 'content' see Mitchell (1969: 20): 'The meanings which the persons in the network attribute to their relationships.'

3. For the sake of brevity I shall only refer to beergifts. For more detailed information on beer exchanges in Burundi, cf. Trouwborst (1970).

4. Concerning the clientship agreements, I shall restrict myself to those gifts which involve cows.

5. For the term 'point of anchorage' see Mitchell (1969: 13).

6. The reader will remember that I discussed in this paper only beer exchanges in the context of ceremonial occasions.

7. There may be exceptions. I have known a rich man who did not have many beer friends. The reason, according to my informants, was that the man, being accused of murder by sorcery, was distrusted and disliked by his neighbours.

An exploration of two first-order zones

JEREMY BOISSEVAIN

1. INTRODUCTION

This paper has grown out of my concern with the relation between social behaviour and environment. Specifically it is an exploration of the relationship between ego-centered, primary or first-order network zones and the environment in which they are encapsulated, on the one hand, and behaviour and personality, on the other. By primary or first-order zone I mean all the persons to which a given person (ego) can trace a social relationship, and has personally met, and the interconnection between these persons (*cf.* Barnes, 1969: 59). (Throughout the rest of this discussion I also refer to primary zones as personal networks or simply networks). Most of the studies to date that have used the analytical concept of network have focused either exclusively on theory, on partial (and therefore limited) networks of workmates, kinsmen, neighbours, or on action sets recruited to solve particular problems (*cf.* Mitchell, 1969). These studies have indicated not only that the partial networks possess certain structural characteristics, but also that these structural characteristics influence behaviour. By and large these studies have not followed up Bott's pioneering effort to relate variations in network structure to environment (1957, Chap. 4). Yet it would seem that the only way meaningful hypotheses regarding the relation between network structure and behaviour can be made is if variations in structure are also related to variations in environment. If it can be shown how environment influences network structure, and how this structure influences behaviour, then it should be possible to trace systematically the connection between environment and social behaviour.

By environment I mean the physical, biological, cultural and social factors which impinge upon and mould behaviour. These environmental factors, plus personality, which in part is genetically determined, influence the composition and structure of a person's primary network zone. This in a sense forms a unique, personal environment in which each person is encapsulated, and of which he forms the centre. While a person's personal network is influenced by and recruited partly out of his total environment, it is conceptually distinct from it. Throughout this discussion I shall thus be concerned with four variables: environment, network (primary zone), behaviour and personality.

As I could not find published data on complete primary zones, I was obliged to attempt to gather this data myself.[1] I began with two informants, on a pilot study basis, planning to branch out and test findings more systematically on a wider sample. Collecting this data proved to be very difficult and very time consuming, as did its analysis. Hence I have data on only two first-order zones. Rather than wait for years until I have the time and funds to gather data on a broader basis, I have chosen to present some of it so that its relevance may be judged and some of the problems associated with it pondered upon before further attempts to collect similar material are made.[2]

The following study is really little more than a first attempt to map and compare two first-order zones and relate the features of these to the observed differences in the environment and aspects of the behavior and personality of the two informants. I try to answer the obvious questions about the personal networks of Cecil and Pietru, my two informants: What is their cultural and social background? What are the objective structural and interactional characteristics of their respective networks? What are their subjective characteristics? Is there a relation between objective and subjective characteristics? What is the influence of the environment on the structure and content of the networks? Finally, what is the relation between network structure and personality?

2. ENVIRONMENT: THE SOCIAL CULTURAL BACKGROUND

Malta

The Maltese archipelago covers 122 square miles. Malta, the largest and southernmost islands, is 17 miles long and 9 miles wide and covers an area of 95 square miles. There are just over 314,000 people on the islands, making the Maltese archipelago, with a population density of just under 2,600 per square mile, one of the most thickly populated countries in the world. Slightly over half of the population lives in the urban area which centres on Valletta and the Grand Harbour; the rest live in clearly separated villages and towns which range in size from 900 to 17,000 inhabitants. No village, however, is more than an hour's bus ride from Valletta, and Gozo is only 30 minutes by ferry from its larger sister island.

The Maltese see the family as the most important institution in their lives. The ideal household is composed of an elementary family living together in a separate house. Maltese have large families and reckon kin relationships equally through males and females. Each person is at the centre of a wide network of blood relatives and relatives by marriage. Though the kinship structure is bilateral, there is a noticeable bias in favour of the mother's/wife's relatives. Maltese families are mother-centred and the contacts with relatives beyond the nuclear family are by and large articulated through women. Kinship obligations extend out to first cousins for men but as far as second cousins for women.

Malta may be said to have a service economy. Until recently the Maltese lived off the income they derived from providing services as civil servants, clerks, soldiers, skilled fitters, semi- and unskilled labourers to the British colonial and military establishments which governed the islands for years. Although Malta has been independent since 1964, she still largely lives off the services she provides, now to the ever-increasing number of tourists visiting the islands in search of sun. The tourist boom and the expanding light manufacturing industry have created what amounts to a situation of full employment in the islands, and there is actually a shortage of labour in the construction and catering sections of the economy. Less than 10 per cent of the islands' inhabitants are full-time agriculturists. Consequently most Maltese travel from their place of residence to their workplace, which is normally located somewhere in the expanding conurbation centred on Valletta.

As may be expected, there are considerable differences between town and country, and, especially, between the residents of the smart, large seaside suburb of Sliema and the inhabitants of small relatively isolated villages such as Farrug. The differences are not only a matter of dialect, but also of behaviour and interests. The Sliema residents regard the religious feasts, processions, and fireworks, so characteristic of village life, with abhorrence. The people in villages have a good deal of informal contact in streets and shops, but rarely visit with non-kinsmen in their homes. Sliema inhabitants, on the other hand, arrange formal visits and frequent large receptions to which non-kinsmen are invited. Villagers deliver personally the invitations to attend their more modest baptismal, betrothal and wedding ceremonies; Sliema people post printed invitations even to kinsmen who live close by. The inhabitants of Sliema consciously as well as unconsciously imitate the behaviour and many of the attitudes of the English, who for so long ruled Malta's fortunes. Even the Maltese spoken in Sliema affects an English accent which contrasts sharply with the broad vowels and gutturals of the countryman. The latter, in turn, patterns his behaviour on the rural elite, the doctors, lawyers, and wealthy merchants, residing in the villages and rural towns.

Most Maltese are fervently practising Roman Catholics and there is traditionally a strong attachment to the Church. This has had an important influence on the moral code. It is especially noticeable in the field of kinship where the large families and strong bonds between members of the elementary family are supported by exhortations and sanctions of the Church. Nevertheless certain ideological divisions exist. These may be characterised as pro- and anti-establishment, for the Church and against the Church. In recent years this cleavage became centred on political parties: respectively the pro-Church Nationalist Party which formed the government from Independence until 1971, and the relatively anti-clerical socialist Malta Labour Party. Much the same cleavage has also been incorporated for a long time at the village level in rival moieties which compete over the festivities in honour of their respective patron saints. The establishment moiety is supported by the Church and includes most of the leading figures of the village and celebrates the official patron of the village. The anti-establishment moiety, composed chiefly of the less influential members of the parish, celebrates a local rival saint, often in contravention to the Church's regulations and interests. These ideological cleavages, at the national level or at the village level, at times actively engage most Maltese villagers. Such ideological commitments influence in no small way the relations between persons. Hence its interest.

Pietru

Pietru lives in Hal-Farrug, a village of just over 1200. Three out of four of the inhabitants work outside the village, chiefly as skilled and unskilled industrial labourers. In Farrug there are no striking differences in the standard of living, as there are in larger villages and towns; there is nonetheless a difference in the circle of acquaintances of a teacher and an unskilled labourer. The village is divided into two ritual moieties which celebrate the feast of Saint Martin, the parish's patron saint, and St. Rocco, his local rival. These moieties in turn focus on rival band clubs. There is also a football club in the village and a number of Catholic lay organisations. The Labour Party is very strong in Hal-Farrug and is centred on the football club. Cleavage for and against Saint Martin and for and against the Labour Party cuts through the village at all levels. It flares into intense rivalry at the time of the annual feasts of the two saints and at election time every five years.

Pietru was born in 1933; thus at the time of the first study he was about 35 years old. He had been married for three years and had one son. Pietru's father, a fairly well-off peasant cultivator, died when Pietru was four years old. His mother, though from the neighbouring village of Qrendi, remained in Hal-Farrug and supported her three daughters and son by continuing to farm the fields she had been left. It was a difficult life and she soon sent one of her daughters to live with her unmarried sisters in Qrendi, where she lives to this day. At the beginning of the war she became ill and, unable to get much help from her husband's brother and sister, both married and by village standards very well off, she and the children moved in with her own family in Qrendi. They returned to Hal-Farrug and her bombed out house after the war.

Through a priest, a friend of the family, Pietru's mother was able to get him a place in a private school run by English monks. She paid what she could towards the cost of schooling from the meagre farming proceeds.

Pietru looks upon this period as one of hard work, for every day after school he had to work long hours in the fields helping his mother and sisters. In 1953, now 18, he tried the highly competitive entrance examination for the Teachers' Training College. Apparently he was unsuccessful. I say 'apparently' because the Rector of his school telephoned the Department of Education in his presence and heard that he had passed the examination and was to be admitted. But when the list of successful candidates was published, Pietru's name was not included. Both he and the Rector assumed that he had been scratched from the list in favour of some better connected candidate from Sliema. The Rector then helped him get a part-time teaching job at an institution run by the same religious order. Two years later he was admitted to the training college. He successfully completed the two year course of studies in 1957.

He was fortunate and immediately found a job in the Government Elementary School in Farrug. He continued to help his mother in the fields after school. He soon became engaged to a fellow teacher, a Valletta girl, who began to occupy his spare time away from teaching and farming. After a difficult year and a half, during which his fiancée persuaded him to abandon his attempts to win a Government scholarship to study agricultural science abroad, but was unsuccessful in getting him to adopt the customs and dress of the city, he broke the engagement.

Freed from his unhappy courtship, Pietru plunged into the social life of his village. He became an extremely active fund raiser for his band club, standard bearer for the confraternity of the Blessed Sacrament, and the leader of the Catholic Action section for unmarried men. He also became the confidant of the new parish priest, supplying him with information about parish affairs and helping him with his numerous fund raising activities. During the political upheaval of 1961 and 1962, he became one of the Church's most vocal advocates in Farrug. At this time he also joined a national anti-Labour Party Church sponsored study group. His militancy and forceful manner alienated many of his former friends and acquaintances in this predominantly Labour village. I first met Pietru in 1960-61 when we lived in the village. He was then in his most active period as a village organizer.

In 1962, Pietru, now 28, became engaged again, this time to a Sliema girl, who had taught for many years in the village school. Having been rather badly bruised during this three year intensive participation in village politics, he withdrew almost entirely from the village arena. He devoted his free time for the next three years to getting to know his fiancée and to building a house.

Pietru has been married since 1965. He is still as active as ever, but he has little time to devote to village politics. Though he helps the new parish priest in his fund-raising activities and takes part in the village processions as the standard bearer of the confraternity of the Blessed Sacrament, he no longer holds office in the band club and shows little interest in its activities. He still continues to help his mother in the fields and grows his own cash crops of potatoes, onions and tomatoes, which he works in the early morning before school begins and in the late afternoon. He also does most of the bookkeeping for the ever-expanding household bazaar run in his mother's house by an unmarried sister. During the last two years he has also been studying intensively to pass his 'A' level examinations in Economics, Social Geography and Maltese so that he may be qualified to teach in secondary schools and, possibly, to begin studying for a University degree. Four afternoons a week during the school year he and his wife run private classes in their home to prepare children from the village for the competitive Government secondary school entrance examination. And last but not least, he devotes a considerable amount of time to his growing family and helps his wife, who has none of her own relations in the village, with many of the household tasks. He also does much of the shopping for the family. In Bott's terms, Pietru and his wife have a complementary – bordering on joint – conjugal role relation.

Owing to his retirement from the front line of the village politics, his continuing studies, and especially, his excellent results in getting his school and fee-paying charges through the secondary school examinations, he has regained some of the goodwill of the village which he lost during the heat of the 1962 political battle. His standing in the villages is complemented enormously by the quiet dignity of his Sliema born wife who, as remarked, taught in the village for many years before her marriage.

Cecil

Cecil, in contrast to Pietru, is Sliema born, thought he now lives in his wife's town of Birkirkara. Sliema is a rapidly expanding residential suburb of some 21,000 persons. It is divided into three parishes and merges imperceptibly with other large suburban parishes to form the northern half of the conurbation centering on Valetta. For the past 40 years it has been regarded as the best residential area of the island and many from the upwardly mobile government, military and business classes have moved there. It is predominantly a white-collar residential area. Many English and other foreign residents live here. Nevertheless there is a sizeable population of industrial labourers. It is thus an area characterised by sharp class divisions.

Birkirkara, where Cecil now lives, is a town of some 17,000. Though it gives the impression of being part of the urban sprawl, it is in fact a separate town and is one of the island's oldest parishes, with intense parochial patriotism. It is a stratified community composed of old established noble and professional families, shopkeepers, artisans and businessmen, industrial labourers both skilled and unskilled, and a fairly sizeable population of farmers. It has two active band clubs and active political party clubs. It is the home base of the former Nationalist Prime Minister and his brother, the former Minister of Education. It has also a strongly organized labour faction which manages to return at least one member of parliament every election.

Cecil was born in 1940. He is the sixth child of a grocer and has eight siblings. He recalls that he was very strictly brought up and was not allowed to play with the children on the street. He thus had little contact with his neighbours. Some of this parental vigilance was temporarily relaxed when his family moved in summer to a seaside house outside the town. From the ages of 6 to 12 he was sent to a strict private elementary school. His father was very ambitious for his sons and obliged them to spend many hours closeted in their rooms studying. This regime was successful. One brother is a Franciscan priest, another a doctor and the third, who is also the only one besides Tony to have married, is a University lecturer in England. His two older sisters have married; his two younger sisters are still unmarried.

At 12 he was sent to an exclusive, Jesuit-run secondary day-school. At 17 he became a Jesuit novice and lived in the school as a boarder, and later transferred to the order's seminary. At 21 he was sent, at his own request, to the order's mission station in India. There he learned and taught Hindi as well as other subjects at primary and secondary level. He also obtained a degree in philosophy at the Jesuit university in Poona. From there he went to one of the order's secondary schools where he ended up as vice rector. In all Cecil spent five years in India before deciding to withdraw from the Jesuit order. At 26 he returned to Malta, where, after a period of searching, he found a teaching position in the government secondary school system.

When he came back to Malta he lived first with his family in Sliema and that summer moved to the family's new seaside house at St. Paul's Bay. There he met the neighbours and discovered that one of them was an ex-Jesuit of about his own age. He soon became engaged to the latter's sister. The next summer, in August 1967, he married and moved to his wife's town of Birkirkara. He told me many times that he finds living in Birkirkara strange in comparison to life in Sliema. By his standards Birkirkara has much of a village about it. In the beginning he found it annoying that people from the neighbourhood into which he and his wife had moved seemed to know a great deal about him. They also seemed to spend so much time talking!

In many respects Cecil is unsatisfied still. The considerable responsibility he held while a Jesuit, his education and the general background of his family leave him with unfulfilled aspirations. For the past few years he has been trying to get a scholarship to study social psychology in England. He seems gradually to be establishing roots in his place of residence, a process helped by the birth of two children. He sees considerably more of his wife's relatives than his own.

Comparative summary

A number of factors relevant to the study of the structure of the networks of Pietru and Cecil emerge from this very brief description of their social environment. To begin with, there is the difference between town and country. Pietru's network is anchored in the rural area whereas that of Cecil in the urban. These differences are of considerable significance.

Cecil comes from an environment in which class differences are pronounced, whereas Pietru comes from what may be called a one-class milieu in which there are differences in styles of life which do not seem to be permanent.

Pietru has climbed many rungs in the economic prestige ladder during his life; he has moved from farmer's son to teacher, married a Sliema teacher and brought her to live in the village. Cecil's upward movement has been much less pronounced.

There is also a striking difference in the range of activities in which the two informants engage. Pietru is not only a teacher who gives private lessons, he also farms, helps his sister run her shop, is a part-time student and takes part in the ritual life of his parish. Cecil's activities are largely restricted to his kinship and formal teaching roles. This difference in activity is of course partly a function of the difference between life in a small village and life in a large centre, that is, of their residential and social niches in Maltese society.

There is also a difference in the geographical mobility of the two. Cecil has travelled widely, both within and outside Malta: between St. Paul's Bay in summer and Sliema in winter, and between Malta and several parts of India. Moreover, as already noted, he has now left his place of birth and moved to his wife's town.

These various factors have combined to make a difference in the personal prestige of Pietru and Cecil in relation to their immediate environment. Pietru is a relatively big fish in a very small pond, whereas Cecil is a smaller fish in a much larger pond. Pietru has high social visibility, whereas Cecil, partly because there are more teachers in his present environment, and also because he plays fewer social roles, has lower social visibility.

Pietru's immediate social environment is riven with ideological cleavages: the festa factions and political parties. These cleavages are not noticeable in Cecil's surroundings. Various factors have combined to influence Pietru to take an unequivocal stand and play a part in these conflicts.

Finally, the differences in personality and character are also significant. Pietru has a hearty outgoing character. He is used to personalizing social relations – in the sense of exchanging small talk and information, in short in getting to know people – with bus conductors, shopkeepers and other strangers met in the course of his expeditions beyond the limits of his village and district. Cecil, though friendly, is more reserved in his dealings with people than Pietru. He is not as garrulous and does not appear to seek to personalize relations with strangers.

3. STRUCTURAL, INTERACTIONAL AND SUBJECTIVE ASPECTS OF THE TWO NETWORKS[3]

a) *Structural characteristics*

Size

The size of the two networks is easily compared. Pietru's network includes 1751 persons and Cecil's 638. These contacts are what we may call first-order contacts: people with whom Cecil and Pietru have or have had some contact. Both have included a few people of whom they know a great deal, but have not actually met. These are persons who have married close kinsmen abroad. They know that they will meet them as soon as they visit Malta. In the meantime they know a great deal about them through letters which are passed to them by family members. Although each has done his best to recall, list and discuss all the persons he knows, quite obviously some have been left out, for the human memory is fallible. Persons under 14 have been excluded. In Pietru's case this involves at least 450 village children whom he knows personally. Except for the few unknown close affines mentioned, no second order contacts were included.

Composition

Who they know is more interesting. The networks can be compared as to sex, age, education, occupation and residence in order to give an indication of the relative spread of contacts throughout a number of important social categories. It is also important to ask in what capacity, that is in which roles, Pietru and Cecil know the members of their networks. In other words, we must compare the relative importance in each network of various activity fields from which the members of the network have been recruited.

Sex. Pietru's network displays a more even spread than Cecil's: 42 % of Pietru's network are women, while only 23 % of Cecil's are. This proportion roughly holds true not only for the total network, but also for the many zones and categories into which it can be divided.

Age. Pietru's network also shows a slightly more even age distribution than does that of Cecil. Pietru knows slightly more young persons – 14-19 year olds – than Cecil. He also knows slightly more older people – 70 years and older – than Cecil. But except for the very old and very young, the distribution of the two networks according to age is similar.

Education. The educational composition of the two networks differs considerably. More than half of Pietru's network has had either no schooling or primary schooling only, as compared to only 14 % for Cecil. By contrast 65 % of Cecil's network has had secondary or higher education (seminary, teacher training, university), compared to only 32 % of Pietru's network.

Occupation. Considering that Cecil's network is on the whole better educated than Pietru's, it is no surprise that religious and white collar workers form just over half Cecil's network, but make up only one quarter of Pietru's network. It is interesting to note, too, that though Cecil knows many more priests than Pietru (145 as compared to 90) the latter knows more in Malta

Table 1. Age

Age	Pietru	Cecil	Malta*
14–19 yr.	9.4	4.5	15.7
20–29	20.7	24.3	21.3
30–39	28.3	31.5	16.9
40–49	15.7	16.6	15.3
50–59	11.0	13.0	12.5
60–67	7.4	8.3	11.9
70 +	2.7	0.6	7.4
unknown	4.8	1.1	—
Total %	100	99.9	100
Number	1751	638	220,447

* Source: *Annual Abstract of Statistics: 1968* (Malta: Central Office of Statistics, 1969), p. 14, Table 4. The figures given for the first age category are 15-19 years rather than the 14-19 years I used.

Table 2. Education

Education	Pietru	Cecil	Malta*
Unknown	10.5	21.0	0.6
None	21.8	2.4	16.6
Primary	36.3	11.3	62.1
Secondary	16.4	32.2	18.6
Higher	15.1	33.1	2.1
Total %	99.1	100	100
Number	1744	637	215,316

* Based on unpublished material from the 1967 census kindly made available by the Central Office of Statistics. The figures for Malta are for the population over 5 years not attending school, which is compulsory from 5 to 14 years. Those for Pietru and Cecil show only persons over 14 years, some of whom may still be at school.

than the former (83 compared to 57). Both, however, know about the same proportion of skilled workers. Unskilled workers, on the other hand, are more important in Pietru's network than in that of Cecil. Not surprisingly, while four out of every hundred persons Pietru knows are farmers, Cecil knows virtually none.

Table 3. Occupation

Occupation	Pietru	Cecil	Malta*
Religious	5.1	22.7	31.6
Professional and white collar	19.2	29.6	
Skilled service (police, broker, shop, etc.)	12.7	12.2	41.9
Unskilled service	28.2	21.5	
Skilled industrial	3.3	2.2	18.7
Unskilled industrial	9.6	0.5	
Agricultural	4.4	0.3	7.7
Other	3.3	1.4	—
Don't know	14.0	9.6	—
Total %	99.8	100	99.9
Number	1751	638	94,367

* Based on unpublished material from the 1967 census for the gainfully occupied population, kindly made available by the Central Office of Statistics.

Table 4. Place of Residence

Place of residence	Pietru	Cecil	Malta*
Farrug (Pietru) or	48.3	—	0.4
Birkirkara (Cecil)	—	20.2	5.5
Villages around Farrug	13.2	0	5.5
Sliema	5.6	21.5	9.0
Urban Malta	13.3	15.0	35.5
Rest of Malta	9.8	10.2	44.1
Abroad	7.3	24.5	—
Don't know	2.6	.6	—
Total %	100.1	100	100
Number	1751	638	314,216

* The figures show the total population and are based on unpublished material from the 1967 census kindly made available to me by the Central Office of Statistics.

Residence. Almost half of Pietru's network live around him in Hal-Farrug. In contrast, only one fifth of Cecil's network live in his place of residence, Birkirkara. Moreover, Pietru's network is clearly rural based, for 73 % of it is located in rural towns and villages, while only 10 % of Cecil's is. As can be seen from table 4, most of Cecil's network is located in various urban centres in Malta, while a full 25 % is situated abroad.

Although this last table shows that the geographical spread of Pietru's network in Malta is greater than that of Cecil, it is even more pronounced than is indicated: Petru knows people in 40 of Malta's 44 parishes, while Cecil has acquaintances in only 27. Moreover, Pietru knows a number of persons in Gozo, while Cecil knows none.

Activity fields

It is now important to ask in what capacity Pietru and Cecil know the members of their networks. Fellow villagers make up the largest segment of Pietru's network. Cecil appears to know most persons in connection with the work that they do or he does. That is, they are part of each other's occupational role sets. Kinsmen, though forming the second largest activity field for both Pietru and Cecil, occupy a relatively larger place for Pietru, for 24 % of the members of his larger network are kinsmen. In contrast, only 17 % of Cecil's network are kinsmen.

Table 5. Activity field

Shared activity	Pietru	Cecil
Occupation	19,9	41.4
School/College	0.5	11.6
Kinship	23.9	16.6
Association and similar interests	6.1	4.1
Village	40.6	0.4
Neighbour	4.8	11.0
Miscellaneous	1.5	14.5
None	2.6	0
Total %	99.9	99.6
Number	2020*	821*

* These totals exceed the number of persons in each network since some relations derive from more than one activity field.

We must not loose sight of the fact that conclusions so far have merely been numerical statements about the composition of the networks. They indicate only that a relation exists between the central ego and a member of his network which may be expressed in terms of a particular activity field. This tells us nothing about the quality of that relation; that is, what the relative importance of that relation is. Phrased differently, how well do Pietru and Cecil know the members of their networks? Is there a relation between the size of a given activity field and the importance of the persons in it to Pietru and Cecil? I attempted to answer these questions by examining the content of their relations in terms of what is exchanged.

Density

By density I mean the extent to which members of a person's primary zone are in touch with each other independently of him. Density is thus a measure of the *potential* communication between members of his network, not of the *actual* flow of information (or exchange content). The density of each network was calculated on the basis of the formula $200\ Na/n(n-1)$ where Na refers to the actual number of links (social relations) in the network excluding those with Ego, and n to the total number of persons in the network including Ego (*cf.* Mitchell, 1969: 18).

The density of Pietru's network is 23.7 % and that of Cecil's 5.2 %. Briefly then, more members of Pietru's primary zone are linked to each other independently of him than is the case with the members of Cecil's primary zone. At least this is the way each perceives the density of his personal network, for it is important to remember that only Pietru and Cecil, and not the members of their primary zones, were asked to indicate which persons knew each other. Thus this density index is their subjective perception of how communication/exchange could potentially take place.[4]

b) *Interactional characteristics*

The type of exchange relations which Pietru and Cecil maintain with members of their network is set out in table 6. From this it would appear that Pietru seems to maintain more personal relations with more members of his network than Cecil, though he ignores a greater portion of his network than Cecil. He also seems more personal; that is, he exchanges conversation. visits and gifts more than Cecil. He seems less noncommittal: while 57 % of Cecil's network are persons with whom he exchanges only greetings or civilities, these categories include only 28 % of Pietru's network. In contrast, Pietru exchanges conversation, information and visits with 40 % of his network, while Cecil maintains these types of exchange relations with only 20 % of his much smaller network.

In table 7 exchange relations are compared to certain activity fields. It is clear that the activity fields which numerically seemed so important to Pietru (village) and to Cecil (occupational role sets) are considerably less important in terms of exchange relations. While the village is proportionally

Table 6. Exchange relations

Type exchange	Number		Per cent	
	Pietru	Cecil	Pietru	Cecil
Ignore	537	138	30,7	21.7
Greet only	288	191	16.4	29.9
Civilities only	204	174	11.7	27.3
Conversation/Information	560	69	32.0	10.3
Visits and gifts	140	59	8.0	9.3
Total	1751	638	100.1	99.4

important for Pietru in terms of his total network, he exchanges conversation and visits with only one out of every four fellow villagers. Thus with three out of four persons in his village he maintains only nominal relations. Pietru also appears to maintain closer relations than Cecil with the persons with whom he shares occupational role relations. Although this category is numerically the most important in terms of Cecil's total network, he maintains only nominal relations with or ignores (does not greet) 80% of the persons within it. Pietru, in contrast, maintains nominal relations with or ignores only one third of the persons with whom he shares occupational role relations and exchanges conversation and visits with two thirds of them.

Table 7. Exchange relations and activity field

Type exchange	Occupation		Kinship		Village	
	Pietru	Cecil	Pietru	Cecil	Pietru	Cecil
Ignore	3.2	20.3	21.3	8.8	41.2	—
Greet only	6.5	29.1	15.7	24.3	23.0	—
Civilities only	21.4	30.1	8.1	36.8	10.8	—
Conversation/information	63.8	14.4	26.9	6.6	21.9	—
Visits and gifts	4.7	5.3	24.8	21.3	2.9	—
Don't know	2.0	0.6	2.9	2.2	0.2	—
Total %	99.8	99.8	99.7	100	100	—
Number	401	340	483	136	846	3

It is also obvious in table 7 that Pietru maintains much more intimate exchange relations with his kinsmen than Cecil. In fact, he exchanges conversation and visits with 51% of his 483 kinsmen, while Cecil does so with only 28% of his 136 kinsmen.

Finally, from table 8 it is evident that most of the people whom Pietru ignores (i.e. does not greet when they meet) are fellow villagers, while most of those Cecil ignores are people who he knows because they are members of each other's occupational role sets. While Pietru and Cecil visit more often with kinsmen than with persons from other activity fields, fully three fourths of the persons Pietru visits are kinsmen, while just under half of Cecil's visits are with kinsmen.

Table 8. Activity field and exchange relations

Shared activity	Ignore		Greeting		Conversation		Visits	
	Pietru	Cecil	Pietru	Cecil	Pietru	Cecil	Pietru	Cecil
Occupation	2.2	41.0	8.0	44.0	36.2	45.8	12.0	22.5
School/College	0.4	9.0	0	5.8	0.1	20.6	0.7	10.0
Kinship	17.9	7.2	23.3	14.7	18.4	8.4	77.3	35.0
Association/similar inter.	4.2	4.2	1.8	2.7	9.8	7.5	2.0	6.3
Village	67.0	0	58.6	0	25.3	0	1.3	0
Neighbour	2.5	16.9	5.5	12.0	5.4	14.0	6.0	6.3
Miscellaneous	0.2	21.7	1.5	20.9	2.5	3.7	0.7	20.0
None	5.6	0	1.2	0	1.4	0	0	0
Total %	100	100	99.9	100.1	99.9	100	100	100.1
Number	552	166	326	225	707	707	150	80

c) *Intimacy zones*

Each informant was asked to separate from his total network those persons who in some way or another meant something special to him. This decision was made on a purely subjective/emotional basis. Although I shall not discuss these categories in any detail here, it is interesting to note that Cecil and Pietru, quite independently, each selected 132 persons from his total personal network. Moreover, each classified 10 persons in a first, the most intimate, category. These include spouse, parents and most siblings. Beyond this intimate cell there is a second zone of approximately 20 persons with whom they maintain especially close relations. While the first zone for both consists mostly of relatives, the second zone, though composed chiefly of relatives for Pietru, is made up largely of non-relatives for Cecil.

Who are the 132 people in each of the zones of intimacy? They reflect closely the relative importance of the various activity fields and, interestingly enough, exchange relations set out in tables 5 and 6. Kinsmen form the largest category for Pietru (45% compared to 21% for Cecil), whereas persons with whom he shares an occupational role are more important for Cecil. Pietru is also more personal with the members of his intimate network than Cecil: he exchanges visits with 52 % of them, while Cecil visits with only 29 %.

4. DISCUSSION

The salient differences between the two networks which emerge from this very cursory comparison include the following. Pietru's network is larger than that of Cecil and appears to have a more even distribution of the sexes, age groups, educational and occupational categories as well as a more even geographical spread in Malta. Kinsmen appear to occupy a more important place in Pietru's network than in that of Cecil, and the density of the former's network is higher than that of the latter. Finally, Pietru has a tendency to personalize a greater proportion of his social relations in the intimate as well as the non-intimate zones of his network than Cecil.

The striking difference in size of the two networks may be explained partly by the fact that Pietru is seven years older than Cecil and thus has had the time to meet and maintain contacts with a large number of persons. But it does not account for the fact that Pietru knows almost three times as many persons as Cecil. A second explanation might be that Pietru plays more occupational roles than Cecil. He is after all schoolteacher, farmer, tutor, informal assistant of the parish priest, member of a confraternity and band club as well as father, son, husband and kinsman. It is apparent, however, that many of these roles derive from his niche in a small village. He is a big fish in a little pond. Furthermore, because he is socially prominent, people seek contact with him, and don't let him forget them. Moreover, by simply being a native of the village, his network is larger than Cecil's by some 846 persons – his fellow villagers. Cecil, as a city dweller, has no comparable ascribed segment in his network. Without this ascribed segment their networks are more nearly comparable: 805 to 638.

Another important factor in explaining the difference in size is Pietru's tendency to personalize his relations to a greater extent than Cecil. The difference in size between the two networks is perhaps also a function of a difference in memory. The explanation for this is not biological but social: Pietru personalizes more relations, therefore has more guide-lines to aid his memory. The details he learns through conversation help to fix persons in his memory. Moreover, by personalizing relations, he creates multiplex ties. Through these he more easily meets new persons. Expressed in another way:

people seem to be more important to Pietru than to Cecil; therefore he knows more.

Finally, it is important to note that Cecil's training as a Jesuit entailed a high measure of isolation, a systematic effort to eliminate or curtail contacts with non-Jesuits – especially family and former friends – and considerable geographical mobility. These all served to limit the number of persons with whom Cecil could maintain contact and remember.

The more even spread of Pietru's network in terms of sex, age, education, occupation and residence can be explained by the fact that he is a villager. This even spread must be seen as an ascribed attribute of his network. There is an even distribution of sexes in the village, as well as of ages. Pietru is well educated, most of the villagers are not, though an ever larger proportion of village teenagers are going to secondary school. Besides this, villages like Farrug are reservoirs of skilled and unskilled labour. Pietru grew up with these persons and still lives at close quarters with them. Cecil has no such bloc of persons who are not white collar workers in his network. Similarly Pietru knows more people in other villages than Cecil, because he is a villager himself: village teachers form blocs in opposition to town teachers in the training college and associations of which Pietru is or was a member (and also in the secondary school where Cecil teaches). Furthermore, his own large kin network is anchored in the villages and through the many kinship ceremonies he meets people from other villages. Moreover, the custom of celebrating the patron saints of villages attracts people from other 'rival' villages who come to enjoy the spectacle and compare notes. Festas are occasions on which old acquaintances are 'serviced' and, through them, new contacts are made. This is perhaps a cultural explanation, but an important one nonetheless, for Pietru attends 10-15 festas a year. Cecil only attends one, that of his wife's parish, and that only since he has been married. Sophisticated inhabitants of Sliema, especially of his generation, regard it as provincial to show great interest in these festas.

How can one explain the greater number of kinsmen in Pietru's network? To begin with, there could be a demographic reason: In his genealogy he listed the decendants of eight married uncles and aunts of his parents. They produced no less than 182 living second cousins. Cecil in contrast could name only two married siblings of his grandparents, and they have produced only three living second cousins. This sound demographic reason for the greater number of kinsmen in Pietru's network would perhaps be sufficient if it were not for two additional factors. First, I strongly suspect that Cecil's grandparents had more married siblings than he in fact knew and therefore listed, for he noted three persons of whose exact relationship he was unsure but whom he guessed were probably second cousins. Secondly, Pietru consistently listed more relatives in every genealogical category than Cecil. For example, Pietru knows 88 of his wife's relatives, whereas Cecil knows only 31 relatives of his wife. Even though Pietru has been married 18 months longer and could have met more affines, it does tend to support my contention that kinsmen are more important to Pietru than they are to Cecil and therefore he knows more. This is also supported by the higher rate of exchange relations that Pietru maintains with his kinsmen (see table 8) and the more important place they occupy in the intimate portion of Pietru's network (45% as opposed to 21% for Cecil).

The question we must answer therefore is why are kinsmen more important – in the sense of a higher social investment – to Pietru than they are to Cecil? Can this be explained by Pietru's more gregarious nature? It could be argued that because people in general seem to be more important to Pietru than to Cecil, and that kinsmen are a special category of people, that they therefore receive proportionately greater attention from Pietru.

Have we reached the point where the essential differences between these two networks have been reduced to a difference in personality between Cecil and Pietru? I think not. In fact, I see personality here as the dependent rather than independent variable. As the differences in sex, age, education, occupation and residence were explained in terms of Pietru's village niche and Cecil's town niche, so the difference between village and town environment also explains why Pietru's network scores higher on density than Cecil's and why kinsmen are more important to him than to Cecil.

Pietru's network scores higher on density than that of Cecil primarily because it includes a compartment (see the contributions of Thoden van Velzen and Niemeijer in this book for a discussion of this concept) of no less than 846 persons that has a density of 100%, namely his fellow villagers, all of whom know each other. If these villagers, and those persons for whom no data was available, are removed from the two networks, it is interesting to note that their respective density scores become almost the same: 5.4% for Pietru's, and 5.3% for that of Cecil. But in spite of the similar density scores, each member of Pietru's corrected primary zone (excluding villagers) is linked with a mean of 42.8 other persons in the primary zone, while the corresponding figure for Cecil is only 31.7 persons. The discrepancy between these two measures of the degree of interrelation between the members of the two primary zones is explained by their different sizes, for as Niemeijer argues (chap. 4 in this book), size is of crucial importance in evaluating the significance of density scores.

The greater degree of interconnection between the (non-village) members of Pietru's network may be attributed principally to the presence in his first-order zone of large, densely interconnected segments or compartments. These include blocs of 170 primary school teachers, 54 policemen, 60 members of the clergy, and nearly 500 relatives.

In short, the greater density of Pietru's network is due principally to the place that fellow villagers occupy in it, as well as to the important place assumed by kinsmen. For if almost half of his primary zone is composed of fellow villagers, almost one quarter consists of relatives, which in turn form segments (his mother's, his father's and his wife's relatives) which have high internal density.

Why are relatives more important to a villager than to a townsman? To answer by saying that kinship is more important in village subculture is to beg the question. To plead culture, I think, is an admission of defeat. It is merely an excuse for stopping analysis. To some extent culture is the normative rationalisation of patterns of behaviour. Though there is feedback, of course, the rationalisation is of less interest than the underlying sociological explanation of those behavioural patterns. Kinship is important in villages because they are moral communities of which membership (in the case of those born there) is ascribed. As a kin network is built up of relations which normatively are morally sanctioned (by church as well as public opinion) – *this is also true in the city* – the kin network is a moral, ascribed segment of the total network. This moral network segment in turn is partly embedded in a larger moral community. This in combination with the many-stranded relations which exist between inhabitants of a small village indicates some of the reasons why the enforcement of kinship norms is much more efficient in a village than in a town. Although the kinship segment of Cecil's network is also a moral network, is is not embedded in a larger moral community of which he is a member. Thus, if he does not honour his kinship obligations, and as I could demonstrate he is indeed very cavalier about these, his offended kinsmen cannot appeal for justice to non-kinsmen who can exert influence on him in several other roles because they are members of the same moral community. In contrast, Pietru lives at relatively close quarters with many of his kinsmen. If he offends them they can appeal to persons who form part of the moral village community of which he and they are members.

Moreover, following Kapferer's line of argument (chap. 6 of this book), a failure to discharge obligations to kinsmen could well jeopardize relations with other villagers, who might well assume that he would also betray the relations he shares with them.

These various reasons combine to ensure that Pietru meets his kin obligations more punctually than does Cecil and that his own kinsmen do likewise.

Thus, the fact that Pietru lives at close quarters in a village with a large number of his relatives ensures that he knows more relatives and sees them more often and that they meet their obligations to each other more faithfully than is the case with Cecil.

Why then does Pietru personalize his social relations to a greater extent than Cecil? Is it because their basic personalities differ? I think that their personalities do differ. The reason for this is less genetically than socially determined. I suggest that the gregarious personality of Pietru is found more often in villages than in towns, and conversely, that the more reserved personality of Cecil is more common in large towns with mobile populations than in nucleated villages. Why do villagers personalize their relations? This is chiefly because most villages are highly interconnected communities. In a village any person with whom one has dealings knows all the other persons in the village (beyond 3,000-4,000 this is no longer true: Farrug has but 1200). They are therefore used to associating with people who have similar backgrounds and know the same people. They thus can exchange information about shared experiences, problems and acquaintances. They do not do so all the time or with all villagers, but it does mean that there are no anonymous persons in the village: everyone knows everyone else.

City people are used to persons with whom they have only single-stranded service relations. In a city there is a category which can be called the anonymous service fringe. These are the people with whom one has relatively frequent dealings, such as bus conductors, shopkeepers, neigbours, etc., but about whom little is known. It is significant, I think, that Cecil did not know the names of 50 non-relatives with whom he had regular dealings while Pietru listed only one case. Pietru begins talking easily to strangers such as bus conductors and shopkeepers, Cecil does not. What I am suggesting is that because Pietru is not used to single-stranded, anonymous relations, he cannot handle them. Consequently, he takes steps to ensure that relations do not remain single-stranded: he begins conversation and searches for common ground. Cecil, on the other hand, used to travelling and the social relations in a relatively impersonal urban centre, is accustomed to such impersonal relations. They form a familiar category. He can handle them. He therefore does not seek to personalize single-stranded relations.

The difference in gregariousness between Cecil and Pietru is similar to the difference between the latter and his city-bred wife. Pietru's wife does not have the personalizing nature of her husband. On her shopping expeditions through the village she does not talk a great deal, although she is not taciturn. Her reserved relations with the shopkeepers and neighbours are regarded as rather unusual by the people of Farrug, while they see nothing unusual about Pietru's talkativeness. In contrast, Pietru's long conversations with strangers are looked on as exceptional behaviour in Sliema, while his wife's reserve is not. I have already pointed to this same contrast in talkativeness between Cecil and his village-bred wife. Cecil is somewhat reserved, and his wife, according to his standards, is very talkative. I know the cases discussed are few. They suggest, however, that there may be evidence to associate an outgoing, talkative personality with a person who is brought up and lives in a highly connected moral community of no more than 3,000 to 4,000 and a reserved personality with a person who has been brought up in an (urban) area with a relatively low density.

5. CONCLUSION

Given the limited data I collected, the conclusions drawn concerning the differences in the network profile of townsman and countryman, the explanation of these, and their effect on their respective personality structures must be seen as hypotheses which should be examined by all readers on the basis of their own experience and by researchers who, hopefully, will subject them to a more rigid examination than I have been able to do. Nevertheless, I do think they indicate the sort of insights into human personality and behaviour which can flow from network analysis. These insights can have more than simply theoretical interest. Network analysis provides important links between social anthropology and other disciplines. For example, this type of analysis could furnish leads for those interested in psychiatric or development work. Would it not be reasonable to examine how far different types of mental illness vary with differences in network structure? If it is found that they do, as I suspect, therapy could conceivably be obtained by manipulating network structure through the environment. Similarly, the developer seeking to introduce innovations might be well advised not to attempt this first in towns of less than 4,000. In these the networks of the inhabitants (unless there is a relatively high degree of mobility) could be such that social control over the innovator/entrepreneur would be so considerable that he would not be able to make profitable decisions which contravene traditional norms and/or adversely affect his relations with others.

The discussion has also raised certain theoretical and methodological questions. If a primary zone is defined as all a person's direct links with people he recalls he interacts or has interacted with, then it can include a staggering number. Yet if an attempt is made to limit these by applying a selective criterion (such as kinship, village membership, a particular exchange content, etc.) the focus is placed on only one particular category of social relations (partial network) from which other significant links have been eliminated. Those eliminated might very well be links which influence behaviour toward persons within the selected partial network or provide channels along with messages can be sent. For example, can we ever fully understand the role that kinship plays without also considering the role that non-kinsmen play? Or, can we ever come to an understanding of why a person activates a particular action-set or communication chain without also considering the alternatives open to him? To eliminate these other social relations which fall outside the partial network under consideration, while useful perhaps for heuristic purposes, does violence to the way in which people manipulate and are manipulated through their networks in real life situations. What I am suggesting thus is that to be able to understand fully the way in which a partial network is operated or impinges upon a person, it must be set into the total first-order zone so that the interconnections between the various partial networks can be traced. This is simply another way of saying that there is a functional relation (in the mathematical sense) between partial networks even as there is between different institutions, and that there is little point in studying them completely in isolation. This however poses a serious problem.

By including the total first-order zone in the analysis the researcher is faced with the problem of gathering the relevant data and processing it. This in my experience is prohibitively time consuming and likely to inundate the researcher with data to the point of immobility. I would suggest therefore that perhaps the most urgent problem confronting those who wish to make use of the network approach is to develop a method of gathering pertinent data rapidly through the use of some form of sampling technique. Until this problem is resolved, the network approach will never be able, as Mayer (1964: 34) suggested, to serve as many and indispensible functions in studies of industrial(izing) communities that the making of geneologies or household surveys do of traditional rural communities.

NOTES

1. Research on which this study was based carried out in Malta in the summers of 1967, 1968 and 1969. It was made possible through the generous assistance of the Wenner-Gren Foundation for Anthropological Research (1967), The Netherlands Association for the Advancement of Pure Scientific Research – Z.W.O. – (1968) and

The University of Michigan Mediterranean Network project directed by Professor Eric Wolf (1969). Francis Mizzi and Anthony Cuschieri devoted most of the summer 1968 to the mind-deadening task of organizing and collecting the network data. Rudo Niemeijer devoted much time to processing the data including the preparation and testing of the computer programme and Jolanthe van Opzeeland-De Tempe helped work out some of the tables. I am most grateful to them and to the University of Amsterdam which made their services and those of the staff and computer of the University's mathematical centre available. Thanks are also due to the Royal University of Malta for the encouragement and facilities it provided during my brief summer visits to Malta. Finally I am grateful to the various discussants of earlier drafts of this paper some of whose criticism I have tried to meet.

2. At this stage it would seem advisable to say a few words about how the research was carried out. I selected Malta because I had already considerable knowledge of the Island and the social customs of the people (Boissevain, 1965, 1969). As informants I chose two school teachers. Pietru is a village teacher, married to a city girl, with whom I had worked before. Cecil, the second informant, is a city teacher, married to a girl from a rural town. I met him the year previous to carrying out the research. Each made out lists of all the people over 14 he knew. As Pietru knew 1751 persons and Cecil, the city-bred informant, 638, this task involved considerable work. After all acquaintances had been listed, each informant filled out an information sheet on every person known. These provided data on the social background, number of shared role relations, frequency of contact, last contact, the actual contents of the relationship and the other acquaintances held in common. Once the data sheets for each of the informant's acquaintances had been completed, I asked Cecil and Pietru to sort the forms according to the affective or emotional importance of their acquaintances to themselves. I then discussed the resulting categorization extensively with them. I also gathered detailed biographical information from each informant and collected case histories on a variety of situations in which segments of the network had been mobilized. This data, which is continually expanding, was typed on some 200 six by eight inch cards. Finally, back in Holland, the data was coded and transferred to punched cards and simple cross tabulations were carried out for each pair of categories of data. A rather more complicated calculation of the density was computed for a number of relevant categories, such as zones of intimacy and activity fields.

3. In setting out the structural and interactional characteristics of the two primary zones I have been greatly aided by the discussions of Mitchell and Kapferer in Mitchell (1969).

4. A more detailed discussion of the density, multiplexity and degree of the personal networks of Pietru and Cecil, an indication of how they are used for problem solving, and a discussion of the forces that keep them constantly in flux are given elsewhere (Boissevain, forthcoming, chap. 5).

Part 3

Network and coalitions

Coalitions in Sicilian peasant society

ANTON BLOK

1. INTRODUCTION

It is unfortunate but true that the concept of corporate groups still dominates a good deal of present discussions on human relations. According to current conceptual usage, corporate structures are generally understood as having permanence, persisting irrespective of the life of the individuals who form them. Families, lineages, villages, religious associations, trade-unions, and what we call 'societies' are perceived in this way. Indeed, linguistic conventions lead us to believe that social structures at large are something abstracted from the individual people who form them and have a separate existence. The limitations of this time-honoured yet essentially static model of human organization become particularly clear when we note the ease with which some anthropoligists and sociologists indulge in question-begging terminologies as 'loosely structured' or 'informal structure' when they are faced with ethnographic data which do not fit their standard conceptions of human relations.[1] Confronted with the study of temporary groups which are subject to continual rearrangement over time, structural-functional theory failed us (*cf.* Boissevain, 1968: 542). We must expect therefore that important organizational features and especially processes of change will be either obscured or misrepresented by approaching the society concerned from a corporate viewpoint. Are there, then, one may ask, other frameworks or theoretical constructions which are more valid and capable of solving these problems?

For a time it appeared that what is called network theory was developing more appropriate tools to come to grips with problems beyond the reach of structural-functional theory. At closer inspection, however, and as far as one can see at the moment, the network approach is still fraught with the conventional conceptual polarity of 'individual' and 'society', which hampers the development of a dynamic model. Two main approaches can be distinguished. On the one hand, networks are understood as egocentric structures which are defined with regard to a single individual. Hence the name personal network. These networks are, as it were, personal creations of an ego and dissolve when ego dies (*cf.* Befu, 1963a, b; Boissevain, 1968, 1971; Mayer, 1966; Srinivas and Béteille, 1964). On the other hand, networks are conceived as ramifying chains of dyadic relationships involving specific fields of activity. Barnes' partial networks, which define particular social fields (e.g. kinship, economic, religious, and political relationships), belong to this realm.[2] The assumption underlying these approaches is that individuals can be separated from the structures which they form with other people. Though this perception is underwritten by ordinary language, it hardly corresponds with what one actually observes. What we call 'individual' and 'society' are aspects of men which belong together. There is no reason therefore to distinguish them for analytical purposes since by analyzing them separately we will not find the links that bind them together. It is precisely one of the main tasks of the anthropologist and the sociologist to study these interconnections and to describe their dynamic character.

The society with which I shall be concerned in this essay is marked by an increasing involvement in relationships transcending its traditional boundaries in the process of which dyadic bonds assumed salient characteristics. In Western Sicily, the impact of the State and the market obscured the contours of rural communities since the early 19th century while, on the other hand, the organizational principles of bilateral kinship, fictive kinship, friendship, and patronage generated temporary coalitions rather than enduring and clearly demarcated groups showing structural persistence over generations. An understanding of these impermanent and composite alliances requires a proper framework of analysis. Like any model, the one employed here seeks to explain what actually happens, but it does so by considering these coalitions in terms of interdependent individuals which have a momentum of their own. It is important to appreciate that these coalitions or whatever one may call pluralities of interdependent people have no separate existence from the individuals who form them. They are neither more nor less real than these people. The basic assumption of the present discussion is that individuals always come in social structures and social structures are always formed by individuals.[3]

2. THE SETTING

Genuardo (a pseudonym) is a small agro-town of about 2,500 people situated in the mountainous hinterland of Western Sicily, some features of which

I have described elsewhere (See Blok, 1966, 1969a, b, c, 1972). The village, or *paese* as it is called, lies off the highways and is geographically rather isolated since secondary roads are few and in bad condition. There is neither tourism nor local industry of any importance. The inland region is predominantly agrarian and characterized by concentrated settlements which, to an extent, separate the peasant cultivators from the land on which they depend for their living.

Until the 1950s when agrarian reform was introduced and large-scale migrant labour began to affect the area, the social structure of Genuardo was closely bound to the prevailing system of land tenure which embraced two main types of farms around which production was organized: the large cereal-pasture holding (*masseria*), for which the large landed estates (*feudi* or *latifondi*) provided the lay-out, and the small peasant holding, often merely strips of land scattered along the fringes of the village and the large estates. The cultivation of wheat was emphasized on both types of farms, but livestock raising was much more important on the *masseria* since the distribution of rainfall made cattle and sheep dependent on the utilization of extensive pastures ranging from lower locations in winter to more elevated areas in summer. All fields were subject to a three-step rotation cycle: every year one field was under crop, a second served as pasture, and the third field would lie fallow. After the harvest, the stubble provided additional pasturage.

The estate owners (*latifondisti*) used to live elsewhere, mostly in Palermo but also in cities on the mainland and abroad. They entrusted the management of their estates to local peasant entrepreneurs (*gabelloti*), who belonged to the tiny segment of relatively well-to-do agriculturalists who owned some land and cattle. The most common form of management was the *gabella* or large lease which involved six years, i.e. two full rotation cycles. The exploitation of the *masseria* included armed supervision by field guards (*campieri*) who were recruited from the ranks of the peasantry. The majority of the population consisted of precariously employed peasants. They performed various occupational tasks ranging from small-holder, sharecropper, and tenant to those of shepherd, occasional land labourer, and artisan. In order to make a living, many peasants had to carry out various combinations of these tasks which brought them in one way or another and to a greater or lesser extent within the orbit of the large estate. In fact, they formed the large reservoir of cheap labour from which the peasant entrepreneurs hired their personnel.

The subordinate position of large sectors of the peasantry reflected their limited control over resources, especially land. This situation should be understood with regard to distinct historical processes that worked on South

Italian society at large. In the early 19th century, feudal jurisdiction was formally replaced by that of the centralized State. The subsequent conversion of land and labour into market commodities alienated the peasants from access to pasture and forest over which they had traditionally exercised common use rights. The development of the market in conjunction with population increase constrained and dislocated the traditional peasant order. On the other hand, this evolution provided opportunities for that small social segment located between lords and peasants which I have called the peasant entrepreneurs. This intermediate peasantry entrenched itself in rural Sicily in the course of the 17th and 18th centuries when the large estate owners became increasingly absentee. By the time that land came up for sale, this stratum of big lease-holders, supervisors, and cattlemen had accumulated sufficient wealth to become a gentry in its own right. In their turn, the members of this new landed class aspired to live in the city and to claim the status of gentlemen (*civili*) thus making room for new entrepreneurs who ran their estates in the countryside. In Sicily and other Mediterranean areas, civilized or seigniorial status involves landownership, permanent urban residence, advanced education, and an emphatic abstinence from manual work. Its counterpart is the way of life of the rustic or peasant (*viddanu*) whose hardship, poverty, ignorance, and low status are related to the general distaste for rural life in this part of the world.

Since the increasing orientation towards commercialization did not imply any significant technical change, the ongoing process of vertical and outward mobility involved the transfer of wealth from the country to the city where it was spent on patronage and leisure. This transfer was realized through a ruthless exploitation of land and labour. If market conditions required it, forests were cut down and turned into grainfields while overgrazing and overcropping led to a steady exhaustion of the soil. There was little effective State control to check these tendencies. Characteristically, efficient power was held by the entrepreneurs themselves, though it was at least partly derived from the influence the estate owners wielded at the national level. Living in the city, the latter were primarily interested in modest though continual revenues rather than investment, let alone improvement of local conditions. The relations between the power domains of the entrepreneur and the estate owner were backed up by the private use of violence which served mainly to keep the proletarianized peasants from engaging in sustained rebellion. Since the State failed to monopolize the use of physical force, people were in a position to take the law into their own hands. To seek a protector and to grant protection involved a dynamic pattern of cooperation and conflict between estate owners, entrepreneurs, peasants, and representatives of the State, who made up the overall configuration of West Sicilian society. I have described elsewhere how the tensions between *civili* and *viddani* provided the setting for the enterpreneurial upstarts or *mafiosi*. It may suffice to stress here that it was chiefly through violence and cunning (*furberìa*) that the succesful peasant entrepreneur could hope to exploit his niche.[4]

Systems like the Sicilian *masseria*, which are based on skimming off the proceeds rather than on production and which de-emphasize long-term employment of capital, have been described as rent capitalistic.[5] Though such systems appear as fundamentally static, they actually possess a dynamic of their own. This can be most readily seen when we examine more closely the *modus operandi* and the careers of some of the Sicilian peasant entrepreneurs.

3. COALITIONS

In this section we will explore, by means of some examples, the ways in which certain people came into coalitions and prevented others from forming them. As specimens of configurations, coalitions may be defined as temporary combinations for special ends between parties that retain distinctive principles.[6]

Between 1902 and 1914, two brothers named Nicola and Michele Jaconi managed a large estate in partnership (*società*) with their father's brother, Domenico, who controlled three adjacent *latifondi*. Upon marriage Domenico moved to the neighbouring town of Bisacquino, but all three belonged to one of the dominant patrinominal families in Genuardo which had held large estates in lease for several generations.[7] The four estates which they exploited as lease-holders covered well over 1,000 hectares and were part of a more extensive and unified complex of *latifondi*, called Baronessa, the owner of which lived in Palermo. As was common for *gabelloti*, the brothers and their uncle were also big cattlemen: their flocks embraced several hundred sheep which utilized the pastures available. At a lower level, they established short-term partnerships with individual herdsmen who brought in their own animals. Like most *gabelloti* in this area at the time, the Jaconi's employed *campieri* who scouted the fields to prevent incursions and thefts from outsiders as well as from the peasants set to work on the estates. As noted above, these armed field-guards on horseback had a reputation for toughness. In local idiom, they were 'men able to make themselves respected'. This orientation involved the use of violence, including killing, when their interests were jeopardized or, even, when they were 'offended'. Broadly speaking, the *campieri* constituted a kind of private police-force which, in the absence of efficient State control, maintained law and order in the countryside.

In early September 1914, bandits unsuccessfully tried to kill Nicola and one of his ploughmen. Their attempt to steal cattle from Domenico remained likewise ineffective. Yet they succeeded in killing fifteen of Domenico's oxen and injuring several others which were ploughing the fields that day. Some time before, Domenico had been blackmailed. Subsequent investigations revealed that all these operations had been undertaken by the Grisafi band and formed part of the strategy plotted by a rival coalition of entrepreneurs from the village of Adernò, located some fifteen miles south of Genuardo. The manoeuvre was intended to remove Domenico from office and to set up some of his own *campieri* as lease-holders. In fact, Domenico eventually retired and his former retainers acquired the lease for the next six years. Before discussing the genesis and structure of the rival coalition, we must first understand the position of the band.

The Grisafi band owed its name to its leader: a former herdsman in his early thirties from Castelbello, another small town in this mountainous border region of the provinces of Palermo, Trapani, and Agrigento. Paolo Grisafi, or Marcuzzo as he was called, had been active as a bandit for well over twelve years before he was arrested together with four of his companions in January 1917. The police-officer who accomplished the round-up provides the following description of Grisafi and his band.

'The outlaw Grisafi, a mountain-dweller of thirty-six years of age, originally a shepherd, who commanded the armed band, was a consummate bandit. Fierce and cautious, most redoutable, up to all the tricks and stratagems of guerilla warfare, and protected by a thick net of local favour strengthened by terror, he had been an outlaw for quite twelve years; and he had set up in the western part of the province of Agrigento a kind of special domain over which he ruled absolutely, interfering in every kind of affair, even the most intimate, making his will felt in every field, including the electoral field, and levying tolls and taxes, blackmailing and committing crimes of bloodshed without stint. Some thirty murders were put down to him, besides an unending series of crimes. Perhaps he had not committed so many; possibly he had committed more; certainly he was ready to go on committing them. They called him Marcuzzo (little Mark), but he was a man of thews and muscles, inclining to stoutness.'

'Aided not only by his boldness but by constant good luck, and being a good shot, he had always succeeded in escaping from the toils of the police;

he had escaped unhurt from several conflicts and had sometimes inflicted loss on his pursuers. Not long after I came to the province of Agrigento, during a raid on the southern part of the province of Palermo, he had run into a group of five police agents with his whole band. Instead of opening fire, as was his wont, he had beaten a hasty retreat over the gentle slope of a small hill, disappearing from view over its shoulder. The police agents had immediately rushed in pursuit, but in their zeal they had not thought of the trap laid for them. Instead of coming on in open order, they had kept closely together. Grisafi and his companions were waiting for them on the other side of the slope: and a well-aimed volley caught the pursuers full at their appearance on the skyline, killing two brave men. [This incident took place in October 1916 in the territory of Genuardo shortly south of Baronessa.]'

'My arrival in the province of Agrigento had aroused some anxiety. I was told that the Grisafi band, which apparently numbered nine men at that time, had been reduced to six. Three of the bandits had preferred to go off on their own affairs. After a little time had elapsed, another bandit had gone away, owing to some dispute with the leader, and the band had been reduced to five – Grisafi, his brother, the two brothers Maniscalco and a certain Santangelo. At that rate there was the risk that the famous band ,would disappear into thin air, and I wanted to capture it, not to break it up' (Mori, 1933: 130-132).

The composition of the Grisafi band was continually subject to modification. Given the relatively long period during which the band maintained itself (1904-1917), the fact that some members were still teenagers suggests that older members were regularly replaced by youngsters.[8] Apart from its core (involving two sets of brothers, who were all from the same town), people from various neighbouring places formed a catchment for the band, though they were not recruited on every occasion. Up to a certain point, membership was intermittent so to speak. This was even more evident for the support on which the band had to rely in order to carry on its activities and to survive. After Grisafi and his men had killed the police-sergeant and a policeman from Genuardo in the incident described above, the band dispersed. Characteristically, the bandits did not take to the mountains, but to different towns where 'friends' hid them from the police for several days. In this respect, the chronicler refers to 'a thick net of local favour' and observes that the Grisafi band 'had eyes everywhere'. This perception of the situation had direct implications for the round-up. Mori sent out his men into the various places:

'that had been the scenes of the bandits' crimes in order to collect – without raising the alarm and so without any official formality – all possible current news on the past activities of the band and especially the necessary indications for identifying their habitual and occasional helpers, whether voluntary accomplices or compelled by fear . . . The network of assistance that had been drawn round the Grisafi band had grown wide, thick and strong in the course of time. The whole system was welded together by complicity in crimes, fear of reprisals, terror, espionage on behalf of the bandits, conflicting interests and equivocal alliances for the most varied ends, to an extent that made it almost impenetrable . . . One night, therefore by sudden simultaneous action in different places, I made an attempt to arrest all the helpers we had identified and against whom – at my own request, which had been kept secret – the judicial authorities had issued warrants of arrests: 357 persons in all, of whom ninety were in Grisafi's hometown alone' (Mori, 1933: 133-134).

This brings us back to the location and composition of the rival coalition that cooperated with Grisafi to intimidate and disrupt the Genuardo partnership – a manoeuvre which forced Domenico eventually to retire. Its location was clear: all members of the coalition were from the village of Adernò and employed as *campieri* on various estates of the Baronessa complex, including the four *latifondi* held in lease by Domenico and his two kinsmen. The Adernò coalition was mainly structured along links of kinship and marriage and contained sections of three patrinominal families represented as A, B, and C in Figure 1.

Figure 1. Composition of the Adernò coalition

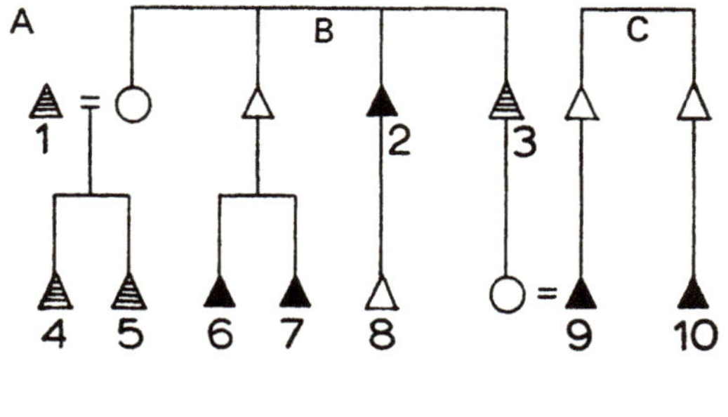

The solid triangles (numbered 2, 6, 7, 9, and 10) designate the *campieri* who supervised the estates leased by the Genuardo partnership. The hatched triangles (1, 3, 4, and 5) represent people who exercised similar functions of surveillance on three other estates of Baronessa held in lease by an impoverished nobleman, a certain Baron Francesco, who had moved from Genuardo to Adernò. His mistress' brother was set up as an additional *campiere* on one of these farms.

As appeared from legal documents and interviews with older people, the leader of the Adernò coalition was Person No. 9, a man called Edoardo, whose father and father's brother had been employed for several years as domestics in the Palermo house of the owner of Baronessa. Confidence between both families was built up during this period. It became clear that Grisafi acted by order of Edoardo, who kept him under cover. As one informant put it: 'Edoardo *garantiva* (protected) Grisafi'. We are here concerned with institutionalized proceedings in which people differentiate between the *mandante* (principal) and the *mandatario* (agent). These specific relationships between bandits and entrepreneurs are somewhat obscured in the otherwise interesting account of Mori, who tends to over-emphasize the role of Grisafi in the area. Though Grisafi interferred in many affairs, it is less correct to ascribe to him qualities like 'absolute control'. Grisafi's power was largely derived from the power domains of *mafiosi*, i.e. people like Edoardo, who were Grisafi's patrons, and who were themselves dependent on the protection provided by the estate owner in exchange for electoral support. As mentioned above, Grisafi was in fact captured as a result of Mori's technique of rolling up the network of support. After the arrest *en masse* of his friends, 'the Grisafi band, now on foot and without support, moved very little, owing to the fewness of houses where it could take refuge, had necessarily to go round the caves . . .' (Mori, 1933: 138).

We may assume that Edoardo already cherished for some time the wish to enter into the estates controlled by Domenico and seriously considered a partnership of leaseholding with some of his kinsmen. As indicated above, Domenico was faced at the time with the choice of either renewing the lease for another term of six years (September 1914 through August 1920) or leaving. Though he had opted for the first alternative (he was in office when Grisafi challenged him in early September 1914), he changed his mind after this violent confrontation with his rival. The fact that Edoardo and some of his kinsmen already established themselves as *campieri* on the very estates they intended to lease facilitated their manoeuvre. Their key-positions as 'men of confidence' supplied them with the intelligence to disrupt the Genuardo partnership from within and brought them into regular contact with the casual labourers set to work on the estates. We know that some of the latter were used by Edoardo to carry out thefts and rustlings suffered by Nicola. Again, these labourers acted under the guise of their role of employee. Likewise, Grisafi must have been informed about the appropriate time and place for his attacks. It is to be noted that these intrigues were by no means unusual as the following frequently quoted proverb illustrates: *Di dintra veni ccu lu voscu tagghia.* (He who cuts down the forest comes from inside.)

Domenico had to accept his defeat; his nephews were allowed to maintain their lease of one estate. For one thing, they lacked the human resources to resist Edoardo who was becoming very prominent at the time. Where Edoardo could rely on several adult male kinsmen, the Jaconis lacked these crucial assets. Domenico, already aging (he died in 1916), had only one son. Though Nicola and Michele had three other brothers, two of them had left for Argentina while the third, though present, was not available. Furthermore, their offspring was very much restricted and in any case too young to provide support. Nor could Domenico depend on other nephews.

Coalitions like the one formed by Edoardo and his kinsmen, which are involved in the control over land and cattle by violent means and which dominate a good deal of the local administration, are called *cosche*.[9] Though we have special names for them, we should resist the temptation to define these social units as clearly demarcated groups, separated as it were from other similar structures and persisting unchanged over time. When we try to stand back and take some distance from the incident described above, we can see this specific coalition in a state of flux and connected with several other units of interdependent individuals: the family of the estate owner, the Genuardo partnership, various clusters of peasants and shepherds, the Grisafi band, the police-squadron, and numerous other units which I was not able to trace out. All these coalitions, units, or whatever one may wish to call them, are interconnected and form an overall network of relationships which has regularities and a momentum of its own. This fluid pattern becomes evident when it is recognized that these interdependencies involve specific forms of cooperation and tension which account for a continual rearrangement of these coalitions seen singly as well as of the overall network. A particular sector of this network was very clearly grasped by Mori, who understood the *changing* structure of the Grisafi band with regard to what he aptly called 'a thick net of local favour'. The band was in a rapid state of flux, partly because of its in-built tensions and partly because of its specific relations with other units. It may be still worth while to point out that when these links were severed by the police, Grisafi and his four companions stopped being active as a band. Similar fluid patterns were formed by the Genuardo partnership and the emerging coalition of Adernò which resulted in the dissolution of the former, largely because its members were unable to join hands with others.

When Edoardo and his kinsmen had entrenched themselves as leaseholders on the Baronessa estates, they became involved in a series of events which can be understood in terms of the model of group dynamics as explored in the present essay. Before looking briefly at some of these episodes, a few crucial features of the setting must be remembered. *Mafiosi* were chiefly engaged in the control over land by violent means. In fact, they may be defined as violent entrepreneurs. Once they got a foothold on the large estate, either as lease-holder, *campiere*, or supervisor of the herds, they sought to accumulate wealth in various ways. Apart from the ordinary revenues from crops and animals and the various levies they imposed upon peasant sharecroppers, the rustling of cattle and sheep was one of the most important modes to social ascent. Ecological conditions strongly favoured the theft of animals. Natural pastures and their relative scarcity entailed a migratory orientation of animal husbandry, and this ruled out fixed boundaries and adequately fenced places where the animals could be effectively kept under surveillance. The same ecological constraints that brought cattle and sheep on long migratory routes and kept the herds roaming over desolate and distant *feudi* included, from the part of the successful owner, a maximum number of relationships with persons on whom he could rely for pastures, accommodation for his herdsmen, transport and marketing of the products, and several other facilities according to the circumstances.[10] These network relations of support and intelligence were not only crucial for the successful pastoralist but also for the successful rustler. It has been argued that in areas like Western Sicily both *métiers* tended to be highly concordant: 'Here bandits meet shepherds, and shepherds consider whether to become bandits'.[11] These networks, then, provided the organizational lay-out for rustling operations as well as the secure disposal of the booty. Not all thefts of animals were organized in this sense, but those which were, especially the large-scale raid, or *abigeato*, required careful preparation. It is to the organization of one particular series of thefts that we now turn.

During the summer of 1915, animals were stolen at three different places adjoining the Baronessa estates. A fourth raid at the end of October of the same year, involving 14 head of cattle, two mares, and one mule, took place near the estate managed by the Cassini family, the core of the *cosca* of Genuardo. Subsequent investigations by the police revealed that the four thefts (all suffered by owners from Genuardo), were organized by one and the same coalition which consisted of 17 *mafiosi* from Genuardo, Adernò, Bisacquino, and several other neigbouring towns, all situated along the borders of the three western provinces of the island. Apart from the *mafiosi*, six of whom acted as accomplices, seven landless labourers from Genuardo and three outlaws from distant towns had an active part in the operations. Each of the four occasions involved a unique combination of interdependent individuals which, however, overlapped on various points. Regarding the participation of the seven casual labourers, we know that they appeared on the estates under the pretext of seeking employment and went off after one or two days right after which a theft took place. The first rustling in June involved A and B; the second in August, C, D, and E; the third in September B and F; and the fourth in October again A and B. The part of the seventh labourer (G) is not specified in the records. The fourth raid, which took place on October 24, was prepared during two banquet meetings: one on September 29 in the house of Cascio Ferro at Bisacquino, one of the most powerful *mafiosi* of the area at the time; the other on October 21, at the *feudo* Misilbesi located in the commune of the neighbouring town of Villamaura, and also presided over by Cascio Ferro. About 16 persons participated in the latter assembly. The six accomplices mentioned above were *gabelloti, campieri,* and livestock supervisors engaged in the management of the Misilbesi estate. It was at this place that a few days after the fourth rustling a third meeting took place during which the money acquired from the sale of the stolen animals was divided.

These fragmented details concerning the raids became known when the police-sergeant of Genuardo tracked down one of the outlaws involved in these thefts and stole in upon him at the Misilbesi estate in the late afternoon of October 30. We have already seen how this ill-starred man met his death at the hands of the bandit Grisafi on one of these reconnoitring tours through the area in October of the next year. Betrayed by one of the stolen mares, the outlaw was identified as a certain Zarzana, 28 years of age and from a place in the province of Trapani some 30 miles west of Genuardo. On account of homicide and extortion, several warrants for his arrest had been issued by the judicial authorities in the area in the course of the past years. A cash reward was offered for his capture. On Zarzana the police found a booklet containing a note regarding the division of the spoils.

As far as the organizers were concerned, we note, apart from the presence of Cascio Ferro, the following persons: Edoardo, his cousin, and three cousins of his wife (represented as 6, 7, 8, 9, and 10 in Figure 1); Giuseppe Cassini and his eldest son Alessandro; and a man called Aloisio Olivieri, also from Genuardo. When we remember the Edoardo-Grisafi alliance which overpowered the Genuardo partnership on Baronessa in the autumn of 1914, we note a striking flexibility in organization of the Adernò coalition as reflected in the considerable range and diversity of relationships in which this coalition was involved. I have described elsewhere how tensions between the *cosche* of Genuardo and Adernò resulted in a series of violent conflicts in the process of which two members of the former were killed. This happened in the early 1920s when Cascio Ferro and Edoardo together with their entourage held down and vassalized the territory of Genuardo. They were protected from exactions of the law by various estate owners, who depended upon these local strongmen for electoral support. Fascism settled accounts with the local *cosche* the power domains of which conflicted openly with the now sustained efforts of the State to monopolize the use of physical force, and thus these specific coalitions of violent entrepreneurs and bandits largely disappeared from the area by the end of the 1920s. With the fall of the régime in 1943, however, they gradually re-emerged. Partly old and partly new *mafiosi* joined together in partnerships to manage and supervise the estates and to dominate again the local administration. As before, these coalitions involved persons from several villages and towns. Regarding the Baronessa complex, three members of the Cassinis and four sons of Olivieri (these two families had become interrelated through marriage in the course of time) joined several younger kinsmen of Edoardo, who himself had set off for America just before the Fascist intervention. The built-in tensions of this coalition were largely controlled by the fact that restive peasants, backed by left-wing parties and trade-unions, invaded and occupied large estates and demanded radical agrarian reform.

The subsequent development of these realignments need not be discussed here. It may suffice to note that coalitions of *mafiosi* were closely bound to the organization of the *masseria* and strongly depended upon the specific position of estate owners at the regional and national level. These specific interdependencies eventually withered after the impact of reform that broke up most of the large estates in recent years.

4. CONCLUSIONS

In the study of human organizations we should refrain from polarizing the individual and the social units he forms with his fellow-men. New conceptual tools are needed to enlarge our understanding of this specific relationship. In this paper I have tried to argue that some fashionable terms as coalition, network, social structure, and society may prove useful when we provide them with a meaning which corresponds more closely with what we actually observe. Among other things, this involves the effort from our part to see these social units as formed by individual people linked to one another in numerous ways: the concatenation of the aim-oriented actions of these people results in a fluid pattern of which the course and product are largely unplanned and unforeseen by the very individuals who help to bring them about. In this theoretical framework there is no room for purely egocentric concepts since they systematically overemphasize the freedom of the individual just as they tend to underrate the significance of the restraints and self-restraints which result from any involvement in chains of interdependencies. If we likewise succeed in disencumbering ourselves from the erroneous belief that social units and societies are something abstracted from the individuals who form them, we can see that social structures have dynamics of their own which result from their in-built tensions and the extent to which the people who form these structures are able to cope with them. It has been noted that, given the basic characteristics of the descriptive concepts we habitually use, there is no way to observe and describe an event of change: in social anthropology, the specification of continuity is highly problematical (See Barth, 1967). The present discussion, which concentrated on coalitions among Sicilian peasant entrepreneurs and on the way in which these temporary groups were connected with other structures and changed with changes in the overall network of relationships, may be considered as an attempt to recover from this *impasse*.

ACKNOWLEDGEMENTS

This paper is a much revised version of the original draft presented at the conference on network approaches in Leiden, September 1969. The material on which it is based was collected in Western Sicily during the period April 1965 to June 1967 while I held a fellowship from the Netherlands Organization for the Advancement of Pure Research (Z.W.O.). For advice and criticism I am indebted to several members of the seminar. My thinking on the specific character of the relationship between the two aspects of men to which we refer as society and individual has been greatly stimulated by the writings of Norbert Elias.

NOTES

1. Firth, for example, distinguishes between strongly and weakly structured kin groups, clarifying the distinction as follows: 'By strongly and weakly structured is meant relatively many or few corporate functions and sanctions, and relatively great or little continuity' (1963: 24).

2. See Barnes (1968). Barnes rejects the terms 'egocentric network' and 'personal network', but introduces new terms ('star' and 'zone') to retain the concept of egocentric structure.

3. This model of configurations has been developed by Norbert Elias in various writings, e.g. Elias and Scotson (1965); Elias and Dunning (1966); and Elias (1969,

1970). Configurational sociology represents a 'sociological realism and stands in contrast to sociological theories which treat societies as if they were mere names, a "flatum voci", an "ideal type", a sociologist's construction, and which are in that sense representative of sociological nominalism... Individuals always come in configurations and configurations are always formed by individuals' (Elias and Dunning 1966: 396-97). Elias demonstrates that these configurations (a group of dancers, players on a football field, a village, a political party, a State organization, and inter-State relations) have regularities, structures, and dynamics of their own. The inherent tensions and conflicts of these changing configurations may be better understood when we consider them as aspects of the purposeless dynamics of groups, for whatever the aims of the people who form them, configurations are at the same time ends in themselves with dynamics of their own.

4. See Barth (1963: 9), who describes a niche as 'the point at which an entrepreneur seeks to exploit the environment: the position which he occupies in relation to resources, competitors and clients'.

5. See Bobek (1962) and Wolf (1966: 55-57), who has considerably expanded the argument on rent capitalism by linking it to specific forms of domains and ecosystems.

6. The Concise Oxford Dictionary of Current English. *Cf.* Boissevain (1971).

7. Regarding patrinominal kin groups, Firth noted that 'in the ordinary European system of patrinominal families the use of the patronymic in successive generations as surnames does allow for the recognition of a kin group (not necessarily *descent* group) of members of two or more generations. A European patrinominal kin group is not exclusive, that is, kin bearing other patronyms combine as working members within the same social entity. But the continuity of common name gives a fairly ready means of identification' (Firth, 1963: 24-25).

8. This trend is consistent with Hobsbawm's statement that 'the most important source of bandits is the age-group of male youth between puberty and marriage, i.e. before the weight of full family responsibilities has begun to bend men's back' (Hobsbawm, 1969: 25).

9. Singular: *cosca,* which etymologically refers to artichoke (It.: *carciofo;* Sic.: *cacocciula*). The term *cacocciula* is also used to denote a local coalition of violent entrepreneurs or *mafiosi: 'E' della cacocciula',* he belongs to the local *mafia.* This subject has received detailed treatment elsewhere (Blok, 1972).

10. The organizational flexibility of pastoralists has been noted by several anthropologists, *cf.* Pehrson (1964); Paine (1970); and Schneider (1971). They suggest that the freedom to form strategic alliances requires a flexible social matrix offering multiple channels of association.

11. Hobsbawm (1969: 28). Several dimensions of brigandage are critically explored in a forthcoming discussion (Blok and Hobsbawm, n.d.).

Politics on the village level

D. G. JONGMANS

1. INTRODUCTION

During my field work in a small village in northern Tunesia[1] I became interested in the field of political structure and political process. While searching for relevant and useful case material I came across a conflict which some ten years ago had kept the village on edge for a considerable period of time. A thorough analysis of this 'extended' case, so it seemed to me, would enlarge and deepen my insight in the political field.

When the conflict broke out between two male inhabitants of the village, each of the two rivals tried to find adherents among the other male inhabitants. The respective factions were formed by exploiting to the utmost the existing relationships, based on kinship, affinity, locality and friendship. For some people the determining forces were straightforward: they had relationships of a more or less obligatory character with only one of the two rivals. They had no option but to do their duty. For others, however, these four determining forces were complex. Relationships of a more or less obligatory type could be traced to both rivals. Through the analysis of such cases, the relative importance of the various determining forces could be worked out.

Another problem which seemed worth solving was by whom adherents of each party were being mobilized – by the two rivals alone or by the two rivals and their supporters together.

Then I wished to investigate in detail the influence of the conflict on the web of existing social relations in the village. Were these relationships affected by the conflict? Were they brought into line according to the adage: my friends' friends are my friends and my enemies' friends are my enemies? If the answer were positive, the factions organized by the rivals would have formed themselves into coalitions. To make a long story short: apart from the conflict itself, I was interested in the first place in the way the web of existing relations was affected by this conflict. This problem constitutes the core of this paper.

Therefore it was essential to collect material pertaining to the network of existing interpersonal relationships prior to the conflict, as well as that illustrating the relations after the conflict had been resolved or settled. The comparison of the two situations might lead to the formulation of a number of answers to my questions.

Moreno[2] has shown how it is possible in a conveniently arranged manner to achieve a semblance of order in the apparent chaos of social relations. First by drawing up sociograms, later by arranging his material in the form of 'matrices'.

In sociology too, matrices, although not used often, were introduced a long time ago. I refer to the excellent study of Festinger, Schachter and Back, *Social Pressures in Informal Groups*, published in 1950.[3]

To me the usefulness of the analysis of matrices seems to be beyond question. I was surprised therefore, that anthropologists, even those who handle the word 'network' – Radcliffe-Brown may serve as an example[4] – hardly if ever adhered to the procedures stipulated by Moreno. Fortunately the first networks have now been diagramatically represented, and here I refer to Kapferer's article 'Norms and the Manipulation of Relationships in a Work Context'.[5] Mitchell is of the opinion that the analysis of networks is a useful tool for social anthropological research in an urban setting.[6] I myself am convinced that this tool has the same merits for analysis in a rural setting, the more so as we proceed from structural and functional analysis to the analysis of social processes, from roles and norms to choice and option, and from the analysis of static societies to the research of rapidly changing communities.

This paper is based on two matrices. The first one represents the mutual relations among the 48 male heads of families immediately prior to the conflict. The second portrays the relations of these family heads after the conflict came to an end. These 'network formations'[7] are the sum total of the 48 total personal networks of the heads of families within the boundaries of the village.

Wherever these personal networks extend beyond the boundaries of the village this has been left out of the picture. I apologise for not being able to map these matrices in their totality, since I have had to handle and map $2 \times 49 \times (49\text{-}1) = 4704$ data. Moreover, the analysis of these network formations will not be exhaustive.

This paper must be considered as an attempt to analyse the two matrices, completed in August 1969. The analysis at home has given rise to a number of questions on details which have to be solved by returning to the field. I am aware of a number of omissions. For instance, I shall not discuss in detail kinship and politics, or marriage and politics, while further no detailed genealogical material will be given. This paper is only meant to give an idea of the type of analysis of a political conflict using the analytical tool of network formations, however.

The research was conducted in Ramlia, a village situated in the Khroumiria, the northernmost mountain region of Tunisia. There is an abundant rainfall and the mountain slopes are grown with the dense forest of oak, cork trees and shrubs so characteristic of the mediterranean area. Primarily the Khroumirians are pastoralists. They give preference to goat breeding. Cattle and sheep, which are more vulnerable in the mediterranean, are only kept in small numbers. In addition, wheat and barley are grown on the lowest parts of the mountain slopes.

The French invasion of 1881 spelt the end of the relatively independent existence of the Khroumirians. The French established a fort at the highest point in Khroumiria and founded Ain Draham in the immediate vicinity. Ain Draham, situated at a distance of less than 3 miles from the village of Ramlia, was turned into a garrison, the centre of the administration of Khroumiria, and a market and shopping centre. At present it has about 5000 inhabitants.

In general, French civilization did not leave a deep impression on the Khroumirians. Admittedly they found work in the French army or with entrepreneurs, or with those involved in the exploitation of cork trees. But in the French period there were no Khroumirians resident in Ain Draham. The French school was only accessible to the sons of tribal sheiks and a few indigenous notables. The French in turn had little if any interest in the Khroumirians or their fertile soil.

After independence, in 1956, there were rapid changes. The government is feverishly trying to raise the material and spiritual standard of Khroumiria. It is interesting to note the measures adopted by the Tunisian government to combat erosion and conserve the soil.

Seriously alarmed by the problem of erosion, which was attributed to the goats – the black locust of North Africa – the Government in 1958 prohibited the population from keeping goats in the middle and northern parts of the country. The people were given a mere four months to get rid of their goats.

Simplified genealogy of Ramlia

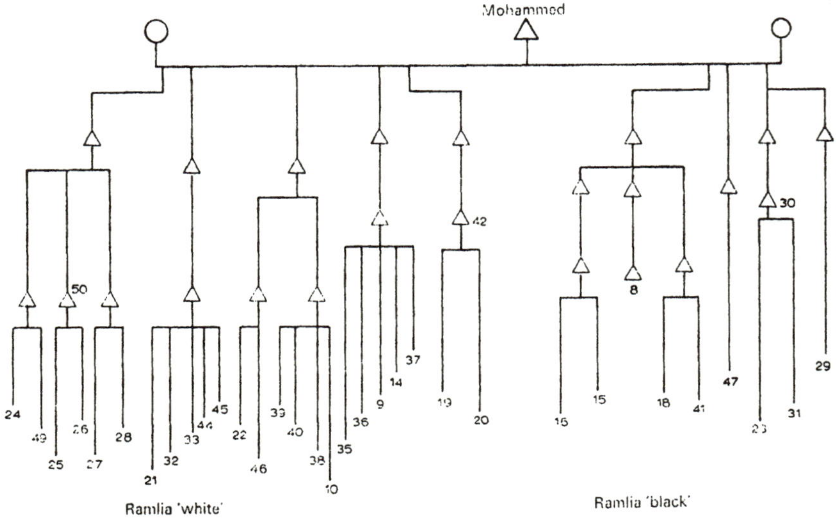

The topographical situation of the houses in Ramlia

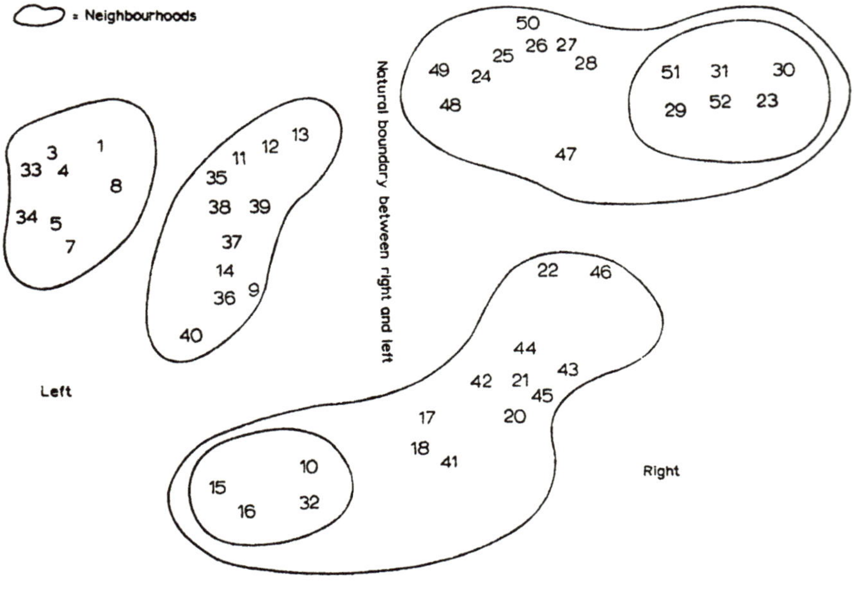

The inflated supply caused the market prices to drop to 40% of the original value. This meant that a herd of 15-20 goats, the average ownership per household, could be exchanged for only one cow. There were other remedial measures. In the interest of soil conservation it was forbidden to cultivate those slopes which were threatened or affected by erosion. To the inhabitants of Ramlia this meant a loss of about 50% of the arable land.

The employment opportunities which were created post haste had to stave off hunger and starvation among the Khroumirians. All those people who did not earn a regular income were put to work at a remuneration of 3.5 D.[8] monthly and a maximum 25 kilos of flour p/m. If one takes into consideration that the price level does not differ much from that in Holland, and adds to this the costs of education for children, then one realizes that the existence of the inhabitants of Khroumiria has been precarious for some scores of years. The happy few included only those who succeeded in finding employment in Ain Draham.

This pauperization has had a serious effect on the whole village, with the exception of those who found sanctuary in Ain Draham at one stage or another. Most of them have turned their backs on their village in order to escape compulsory participation in the state of dire penury. At the time of the disaster Ramlia had 49 families. Now it only boasts a paltry 32. The rest of the population unanimously agree that social life has been corroded, that individualism and egotism have increased and that conflicts are more prevalent than before.

The conflict

The conflict in question must be seen against the background of the prohibition on goats and the withdrawal of 50% of the arable land. Once the inhabitants were fully aware of the government's plans, land became an even more precious commodity. Khadar, one of the 'informal' village chiefs (he will later be indicated as no. 30) decided to cash in on the deal by trying to gain control in advance of a piece of land which formed part of the public domain. This was the place where the men tarried a while with their cattle in the afternoons or held their meetings. It was not affected by the ban. He appointed his 'opulent' son (indicated in the matrix as no. 23), who was generally known as an extremely egoistic person, to accomplish the assignment. No. 23 proceeded to put the public area under the plough without prior consultation.

Most of the villagers took this development quietly. After all, no. 30 was the village chief and they were appeased with promises that they would share in the produce. However, ben Mosbah Tounsi (no. 12), flew into a rage and would not take this arbitrary action lying down. He was not so much angry about the cultivation of the land as he was at the affront offered him. No. 30 was, after all, of the opinion that no. 12 and his kin could lay no claim to any land whatever in Ramlia, let alone land which was public property. By reclaiming the land himself, he had made himself clear in no uncertain terms.

In order to grasp the meaning of no. 30's action, it is necessary to know a little about the history of the village of Ramlia. The village was established about 80 years ago by Mohammed and his sons. They had been given the right to settle and develop it by Ouled el Haj, the owners of the valley in which Ramlia is situated. The boundaries within which Mohammed and his sons could begin their work of development were indicated precisely. Mohammed and his sons set their shoulders to the wheel. Their anger was aroused, however, when strangers also began to develop land in the area assigned to them. They disputed this right, but Nasser would not submit, not even in the face of violence. The case was put before some wise men who were neutral, who were forced to conclude that Nasser was within his legal rights because he, too, had been granted permission by Ouled el Haj to reclaim and develop land.

Mohammed and his followers were then forced by the Ouled el Haj to accept Nasser and his supporters (together they formed the Nasseria) and to respect their rights. A wild race to outbid each other in developing the land ensued. The conflict between no. 30 and no. 12 is a continuation of an age-old family feud. After all, no. 12 is a descendant of Nasser and no. 30 one of Mohammed.

In order to gain a clear insight into the conflict it is also necessary to examine the mutual relations between the descendants of Mohammed. (In Khroumiria descent is patrilineal.)

Mohammed had two wives. The first was the daughter of a rich and influential man; the second was a 'plain Jane' of poor parentage. The sons of these two women (i.e., the half-brothers) did not see eye to eye with each other. The sons of the more affluent mother considered themselves superior to the sons of the poorer wife and made no bones about it. Spurred on by this rivalry, the sons of the poorer wife tried to develop as much land as possible in the area assigned to Mohammed. The sons of the richer wife were not to be outdone, however. This reclamation squabble was conducted with more prudence and tactical insight by the wealthier offspring, so that the 'inferior branch' was forced to seek alliance with Nasser. Ramlia, at the time of the big conflict between no. 30 and no. 12, counted among its inhabitants:

1a) 'black' Ramlia, the descendants of Mohammed and his wealthy spouse, indicated on the matrices as nos. 8, 15, 16, 17, 18, 41, 47, 29, 30, 31, 23;

1b) 'white' Ramlia, the patrilineal descendants of Mohammed and his impecunious spouse, indicated on the matrices as nos. 24, 25, 26, 27, 28, 49, 50, 21, 32, 44, 45, 43, 22, 46, 20, 40, 39, 38, 10, 35, 36, 6, 9, 14, 37, 20, 42.

2) The descendants of Nasser, indicated on the matrices as nos. 5, 7, 11, 12, 13.

3) Immigrants.

a) The sons of 'white' and 'black' women married off to men in other villages. Once these sons are mature, they petition their mothers' brothers, be they 'black' or 'white', for the right to settle in Ramlia (i.e., the village from which their mother hails) on the land ceded by their mothers to their brothers on the occasion of their marriage and departure. This request can hardly be refused.

In the matrices the 'black' sisters' sons are nos. 3, 33, 51, 52; the 'white' sisters' sons are nos. 4, 34.

b) Those immigrants who have married women from Ramlia and have asked their father-in-law the right to move in with him, indicated in the matrices as no. 1 (who is at the same time the son of a mother from Ramlia).

'Black' and 'white' local labels differ in their historical development. 'Black', tinged with a feeling of superiority, has taken a traditional standpoint. To the members of 'black', agriculture and pastoral farming are virtually the only sources of existence. Any person with insufficient lands at his disposal would try to acquire land elsewhere and would not hesitate to move. In contrast, 'white' did not seek a solution in the continuation of the traditional pattern, nor did they embark on new courses when they encountered similar problems. They concentrated especially on the cultivation of contacts in Ain Draham and the acquisition of lucrative positions. The greater attachment of the 'white' inhabitants to Ramlia is reflected in their numerical strength over the 'black' inhabitants. To every 11 'blacks' we find 26 'whites'.[9]

But let us return to the conflict. No. 30, an intelligent and shrewd man in business affairs and inter-human relations realized very well that the black Ramlia would suffer more than the white Ramlia and the Nasseria from the ban on goats or the freezing of half the arable land. After all, the basis of their existence was land and livestock.

'White', already regarded as inferior, would not be so seriously affected. They had less land and livestock at their disposal per head. This new turn of events could easily lead to a reversal in the 'black-white' relationship. More aggravating was the fact that the Nasseria, who were already wealthy, would lose relatively little. The favourable layout of their lands and the fact that no. 12, Mosbah, was working for wages in Ain Draham and, as a result of the departure of the French, had nothing to lose, were important factors favouring Nasseria. No. 30 the 'black' village chief, especially feared that Mosbah, no. 12, who was known among his relatives and neighbours for his magnanimity, wisdom and ability to arbitrate in times of conflict, could at some stage or other emerge as village chief and find easy recognition.

In such a case his wealth could be an added boon to the inhabitants of Ramlia, who might suffer under the new government measures. Up to this point the two informal village chiefs had always been 'supplied' by 'black' and 'white'. But if 'black' should be seriously impoverished, and this seemed to be the general expectation, then it would perhaps have to do without the material resources which are so essential for effectively exercising authority and for the strength of leadership. For this reason no. 30 decided to attack no. 12. In the land-developing issue no. 30 made it quite clear that as far as he was concerned no. 12 was without any rights, and that he should not put on any airs.

No. 30 speculated on the unanimous support of black by making reference to 'stealing the land' and because of his hopes that black would have no difficulty in perceiving the danger spelt by no. 12.

Moreover, he hoped that white would also take his side if he manipulated his ideological weapons well. Then no. 12 would be defenceless, exposed to all and sundry, and forced to admit in his hour of affliction that only a few people supported him. This would throw a decisive spanner in no. 12's village chieftaincy aspirations.

Meziaa[10]

For a thorough understanding of the political structure and processes in Ramlia it is essential to give a brief account of the concept known as *meziaa*. The world view of the Khroumirians is permeated with the idea of mutual service. The word for this is *meziaa*, 'service'. Everyone in Ramlia renders favours to kin, neighbours, fellow villagers of foreign origin and to inhabitants of other villages. The many proverbs making reference to the *meziaa*-concept underscore its importance. My chief informant summarized the following: 'Help me today, I shall help you tomorrow'; 'He who renders many a *meziaa*, lives on after death'; 'With *meziaa* one forges a bridge across the ocean' (i.e., achieves the impossible); 'With *meziaa* you turn people into brothers'; 'The *meziaa* is like a saw, it goes once in your direction, once in mine'.

Not only human beings are in each other's service; men and livestock also are, men providing food and shelter for the livestock, the animals giving milk.

The earth and humans also help each other. Man ploughs the fields (the earth is like a woman; man sees to it that the field woman becomes fertile). The land provides food for the cultivator's family. The saint intercedes with Allah on man's behalf; the followers of a *marabout* pay him 'homage' (to show someone respect and honour is considered a very important service). Even the earth and the sea stand in a *meziaa*-relation to one another. The earth carries the sea, and in return the sea supplies the earth with rain. The word also has a political connotation. Followers perform services for their leaders, and vice-versa the leader reciprocates.

According to Khroumirian concepts, a service is only a *meziaa* if:

1. It is done 'with a good heart' (with the right disposition);
2. There is question of reciprocity;
3. Those who have once been recipients of *meziaa's* do more in return than they have received;
4. He who has rendered a *meziaa* to someone else does not talk to others or boast about it.

In actual practice, the Khroumirians consider all services as *meziaa's*. They distinguish five types of *meziaa's*.

1. The *meziaa* 'with the good heart'. This is a *meziaa* in the true sense of the word. The basis is complete confidence.
2. The *meziaa* reserved for a later stage. Such *meziaa's* are also performed in good faith, but in smaller numbers. Here, too, trust forms the basis. Whereas the partners may feel the need to perform a *meziaa* for each other as often as possible, circumstances may act against it. Mutual quarrels between their respective children cause the *meziaa*-partners to fear that their relations may suffer. They limit their contact, therefore, which in essence implies a diminishing of *meziaa's*. Later, when the children have learnt to tolerate one another better they can switch over to showing *meziaa* 'with a good heart'.
3. The *pro forma meziaa*. The partners dare not break off relations out of considerations of respectability and pretend that it is a *meziaa* 'with a good heart' or one intended for a later stage. This requires, according to popular Khroumirian usage, 'a confidence like the sun shining in January' (hidden behind the clouds).
4. The *meziaa* 'with the bad heart'. Like that listed under 3 it also is a *contradiction in terms*. Such a *meziaa* is performed with the aim of causing damage at the appropriate moment. The attitude which forms the basis for this is known as 'lip-service'.

5. The compulsory *meziaa*. This is grafted onto the '*laazem*', that obligation resulting from kinship and relationship by affinity and/or proximity. He who adheres to such 'bare' *laazem*, runs the risk of incurring punishment for being party to a *meziaa* 'with a bad heart'. Relatives neighbours, etc., are therefore expected to do more than that, as prescribed by the '*laazem*'.

The system of *meziaa's* forms a very important part of the basis of the village chief's authority. At the time of the conflict in 1958, no. 50 (white) and no. 30 (black) were *kebir douar* (literally: village elders) of Ramlia.

The requirements made of such a *kebir douar* on informal leader are that

1. He is wise and of sober character, with a good ability to judge. In general a certain age is a prerequisite;
2. He knows the history of the village thoroughly; more specifically, that he is aware of the problems relating to the possession of land;
3. He is capable of settling disputes.

Apart from these qualities, he must also excel in Khroumirian virtues. He must be generous, a source of strength to widows and orphans, a haven of refuge to the poor, i.e. he must excel in those *meziaa's* which are highly rated on the *meziaa* market. Of cardinal importance, too, is the fact that he must excel in the number of *meziaa* relations which he maintains in his village or outside it.

The *kebir douar* does not possess any formal authority. He has to justify his role, his importance, time and again. If he fails, and his advice is not useful, and if he can no longer reconcile antagonists, he becomes redundant.

The villagers then drop him and seek a replacement. The *meziaa* relationship is of fundamental importance. A person involved in such a *meziaa* relationship may expect of his opposite number that he will help and support him and take his side in difficult issues during the discussions in the men's meeting-place. If this does not happen there is the danger that the *kebir douar* may sever his *meziaa* relationship with such an unfaithful partner. Due to a number of carefully selected *meziaa* relations, a *kebir* who plays his part well is in a position to influence public opinion or find support for his point of view. Services rendered imply counter-favours. The *kebir douar* can only expect help if he invests in his relations. To the poor he gives food and clothing; he puts in a good word for other persons with the sheik.

He can enhance the prestige of the *meziaa* relation among his *meziaa* associates by inviting them to his house and liberally providing them with tea, food and smoking materials. In order to invest he also has to be rich and generous with his surplus. By intensifying his relationship and increasing his investment per relationship he strengthens his position. By diminishing the number of his relationships and decreasing his investment he undermines his own position. In short, one can easily approach the political structure and process in Khroumiria by means of the theory of exchange evolved by Homans, Thibault and Kelly, and Blau.[11]

When the conflict erupted nos. 30 and 12 tried to mobilize as large a number of their *meziaa* relations as possible. Nos. 12 and 30 were in the good books of some inhabitants and in the bad of others. Thus many were placed in an awkward predicament.

No. 30 would be the victor if no. 12 should lose, numerically speaking. In the case of a numerical balance, no. 12 would not emerge as the loser. The result was practically a 'draw'.

No. 12 had the unqualified support of 18 villagers, and with some reservations that of three others. No. 30 could depend on the unqualified support of 18 villagers, and possibly one more. Double roles (N.B. two-faction struggles) were played by five persons among whom was the 'white' village chief. In addition there were three neutrals. No. 12 was not to disappoint his supporters.

When the second village chief, who was and continued to be a friend of both no. 12 and no. 30, but who was not fully trusted by no. 12, failed to supply a solution the tribal sheik was consulted. The tribal sheik availed himself of a committee of sage, experienced men who did not hail from Ramlia. They concluded that the actions of no. 30 were arbitrary and that the right of no. 12 had been violated. No. 30 was not forced to cede his developed land.

No. 12 was given the right to develop a piece of the public domain. He, however, very proudly declined the offer. Undoubtedly he considered the fact that his villagers could hardly do without a public area. If no. 30 was the de facto winner, no. 12 certainly was the moral and real victor.

2. MAPPING

One by one the 49 nuclear family heads were asked to describe their relations with the rest of the villagers in terms of Khroumirian *meziaa* relations. Even when we were forced to go back eleven years in time we did not encounter many problems, for this conflict was still fresh in the minds of most people. As each villager was subjected to questioning, information on every *meziaa* relation was obtained from both partners. There was hardly any disagreement on the quality of their relationships between the partners.[12]

In the following tables denotes:

B or Bc = *meziaa* relations 'with a good heart'
P = *meziaa* relations reserved for a later stage
F = *meziaa* relations *pro forma*
m = *meziaa* relations 'with a bad heart'

In addition we have included:

N = a neutral relation
E = enmity relation between any two inhabitants of the village

3. SOME NUMERICAL RESULTS

Comparisons of the two matrices reveal that a real shift has taken place in the nature of the relationships.

	B	P	F	N	m	E
Before	704	527	443	611	62	5
After	662	143	289	636	9	613

One may conclude that:

1. The relations 'with a good heart' are considerably reduced;
2. The number of neutral relations has remained relatively stable, while the inimical relations have increased to such an extent that they are almost as numerous as those 'with a good heart'.

Taking into consideration the decreases in categories P and F (there is no room for those who assume a midway position), one may speak of a certain polarisation in the relations.

In my opinion some simple calculations may be useful in arriving at a better understanding of the changes which have occurred. A number of relations did not undergo any change. Scrutinizing the categories of relations which remained unchanged we arrive at the following result:

375 out of 704 original B relations did not undergo a change
464 out of 527 original P relations did not undergo a change
(a confirmation of the instability of the P relations)
90 out of 443 original F relations did not undergo a change
303 out of 611 original N relations did not undergo a change
0 out of 62 original m relations did not undergo a change.

Expressing the degree of stability in percentages and arranging the categories from the highest to the lowest according to the stability, we arrive at the following measure of stability (in %):

B	N	F	P	m
53	50	20	12	0

It would be going too far to deal extensively with the material on the devaluated categories, as all the material has not yet been worked out properly and a great deal of research still has to be undertaken in the field. But we find here a survey of the frequency of the different types of devaluation. The 704 B relations gave rise to the development of:

34	P relations
109	F relations
5	m relations
99	N relations
82	E relations
329	relations

The chance that P relations would develop from a B relation is more remote than the possibility of a change from B to F, or B to N, or B to E. In which cases and under what circumstances does a B relation change into a P relation and what is the difference between a P relation and an F relation under different conditions?

I hope to gain some clarity through a precise and thorough analysis of the material. It would be even more expedient to re-open the issue with the inhabitants of the village after formulating precise questions. Before the conflict broke out there were 527 P relations. Only 64 P relations did not undergo any change and 374 relations were devalued:

74	P relations changed into F relations
2	P relations changed into m relations
143	P relations changed into N relations
155	P relations changed into E relations
374	relations changed into other relations

If we compare the two tables above, we learn that the instability of the P relations finds reflection in the fact that there are proportionately more P than B relations which develop into N or E relations. When and in which cases would this be otherwise? If P and F are both unstable relations, what is the difference?

Of the 349 cases which show an improvement in relations we have the following crystallisation:

144 improved from F to B
89 improved from P to B
57 improved from F to P
12 improved from N to F
20 improved from N to P
16 improved from N to B
4 improved from m to F
3 improved from m to P
4 improved from m to B

Improvements from E to N, E to m, E to F, E to P and E to B are not to be found. In general, category N showed an improvement in relation on a moderate scale. This is indeed also the case in categories F and P. Under what conditions are these changes likely to occur?

There is the possibility of viewing the stability and change per family head. Let us compare the numbers 10 and 32, close neighbours and both belonging to the 'white' party. Before the conflict no. 10 and no. 32 could claim the following number of relations:

	B	P	F	N	m	E	Total
No. 10	17	10	9	10	2	–	48
No. 32	15	17	10	6	–	–	48

No. 10 succeeded in 15 cases in keeping his relations constant; no. 32, however, in 18. No. 10 lost more in terms of relations than no. 32. For no. 10 there were 28 cases of devalued relationships, for no. 32 only 22 cases. If we count a change from B to P as one step, a change from P to F as one step, a change from B to F as 2 steps, a change from B to E as 5 steps, and so on, then no. 10 in 28 cases devalued 63 steps, but no. 32 in 22 cases only 44 steps. No. 10 succeeded in improving the quality of 5 partnerships; no. 32 succeeded in improving 8 partnerships, however.

The new relationships of nos. 10 and 32 are shown in the following table.

	B	P	F	N	m	E	Total
No. 10	10	1	15	10	–	12	48
No. 32	13	5	10	19	–	1	48

If we accept that no. 32 showed a slightly better pattern of relationships than no. 10 before the conflict broke out, then we can also conclude that no. 10 has lost more in terms of relations than no. 32. While no. 32 had to face only one enemy, no. 10 was surrounded with 12 enemies!

The explanation of these cases is not difficult. No. 32 and no. 10 were close neighbours and both of 'white' descent. Although they lived in the *left* part of the village, they are nowhere near no. 12. No. 10 is the brother of no. 12's wife and thus a mother's brother of nos. 11 and 13, the sons of his sister and no. 12. He was thus forced to support no. 12. But no. 10 had to pay dearly for it even in a neighbourhood which partly adopts a neutral position between nos. 30 and 12. No. 10 can be considered a victim because he is a member of Nasseria, the party of no. 12. He is even more of a sitting duck because he finds himself in a foreign environment far from Nasseria and did not share in the improvement in relations between Nasseria and its close neighbours.

No. 32 is of 'white' descent, too. Before the outbreak of the conflict his relations with no. 12 were excellent (B). He was married to the sister of no. 12's wife and thus forced by his wife to come to the support of no. 12. Why, then, being a neighbour of no. 10, did he not suffer in the same way? Because no. 32 was the local shopkeeper who, for the sake of his shop, devalued his relations with no. 12 from B to F (as a token for the 'black' party that he did not fully agree with no. 12). The 'black' party and the other villagers did not want to devalue their relations with no. 32 to any great extent (he had only one enemy) because in the interest of his shop he was prepared to sell on credit. And that was a *meziaa* of great importance.

No. 32 was 'excused', the more so as his elder brother, no. 21, gave his full support to no. 12. But no. 10, who had neither a brother nor a shop, was forced to support no. 12 and had to pay for it.

I think that if we compare the stability and changes per family head for a number of persons, and trace who devalued and who did not, then we may arrive at an adequate insight in the conflict that shook Ramlia.

4. THE FORMATION OF FACTIONS

If up to this point we have only made calculations, it is useful to remember that the matrices can also be analysed differently. No. 23 appropriated the land, which was interpreted by no. 12 as an affront, and he was right. No. 12 knew very well that no. 30 had a finger in the pie. He felt that it was a personal attack on him and the whole of Nasseria.

What happened to Nasseria? They closed their ranks, which is deducible from the matrices indicating the dispositions of the members of Nasseria towards one another before and after the conflict. These are the numbers 11, 12, 13 and 5. One F relation is converted into a B relation, so that between the members of Nasseria integration on the highest level has taken place.

Matrix 1

	Before				After			
	12	13	11	5	12	13	11	5
12	.	B	B	B	.	B	B	B
13		.	B	B		.	B	B
11			.	F			.	B
5				.				.

No. 7 is a descendant of Brinis who came to the village as a herdsman of Nasser, who gave his name to Nasseria. Then Brinis married a daughter of Nasser and settled on a piece of land given him by Nasser. Making a living on part of Nasser's estate bears the implication of political assistance to Nasser's male descendants – heirs – as though no. 7 were one of Nasser's sons or grandsons. No. 7 behaves according to this binding obligation and closes ranks with Nasseria. The relations of 7 before and after the conflict are shown in the following table.

7 –	11	12	13	5
Before	F	B	P	B
After	B	B	B	B

No. 1 is the sister's son of no. 12 and lives on the land of no. 12. Apart from other obligations – he has married a stepdaughter of no. 12 – he is obliged to give full support to his mother's brother and numbers 11, 13, 5 and 7 who live on the estate of Nasser.

1	11	12	13	5	7
Before	B	B	B	B	P
After	B	B	B	B	B

An attack on the honour of no. 12 is an attack on the honour of all the heirs of Nasser. This honour has to be defended collectively. The acknowledgement of this duty is expressed by mutual cooperation on the highest level, that of relations with a good heart based on complete mutual trust.

Matrix 2

	Before						After					
	11	12	13	5	7	1	11	12	13	5	7	1
11	.	B	B	F	F	B	.	B	B	B	B	B
12		.	B	B	B	B		.	B	B	B	B
13			.	B	P	B			.	B	B	B
5				.	B	B				.	B	B
7					.	P					.	B
1						.						.

An attack on land is an attack on honour. This, according to Khroumirian concepts, means that the neighbours of Nasseria (i.e., nos. 9, 14, 35, 36 and 37) must also feel offended and join the ranks of Nasseria. Matrix 3 indicates the relationship of the neighbours and members of Nasseria before and after the conflict.

Matrix 3

	Before						After					
	11	12	13	5	7	1	11	12	13	5	7	1
9	P	P	F	N	B	B	P	B	B	P	N	P
14	P	F	P	N	F	P	m	P	B	N	N	N
35	B	P	B	P	F	N	N	B	B	B	B	E
36	P	B	F	P	B	N	B	B	B	N	B	N
37	F	B	P	N	P	F	m	B	B	P	N	N

But they have done so only partly. No. 12 and his neighbours, with the exception of no. 14, changed to B relations. The contacts between no. 13 and his neighbours also improved. No. 14, however, seems to feel a hidden resentment against, or if one wishes, hostility towards his neighbours nos. 11, 12 and 13, the core of Nasseria.

Besides improvements in relationships we also find relations which have deteriorated: 37-11 from P to m, 35-11 from B to N, 37-11 from F to m. There is one obvious conclusion. The relations between the neighbours and nos. 1, 10, 5 and 7 are not in line with the principle of the closing of ranks between Nasseria and their neighbours. It is interesting to note that such assistance of neighbours to the offended party was explained to me as one of the basic principles of the Khroumirian 'political theory' on the formation of factions. How is this discrepancy to be explained?

A number of brothers-in-law of no. 12 live in Ramlia, namely numbers 10, 38, 39 and 40. These men are mother's brothers of numbers 11 and 13 and no. 1's wife. The only thing they can do is support their sister's children.

Matrix 4

	Before				After			
	11	12	13	1	11	12	13	1
10	F	B	B	B	B	B	B	B
38	B	B	B	F	B	B	B	F
39	B	F	B	B	B	B	B	B
40	B	F	F	F	B	B	F	B

Their alliance with no. 12 is not of an obligatory nature. The relationships between brothers-in-law has no political implications of an absolute character. But it is out of question that they should not have given their full support to no. 12. Before the outbreak of the conflict they happened to have very positive relations with their neighbours 11, 12, 13 and 1. They could not feel much sympathy for the actions of no. 23 and no. 30, the traditional opponents of white Ramlia in connection with land. Being mother's brothers of 11 and 13 and no. 1's wife, and not giving full support to no. 12 would imply a heavy blow to the honour and position of no. 12. As there were no good reasons for neutrality, there was only one thing left to do: give full support to no. 12. Because all these mother's brothers could have counted on severe sanctions from the relatively well-to-do number 12 once the conflict was over. At least the relation of mutual cooperation between neighbours could be endangered, and this price was too high to pay, the more so as they were opponents of no. 30 and not in danger of reprisals from 'black' Ramlia.

Apart from two constant F-F relationships between 13-40 and 1-38 (notwithstanding the fact that these relationships are not free but binding), there is integration on the level of cooperation with a good heart.

Although full support is given to no. 12, numbers 5 and 7 seem to remain apart in this process of closing of ranks (see matrix 5). This fact may be explained by the absence of any obligatory type of relationship between 5 and 7 on the one hand and numbers 10, 38, 39 and 40 on the other. Therefore these relations may develop into relations of any type, with the exception of relations of enmity. The matrix shows that all sorts of relations have developed between them: B, P, and N.

Matrix 5

	Before						After					
	11	12	13	1	5	7	11	12	13	1	5	7
10	F	B	B	B	B	B	B	B	B	B	N	N
38	B	B	B	F	P	N	B	B	B	F	F	P
39	B	F	B	B	B	N	B	B	B	B	B	B
40	B	F	F	F	P	B	B	B	F	B	B	N

What is the reaction of Nasseria towards everything that is 'black' Ramlia?

Matrix 6 reveals that the relations, already shaky, have developed into enmity with the reservation that with respect to no. 5, no. 16 assumes not a hostile but a neutral attitude. Between numbers 33, 3 and 8 on the one hand and Nasseria on the other, not all relations changed into enmity. The difference between numbers 33, 3 and 8 and the rest of black Ramlia is easily explained by the fact that 33, 3 and 8 live 'far away' from the rest of black Ramlia, situated in the other half of the village. Though not close neighbours, 33, 3 and 8 live in the domain of Nasseria and their friends.

Another fact to be explained is the positive and neutral relations of 5 members of Nasseria in respect of no. 8 (who is 'black'), and the hint of a neutral attitude towards no. 16. The explanation is that no. 8, although not belonging to Nasseria's immediate neighbours, nevertheless does not live far off, and that no. 16 also lives in the left half. Not even this fact gives complete clarity, for nos. 17, 18 and 41 also reside in the left half. The relationship towards no. 30 in particular will provide a clue to the attitudes of some members of Nasseria towards nos. 8 and 16.

Nos. 8, 15 and 16 were deliberately treated unfairly by no. 30. Moreover,

Matrix 6

	Before														
	15	16	17	18	41	47	29	30	31	23	51	52	33	3	8
11	N	P	N	F	P	B	B	P	N	N	N	N	P	N	N
12	B	F	B	P	N	N	P	P	F	B	N	m	P	P	P
13	N	P	F	B	F	P	F	F	P	P	P	N	N	B	P
5	F	N	m	N	m	N	m	P	N	N	N	F	B	P	B
1	N	N	P	N	N	N	B	B	N	N	P	N	B	P	P
7	N	P	P	N	P	P	P	P	N	F	N	N	P	N	B

	After														
	15	16	17	18	41	47	29	30	31	23	51	52	33	3	8
11	E	E	E	E	E	E	E	E	E	E	E	E	E	E	E
12	E	N	E	E	E	E	E	E	E	E	E	E	E	E	P
13	E	E	E	E	E	E	E	E	E	E	E	E	E	E	N
5	E	N	E	E	E	E	E	E	E	E	E	E	F	F	N
1	E	E	E	E	E	E	E	E	E	E	E	E	F	F	F
7	E	E	E	E	E	E	E	E	E	E	E	E	F	F	F

they lived far away and could be put under pressure by no. 30's close associates or even no. 30 himself only with great difficulty. It was no. 12 who succeeded in maintaining a good relationship, i.e., a P relation, towards no. 8. The importance of no. 8 for no. 12 is crystal clear. This way no. 8 is neutralized by no. 12; the 'black' party is weakened by the 12-8 P relationship. It is remarkable that no. 13, who is an obedient son to his father in almost everything (this is also apparent in the matrices) could not come to more than a mere N relation with no. 8. Perhaps no. 12, who would have benefited from a positive 13-8 relation, is incapable of it. Perhaps there are other reasons. I think that an answer based on the mathematical theory of balance, to which I shall turn later, could possibly supply the answer. The reactions of the mother's brothers of 11 and 13 are shown in matrix 7. In their negative reactions they are in line with Nasseria. Only the neutral relations are exceptional and call for a satisfactory explanation, which is only to be found for no. 10. With regard to him one must bear in mind that he belongs to the immediate neighbours of nos. 15 and 16 and cannot therefore easily adopt a hostile attitude. That would disturb the relations in the neighbourhood. On the other hand, positive relations would be a thorn in the flesh of no. 12, who, being a brother-in-law, could exercise pressure on no. 10. An N relation seems to be the ideal solution.

Matrix 7

							Before								
	15	16	17	18	41	47	29	30	31	23	51	52	33	3	8
10	P	P	B	m	N	P	P	P	N	m	N	N	B	N	F
38	N	B	N	P	N	N	F	P	P	P	P	N	N	P	P
39	P	F	F	B	N	P	N	B	P	B	N	F	N	F	m
40	P	F	B	F	P	F	N	B	N	N	N	N	N	N	N
							After								
	15	16	17	18	41	47	29	30	31	23	51	52	33	3	8
10	N	N	E	E	E	N	N	E	E	E	E	E	E	E	E
38	E	E	E	E	E	E	E	E	E	E	E	E	E	E	E
39	E	E	E	E	E	N	E	E	E	E	N	N	E	E	E
40	E	E	E	E	E	E	N	E	E	E	E	E	E	E	E

What was the reaction of 'black' and the four sister's sons of 'black' to the conflict? Matrix 8, which represents the situation among 'black' before and after the conflict, reveals that the endeavours of no. 30 to obtain the support of everyone are relatively successful. Only nos. 15 and 16 assume attitude P. No. 23 continues on level F. This may be a fake relationship for political reasons, since we do know whether no. 30 fully agreed with the outrageous behaviour of no. 23. Here, too, there is integration, albeit not so complete as

Matrix 8

	Before														
	8	15	16	17	18	41	47	29	30	31	23	33	3	51	52
8		B	B	F	B	F	P	P	B	P	F	P	B	B	F
15	B	.	B	F	B	F	P	P	B	P	B	P	N	N	F
16	B	B	.	F	F	F	P	P	F	m	F	F	F	P	F
17	F	F	F	.	B	F	P	F	B	N	F	P	B	P	N
18	B	B	F	B	.	F	F	N	P	F	N	P	F	N	F
41	F	F	F	B	F	.	m	F	P	F	P	F	B	F	N
47	P	P	P	P	F	m	.	F	F	F	m	B	B	P	F
29	P	F	F	F	N	F	F	.	B	P	F	B	B	F	F
30	B	F	F	B	P	P	B	B	.	B	F	B	B	B	B
31	P	N	m	N	F	F	F	P	B	.	F	P	P	B	F
23	F	m	F	F	N	P	m	F	F	F	.	F	F	F	F
33	P	P	F	P	P	F	B	B	B	P	F	.	F	B	F
3	B	N	F	B	F	B	F	B	B	P	F	F	.	F	N
51	B	P	P	P	N	F	P	F	B	B	F	B	F	.	B
52	F	N	F	N	F	N	F	F	B	F	F	F	N	B	.

	After														
	8	15	16	17	18	41	47	29	30	31	23	33	3	51	52
8	.	B	B	B	B	B	B	P	B	B	N	F	E	F	B
15	B	.	B	B	B	B	E	P	P	F	P	B	N	P	N
16	B	B	.	B	F	F	N	B	P	B	P	B	B	B	N
17	B	B	B	.	B	B	B	P	B	N	P	B	B	B	F
18	B	B	F	B	.	B	P	B	B	P	N	N	B	N	P
41	B	F	F	F	F	.	E	P	B	B	B	B	B	N	E
47	B	E	N	B	P	E	.	B	B	P	B	B	B	B	P
29	P	P	B	P	B	P	B	.	B	B	B	F	B	B	P
30	B	P	P	B	B	B	B	B	.	B	F	B	B	B	B
31	B	F	B	N	P	B	P	B	B	.	F	B	B	B	F
23	N	P	P	P	N	B	B	B	F	B	.	B	F	F	F
33	F	B	B	B	N	B	B	F	B	B	B	.	F	B	B
3	E	N	B	B	B	B	B	F	B	B	F	F	.	B	P
51	F	P	B	B	N	N	B	B	B	B	F	B	B	.	F
52	B	N	N	F	P	E	P	P	B	B	F	B	P	F	.

in the case of Nasseria (see matrix 2). It is noteworthy that we find not only N relations (what do N relations signify in this context?), e.g., between 8-23, 16-47, 18-23, 41-51, but even E relations, e.g., between 8-3, 41-47, 41-52. There are also relatively more F relations which, if we consider the cooperation among the members of 'black', give food for thought. There is less closing of the ranks among the 'blacks' than among the members of Nasseria.

The following points can be added to the explanation:

1. The 'blacks' are locally dispersed;
2. The genealogical distances among the 'blacks' are sometimes greater than among the members of Nasseria. Nos. 8, 15 and 16 are genealogically further removed from no. 30 than nos. 29, 30, 23, 18 and 17;
3. Former serious conflicts stood in the way of integration.

In my opinion, two groups are readily distinguishable, namely nos. 15, 16, 17, 18 and 41 who all live together in the bottommost part of the village, and nos. 30, 29, 31, 47 and 23 who live slightly higher up (see map). What is the reaction of the neighbours of Nasseria towards 'black' Ramlia? Matrix 9 indicates the relations of the neighbours (nos. 9, 14, 35, 36 and 37) with regard to 'black'.

The solidarity of the neighbours is reflected in the high proportion of E relations. There is only one positive relation, namely 35-8, while there are very definitely 26 N relations. Positive relations would without a doubt be a disadvantage to no. 12 and spell danger in respect of the relation to no. 12. Conspicuous is the high number of N relations of no. 14 (i.e., 10 out of the 26 N relations). This phenomenon must not be viewed outside the context of his relations to nos. 12, 11 and 13. The N relations with 'black' are another means of criticism of no. 12. In my opinion, N here signifies more than mere neutrality. No positive support of 'black', but definitely criticism of no. 12. No. 14 thus shows that he is not averse to being bought off, if the price is right. No. 8 also has 4 N relations to his account. Admittedly he is 'black', but no. 12 maintains positive contacts with him (which permits 35-8 to be positive: B), with the result that N seems to be an excellent solution, poised between attraction and repulsion.

'Black' also has neighbours. They are nos. 50, the former 'white' village head, 49, 25, 26, 27, 28 and 24. Together they form Hasseynia. Through marriage ties they have developed relations of cooperation with their 'black' neighbours, nos. 29, 30, 31, 47 and 23. During the conflict the ties with some of the 'blacks' were intensified and those with others weakened. Generally they responded positively to their immediate 'black' neighbours. The relations

Matrix 9

	15	16	17	18	41	47	29	30	31	23	51	52	33	3	8
9	N	E	E	E	E	E	N	E	E	E	E	E	N	N	N
14	E	N	N	E	N	N	N	E	E	N	E	N	N	N	N
35	E	E	N	N	E	N	E	E	E	E	E	E	E	N	B
36	E	E	E	E	E	E	E	E	N	E	E	E	N	E	N
37	E	N	E	E	E	E	E	E	E	E	E	E	N	N	N

with those 'blacks' living in remote areas tend to become neutral if not completely negative. Why? It may point to a policy of avoiding the formation of political blocs (matrix 10).

Matrix 10

	Before														
	29	30	31	23	47	15	16	17	18	41	8	33	3	51	52
50	P	B	B	F	B	B	N	B	N	B	P	P	B	P	B
49	P	F	P	B	P	F	P	N	N	N	N	P	N	B	P
25	B	B	B	B	B	P	B	B	B	B	N	F	P	B	F
26	B	B	P	B	F	N	E	N	P	N	N	N	m	B	F
27	B	B	P	B	B	F	P	B	B	N	N	N	B	P	B
28	B	B	F	B	P	N	N	N	F	N	N	N	N	F	N
24	F	B	P	P	B	N	N	B	N	P	F	B	N	F	F
	After														
	29	30	31	23	47	15	16	17	18	41	8	33	3	51	52
50	B	B	P	F	B	N	N	B	N	P	N	N	B	B	F
49	B	B	P	F	F	E	N	E	E	N	E	N	E	B	F
25	B	B	B	P	B	E	N	P	F	P	E	N	P	F	F
26	B	B	F	F	F	E	E	N	P	N	E	N	F	P	B
27	P	B	B	B	F	E	F	P	B	N	N	E	B	F	P
28	B	B	P	F	F	E	N	N	P	N	N	N	N	P	F
24	P	B	F	P	B	N	N	F	E	P	E	N	P	B	P

If Hasseynia adopts such a positive stand with regard to her 'black' neighbours, what is the reaction of Nasseria to Hasseynia (the friends of 'black)?

Generally neutral to hostile except in the case of no. 12, who besides two neutral and two hostile relations still manages to retain a B relation with no. 50, the former 'white' village head, and P and B with nos. 25 and 24. Furthermore, only 24, the son-in-law of no. 12, succeeds in maintaining positive relations, yet is unable to exert any influence on the other relations in respect of either 'black' or Nasseria.

Matrix 11

	Before						After					
	12	13	11	1	5	7	12	13	11	1	5	7
50	B	B	P	B	N	N	B	N	N	E	N	F
49	P	B	F	P	N	N	N	N	N	N	N	N
25	P	B	N	N	P	B	P	N	N	N	E	E
26	N	B	m	P	P	P	N	N	N	E	N	N
27	F	B	P	E	F	N	E	E	E	E	E	E
28	N	N	N	N	N	N	E	E	E	E	E	E
24	B	F	B	F	P	P	B	B	F	F	B	F

One could also ask how the 'white' neighbours (nos. 50, 49, 25, 26, 27, 28 and 24) of 'black' (nos. 30, 29, 23, 31, 47) behave towards the neigbours of Nasseria, 9, 14, 35, 36, 37, and mother's brothers 10, 38, 39, 40 (matrix 12).

Matrix 12

	Before									After								
	10	38	39	40	9	14	35	36	37	10	38	39	40	9	14	35	36	37
50	B	B	P	B	B	B	B	P	P	B	N	F	N	B	B	N	B	B
49	P	B	P	P	B	B	P	F	B	N	B	N	N	F	F	N	B	B
25	N	P	B	N	B	P	B	F	B	P	F	m	N	B	F	N	B	B
26	N	N	N	F	N	F	B	N	B	N	N	N	E	N	F	N	N	B
27	P	P	B	B	P	B	B	N	B	E	P	N	E	F	F	E	N	B
28	N	P	N	N	N	P	N	N	F	E	P	N	N	N	P	E	N	P
24	B	B	B	N	B	N	B	B	P	B	B	N	N	B	N	B	N	B

I will not comment extensively on these matrices. It is true that Hasseynia, considered as a whole, is developing deteriorating relations with nos. 10, 38, 39 and 40 and the group of brothers 9, 14, 35, 36 and 37. *Ça va sans dire*! because the first and second set are supporting Nasseria and Hasseynia is supporting 'black' Ramlia. Further, we count more deteriorating relations and greater changes for the first than for the second set. This may be explained by the fact that in the first set more types of relations towards Nasseria are involved than in the second set. The first set consists of men who are both neighbours of Nasseria and mother's brothers of numbers 11 and 13 and the wife of no. 1. The second set consists of men who are merely neighbours of Nasseria.

These matrices, however, pose some increasingly interesting problems.

1. Why do we find such a small number of E relations developing between these sets and Hasseynia? Only two of these relations ended in the development of hostile relationships. This is the problem. Why are my enemies' friends still my friends' friends?

2. We notice, too, that the brothers 10, 38, 39 and 40 did not develop identical relations, although these brothers occupy exactly the same position towards Nasseria. The same holds true for the brothers forming the second set. They did not develop identical relations with Hasseynia either.

3. They are not only acting as a group. Even for the duration of the conflict they fail to arrive at the same level of relationship, nor do they all move in the same direction. Some of the members of these two groups even move in opposite directions. No. 38 has devalued only two relations, one from B-N, the other from P-F. The rest of his relations do not seem to be affected by the conflict. No. 40, on the other hand, devalues from B-N, P-N, F-E, B-E and arrives only at neutral and hostile relations. No. 37 even arrives at a higher level of cooperation with Hasseynia at the end of the conflict. But his brother, 14, arrives at a lower level of *meziaa* relations.

The first problem is easily solved. Numbers 10, 38, 39 and 40 and 9, 14, 35, 36 and 37 do not break off their relations with Hasseynia, because Nasseria, led by no. 12, does not do so itself. Although on the whole the relations are deteriorating, 50, 24 and 25 retain positive relations with some members of Nasseria: 50-12 B, 25-12 P, 24-12 B, 24-13 B and 24-11 F, because there is an affinal relationship between Nasseria and Hasseynia. No. 24 is married to the sister of 11 and 13, and 11 and 13 are brothers-in-law of no. 24. Now I do not think that in such an internal village strife political assistance is due to a brother-in-law, nor to his father. No. 24 did not build his hut on a piece of land belonging to 12, nor did he live on the rent of a piece of land belonging to 12, nor was he a member of the household of no. 12. If however such assistance is not obligatory and Hasseynia is tied to 'black' Ramlia, then why does not Hasseynia cut off its relations with Nasseria and bring these relations into line with its political obligations towards 'black' Ramlia?

On the other hand, the same might be done by no. 12. The continuation of the existing relationships means – and cannot mean anything else – that the interests of Nasseria are served by the continuation of these positive relationships. As Simmel says: 'You need two persons to start a relationship but only one to cut it'. Thus for the continuation of an existing relationship two persons are needed.

Why, then, does not Hasseynia cut? It seems to me that there are some indications of a not entirely whole-hearted integral support given by Hasseynia to 'black' Ramlia. Matrix 10 (Hasseynia – 'black' Ramlia) reveals that not all the relations have arrived at level B. The same matrix reveals another interesting fact. The relations between 'black' Ramlia at the bottommost part of the valley (17, 18, 15, 16, and 41) and Hasseynia have deteriorated. The devaluing relations between Hasseynia and this part of 'black' Ramlia are a hint – even a sign – that Hasseynia is not the personal enemy of 12, and therefore he can stay in contact with it. Why should he break? This conflict implies that almost everyone will lose a number of relations which may be considered a disadvantage. But this contact between Hasseynia and Nasseria is a sign for 'black' Ramlia (23, 29, 30, 31 and 47) that Hasseynia is not giving its full support and cannot be trusted completely, which fact is indicated by the lack of complete integration between Hasseynia and no. 30's party. The same reasoning may be applied the other way round.

If this explanation is correct, the definite positions, as indicated in the second total matrix (see p. 179), can only be reached after taking a series of steps in connection with the problems posed by the different parties.[13] The advantage for no. 12 is that he helped loosen the links between Hasseynia and 'black' Ramlia a little. The advantage for Hasseynia is that for such a conflict, which is not their proper concern, they do not want to risk their important *meziaa* relationships.

The second problem is: why don't the brothers act in identical ways? We have shown this for numbers 10, 38, 39 and 40 (40 being the exception in moving in an opposite direction) and for numbers 9, 14, 35, 36 and 37 (37 being the exception and arriving at a higher level of *meziaa* relationships than before and than the others).

Acting in identical ways as brothers is not contrary to Khroumirian values. On the contrary. It is the eldest brother who, in the absence of a father, represents his brothers in the outside world. It is the eldest brother who represents them in the council of the elders, the *djemaa*. It is the absence of an identical reaction of a group of brothers in politics which is astonishing and therefore has to be explained. In addition to private interests, individual persons and groups of brothers, too, (because from a structural social point of view they occupy some identical positions) may have not only one-sided, but two-sided obligations as well. If they should behave as a block between two groups who are in conflict, and have obligations towards both factions, and if these obligations carry the same weight, there seems to be only the solution of the development of either neutral or F relations. But how to react if these two-sided relations are not of the same quality or weight? If the difference should be expressed by handling the different terms of *meziaa,* the N, B, P and F may not be the proper 'instruments' for expressing the sometimes subtle differences between the two parties, since the differences between B and P and F are too great. Freedom of movement in individual manoeuvering would offer that possibility, however. Five brothers with dual obligations and with five different types of *meziaa* relationships at their disposal have a choice from a large number of combinations for expressing their standpoint with respect to both parties in a subtle way.

If it is true that the political process consists in a long period of mutual adaptations of interpersonal relations, then individual freedom of movement is an invaluable asset. If the political process can be considered as a game or a series of games (a combination of zero sum games, non zero sum games and cooperative games), then individual manoeuvring may be considered as a *conditio sine qua non.*

Now we arrive at the point of the individual differences within the different groups of brothers. While the brothers 10, 38, 39 and 40 on the whole are diminishing their relations with Hasseynia, it is 40 who carries on at a higher level. This can be explained by the necessity of certain moves while playing the subtle game of politics. A pragmatic explanation is that in general it is a good thing not to put all your money on the same horse. Diminishing the risks by dividing one's interests is, from a game theoretical point of view, considered as rational behaviour.

In the matrix there are a number of examples of the game of dividing and spreading interests. One example is the numbers 32, 21, 43, 44 and 45. Other examples are nos. 25 and 26, 27 and 28. Even 33 and 3 are good examples of the use that is made of this principle. I am convinced that this material cannot be interpreted in any other way. In another context the Khroumirians explained to me that often a man and his wife occupied different, almost opposite, positions on different levels. A man who does lots of *meziaas* is usually married, so they say, to a tight-fisted wife, and a wife who gives *meziaas* to everyone is married to a man whose behaviour is egotistical.

From the conscious playing of such opposite roles *il n'y a qu'un pas* to the explanation given above.

If the political process consists of numerous gradual, individual, reciprocal adaptations, the study of the political process in the form of successive matrices of interpersonal relations, dispersed in time, may be a useful tool for obtaining a detailed insight into politics at the micro level.

Why it is 37 who develops positive relations with Hasseynia and why it is 14 who diminishes his relationships with Hasseynia, etc., are problems that have to be tackled in the field.

In the beginning the analyses of the matrices seemed to lead to the conclusion that, apart from some very important clear lines, in the case of a great number of changes in relationships we are confronted with a chaos of changes. This chaos would be explained by the diversity of personal interests, by the fact that outsiders are not affected by the conflict in their mutual relations, and so on. Going on with our closer reading, however (e.g., by following and comparing all the reactions of different pairs of brothers), we gain insight into a certain system: such a partly systematic chaos cannot be explained by absence of interest in the conflict, nor by chance, because to a certain extent it seems well organized. Groups of brothers, for example, want to give the impression that their reactions are individual reactions. In reality, however, the brothers must have come to an agreement on the strategy to be followed and the roles to be played by each of them. This means that the brothers not only have to define their position, interest, and role after the outbreak of the conflict, but also have to be always on the alert. They have to remain in contact as long as the conflict goes on, for their position, interests and strength and therefore their strategies may be in need of redefinition as a consequence of certain steps taken in relation to the conflict by one or more villagers.

If this is right, then, we are dealing here with the phenomenon of the group-binding functions of conflict, not only for the cores of the two rival factions, but even for those who are not directly involved, as, for instance, numbers 21, 32, 43, 44, 45 and Hasseynia.[14]

From a Khroumirian ideological point of view there are no better relations than those between brothers, who like and trust each other completely and support one another because they have been given milk from the same breast. In reality, however, a 'true milk' relationship of this type between brothers is a rare phenomenon. The opposite seems to be nearer to real life situations. In fact, they often act as rivals, prefer not to live together after the death of their father, and even choose to cease living as close neighbours. Even if from fear of disgrace they remain in a *meziaa* relationship, they often evaluate their own *meziaas* towards each other as *pro forma meziaas*. This is indicated by a number of matrices made in 1965, 1968 and 1969.[15] In short, relationships between brothers are obligatory. Out of fear for disgrace and other practical consequences they are honoured, though *contre coeur*. In politics, however, they seem to be in need of cooperation, of acting in concert. What, then, are their collective interests? In my opinion, these have to do with the 'right to a place under the sun'. Such a place can only be obtained and defended by acting in unison in politics. If they do not want to become lost in the jungle, or the sphere of competition of the village, and if they do not want to be deprived of influence and power, now and for later, the brothers have to cooperate. There does not seem to be any other way of arriving at a safe place under the sun than by practising political cooperation along agnatic lines.

This necessity to stick together may be explained by the still existing, uncorroded authority and influence of the eldest brother. It is he who succeeds as leader of the extended family, after the death of their father, if the father has no living brothers who are members of the extended family. But even if these brothers do not stay together as an extended family, the eldest brother retains authority over his other brothers, a phenomenon which has often puzzled me. It is he who guards the interests of his brothers. He represents them in the world outside. He has to make marriage arrangements on behalf of his younger brothers and, in spite of a rapid growing individualism, these rights and obligations are still accepted and respected. He also represents them in the *djemaa*, the informal village council consisting of a representative of each family. It is invariably the eldest brother who is the best informed and who will lead his other brothers in adopting a collective policy and strategy and in giving each of them his special task.

The Khroumirians will not object to the thesis that there does not seem to be a safe place under the sun other than by practising political cooperation along agnatic lines. They are convinced that only by standing close by one another and by living as an extended family are close agnates able to overcome all their problems and arrive at a state of material well-being. Hand in hand all problems can be overcome. Seldom, however, is a pure form of extended family realized; it is the nuclear family that is preferred by almost everybody, at least if people are able to make their own living. The lack of cooperation between agnates in this village was and is considerable. Obligatory types of relationships are accepted as a must but not honoured wholeheartedly. Then if in all these fields they fail to arrive at cooperation, why do they succeed in practising it in politics? I think the answer is that having a place under the sun is a problem of influence and power, if necessary.

Apart from influence based on an exemplary moral life – which implies the cooperation and mutual support of brothers – power is a necessary attribute even for people whose lives can be considered good from a Khroumirian moral point of view.

Even good *kebirs douar* defend their position and augment their influence by being rude from time to time. By showing that they are bold and strong and vigorous, they add to their moral claim to being followed and obeyed and respected a demonstration that if necessary they will enforce obedience and respect by the use of force. The Khroumirians are realists in politics and know very well that power grows in proportion with the increase of material and human resources. The more you stick together, the more you make yourself felt, the less chance there is of your interests not being served, and the greater chance that you will be respected. From their stories about the life of the Khroumirians before the protectorate, and even a long time after the establishment of the French in Ain Draham, I gathered that brute force played not the role of *prima donna* but that of an effective means of defending one's own interests. This law of the segmentary jungle kept agnates together.

The use of force diminished considerably during the French protectorate. The Tunisian government itself is very strict about this. It tries to do everything possible to prevent the application of brute force by the inhabitants and on the whole the policy is successful. Nevertheless, I have heard and seen enough interesting cases of the use of brute force during six half years in Khroumiria to be convinced that such brute force still has to be reckoned with. But in politics it has become exceptional nowadays, so that this is not the reason why brothers or close agnates have to stick together.

Other effective means have replaced brute force, however. Respect is now won by an almost scientific knowledge and practice of human manipulation: by playing 'good' and 'bad' tricks upon one's enemies and by arranging things in such a way that their resources diminish and that the public will be convinced as to who is the more intelligent of the two and who should be feared and respected. Nowadays, they say, everybody has to be careful that other people do not play bad tricks upon one. He who isolates himself too much will be attacked one day and if there is no one to extend a helping hand he will be a sitting duck. There is only one means of defending oneself in a positive and effective way. That is by doing a lot of *meziaas*, and by making many friends. You have to rely on friends who can extend a helping hand by spying on your behalf and passing on information on what is going on against you in the village. It is a must to have trustworthy people around you who can assist in playing bad tricks upon your opponents.

The problem is why in matters of serious attacks on 'honour' people still cling to their close agnates, although these relations with close agnates are enduring much strain and are endangered by jealousy and egotism. Real friendship based on mutual trust is to be found more outside the domain of obligatory relationships. Why then do the villagers depend on close kin for their defense in serious attacks on *hormaa* (prestige) and attacks on their material resources. If friends are important for the needs of everyday life, why then do they not function in political matters?

The greatest disadvantage of free relationships is their instability. A comparison of the network formations of 1965, 1968 and 1969 shows the following rates of stability and instability.

Of all the relationships existing in 1965 only 61% survived in 1968, notwithstanding the fact that in 1968 the total number of relationships had largely increased. After 1968 the number of relationships had shrunk to almost the same level as that of 1965. Of all the relationships of 1968 only 50% were stable. Comparing the network formations of 1965 and 1969 only 50% proved to be constant. 37% of the relations were constant through the years; 46% of the latter were formed by obligatory relationships, as between close kin. Although the obligatory relations are not always perfect, they are at least stable.

Free partnerships easily break off if one of the partners is too demanding in terms of material goods or risky services. The following case is an example of the breaking up of a relationship after one of the partners falling ill.

'Khmis and Mabrouk were good friends for many years. They exchanged many important *meziaas*. One day, however, Khmis fell ill and it turned out to be a serious illness which would last for some time. As soon as the sick man asked him to lend him some dinars the other excused himself on the grounds that he was not at all able to render this service. That was the last visit he paid to the sick man! To us Mabrouk explained that Khmis could not be trusted at all. For years he had shown himself to be a man who refused to honour his relations or pay visits to people who were ill, so that he should be punished. That is why he stopped visiting his friend. Khmis, who was not lacking in understanding for the behaviour of his friend – visiting sick friends is an obligatory *meziaa* – soon after his recovery dissolved his relationship with this man, who had been afraid to risk his money when he had to help a friend who was in need of it'.

What is true for illness may also hold true for political matters if they are considered risky.

Relations with close kin have at least the advantage that they are not supposed to break off. Although obligatory relationships between close agnates do not function smoothly in daily life, how is it that they function in times of extreme conflict? The matrices of 1958 show that all the members of Nasseria lived up to their obligations and integrated themselves on a B level of mutual support. This case, however, is not convincing because before the conflict broke out they were already well integrated and formed a group of almost maximal cohesion. The other core group offers a better example because the initial level of integration, or the level of cohesion, was considerably lower. Here, too, we notice a closing of the ranks during the conflict and the operation of *meziaa* partnership on a much higher, though not the highest level.

By studying the Khroumirians I learnt that they are masters at evading obligations. People wanting to evade obligations will look for watertight reasons why they cannot or do not need to fulfil their obligations. They are clever at finding reasons why the general rule does not need to be applied in this special case. Often they base themselves upon a number of more or less similar cases and try to convince the public opinion that they are right. But in matters with which we are concerned here I hardly ever heard of a search for excuses. The system of values concerning the obligation of the right hand is a very strict and precise one.

Brothers have not only a 'milk' relationship but also a blood relationship. The domain of binding obligations related to blood is that of the right hand. The name, prestige, or *hormaa* in short, of those who have the same blood – the same agnatic descent – is a collective affair. An attack on a person's right-hand elements is an attack on those of the same blood. These elements consist of *hormaa* (prestige) and *qdar* (respect), elements of extreme importance in public life. If *hormaa* or *qdar* are seriously attacked with the end of devaluing a person's status in public life (and that means a diminishing political influence), possession of the same blood is equated with the obligation to assist. Such an attack on *hormaa* and *qdar* is also an attack on the wives, land and flocks of a man. This is the general, absolute rule, but in practical, daily life we are faced with the notion of relativity. Not all the attacks have the same weight in this respect.

Whether an attack can be considered a more or less serious one, involving the problem of whether or not assistance is obligatory, depends on the relative status of the attacker, on the ends he has in view and on the status of the man being attacked.[16] Another variable is the effect of such a deed on the public opinion. The seriousness of such an attack also depends on the interpretation of those concerned and the interpretation by the other inhabitants of the village. Any attack intended to devalue the public status of a man in relation to his ability to exercise influence, may, I think, be considered a serious attack. That is why an attack on those in a leading position, such as elders, their respective families and those who represent them in the world outside and in the *djemaa*, is a more serious attack than that on a mere member of a family. An attack on a *kebir douar* with the effect of deminishing his *hormaa*, which has to excel that of everyone else in the village, is one such serious deed. But the same attack coming from someone who has no great prestige in the village may be overlooked as an insult and punished privately. In reality the attack on 12 came from no. 23, a man who has hardly any prestige at all according to public opinion in the village. Still it was considered by no. 12 as a heavy blow to his public status because he knew very well how it had to be interpreted. It was no. 30 who was behind the affair and in essence it was an attack by 30. But that 23 made the attack was even more damaging to the prestige of no. 12.

Values can only serve as explanation if we take into account the sanctions on obligations which are not fulfilled, however. And these sanctions may explain why people comply with their obligations in cases of serious attacks on their leaders, who are of the same blood.

1. In the first place he who does not assist while everyone else lives up to his obligations damages his own public image. He is not much of a man; he has not the courage to stand up for basic principles.

2. Apart from such considerations he is showing that he is not a trustworthy man and that if seriously attacked himself one day, he may be considered a sitting duck because assistance, if rendered at all, will be given him in a reluctant and formal way.

3. The withholding of assistance is interpreted unfavourably by all those with whom he has or might have *meziaa* relationships. If he is a poor man everyone will get rid of him, if he is a middle class man the rich people who like to select their *meziaa* partners from the middle class will not consider him a reliable partner. The result is that he will make himself an isolated person who can be easily attacked. There may be only one exception. If such a person is rich and not interested in making a political career in the village and is uninterested in the political future of his close agnates, his material well-being will enable him to buy poor people as relations. His material well-being may serve as a mighty shield against attacks.

4. In affairs of daily life he will be punished by the people whom he had to assist. This is a rather severe punishment because in times of illness his friends will find excuses for not assisting him. This will be more difficult for close agnates, unless he has made the first major mistake himself.

5. For such serious misconduct, by failing to honour obligations which have an almost supernatural aspect, he can be sure of punishment by super-

natural forces. He will lose his material wealth, he will die a painful death, or his sons will die in childhood, and even if he need not fear this, a later generation will be severely punished.

What are the sanctions on breaking a free relationship? He who breaks a free relationship is not disgraced by such a deed. The only sanction is that if he was in the wrong in breaking off the relationship other people will have a negative opinion of his trustworthiness.[17]

5. EQUILIBRIUM AND INTEGRATION

Theories on factions sometimes hold[18] that factions are supposed to be exclusive groupings. This is not true of Ramlia, however. No. 8, a member of 'black', has positive relations with 'black', but at the same time stands in a positive relation towards no. 12.

8 –	30	29	31	23	47
Before	B	P	P	F	P
After	B	P	B	N	B

8 –	1	5	7	11	12	13
Before	P	B	B	N	P	P
After	F	N	F	E	P	N

Number 3 is a different case:

3	30	29	31	23	47
Before	B	B	P	F	B
After	B	B	B	F	B

No. 3 is a 'black' sister's son who obtained land from no. 30. But he lives far away, surrounded by people who assist no. 12. This makes it difficult for no. 30 to exert too much pressure.

No. 3 stands in relation to Nasseria, before and after the conflicts, as follows.

3	1	5	7	11	12	13
Before	P	P	N	N	P	B
After	F	F	F	E	E	E

There is, however, an alienation of his relations from nos. 11, 12 and 13. Yet he remains in an F relation with nos. 1, 5 and 7.

The fact that he is a neighbour and lives in the same neighbourhood, is sufficient explanation. The conflict of no. 12 with no. 30 is apparently not enough to disrupt mutual relations among the neighbours. Moreover, no. 3 does not profit from such a state of affairs. As an immigrant he is in need of friendly relations with everyone, including Nasseria. After all, the neighbourhood is more well-disposed to Nasseria than towards 'black'.

The explanation in terms of neighbourhood ties is also applicable to no. 8. He, too, is a neighbour of nos. 1, 5 and 7, and feels no inclination to sever his relations. For various reasons, however, the relations have deteriorated on both sides from P, B and B to F, N and F.

Locality (matrix 13) is an important factor in Ramlia. It is useful, therefore, to examine the relations in the neighbourhood to which nos. 1, 5, 7, 3 and 8 belong. Nos. 33, 3, 4 and 34, and 1, 5, 7 and 8 are neighbours, with the exception that 33, 3, 4 and 34 form one sub-neighbourhood, and 1, 5 and 7 belong to a second sub-neighbourhood.

Matrix 13

	Before								After							
	33	3	4	34	1	5	7	8	33	3	4	34	1	5	7	8
33	.	F	P	B	B	B	P	P	.	F	B	B	F	B	B	F
3	F	.	B	B	P	P	N	B	F	.	F	B	F	F	F	**E**
4	P	B	.	B	B	P	N	B	F	B	.	B	B	B	F	B
34	P	B	B	.	P	F	N	P	B	B	B	.	B	B	B	**E**
1	B	P	B	P	.	B	P	P	F	F	B	B	.	B	B	F
5	B	P	P	F	B	.	B	B	F	F	B	B	B	.	B	N
7	P	N	N	N	P	B	.	B	F	F	B	B	B	B	.	F
8	P	B	B	P	P	B	B	.	F	**E**	B	**E**	F	N	F	.

For purposes of analysis it is an interesting neighbourhood, because nos. 1, 5 and 7 belong to Nasseria (they have closed ranks mutually); 3 and 8 are 'black'; 34 and 4 'white'.

The picture of the 56 relations in the neighbourhood was as follows:

	B	P	F	N	E
Before	25	20	5	6	0
After	29	0	21	2	4

While the F relations in the whole of Ramlia underwent a decline from 443 to 289,[19] the F relations in the neighbourhood increased from 5 to 21. According to the Khroumirians, this relation is 'neither hot nor cold'. 'It is one like the sun shining in January, very often concealed by the clouds'. This F relation is apparently intended to express that 'I cannot be wholly for you, and I cannot afford the liberty of being against you, because you are my neighbour. I would not like to put my relationship with neighbour in the balance because 12 and 30 are involved in a serious conflict. I therefore assume a temporary F relation towards you. That will satisfy my faction associates, and will not place me in a precarious position towards you'.

Nos. 1, 5 and 7 (Nasseria) assumed F relations in two cases, and an N relation, with regard to no. 8, in one case, but there is no question of an E relation. No. 3 also assumed an F relation in respect of nos. 1, 5 and 7. Interestingly enough, even no. 7 changed from an F to an N relation with no. 3.

What disturbed me most in these relationships within the hamlet was that nos. 8 and 3, who are 'black' and sister's sons of 'black' respectively, have changed their relations from B to E. I have the impression that it is intended purely as a *besoin pour la cause*, i.e., as a demonstration to everyone in the neighbourhood that their intentions are good, but that neither of them is in a position to deny their obligations in respect of no. 30.

For the change of 34-8 from P to E, I have not yet found a satisfactory explanation. 33-8 is also worthy of analysis. No. 33 is pro 'black', and so is no. 8. They have changed from P to F relations, which strengthens the case of 3-8.

It is on the basis of the structural or mathematical theory of balance that a number of these astonishing facts may be explained in a satisfactory way.

Social equilibrium and social balance are well-known concepts in social and cultural anthropology as well as in other social sciences. In spite of its physical origin and in spite of the use that is made of an impressive number of sub-concepts such as static and dynamic equilibrium, we cannot deny that we are dealing with a metaphor.[20]

It seems to be the social psychologist Heider who started the process of operationalisation of the concept.[21] In 1946 he succeeded in formulating in a systematic way what is to be understood by balance and unbalance. Ten years later Cartwright and Harary succeeded in mathematizing the ideas of Heider.[22]

The theory of Heider is based on pleasant and unpleasant states between three elements. These elements may be represented by three persons or by at least one person and two objects. If the three elements are represented by three persons, there are three relations which may be defined as pleasant or unpleasant between these persons. In terms of algebraic graphs they may be given a positive and negative sign.

The different combinations of positive and negative relationships lead, according to the theory, to states of pleasantness or unpleasantness, or in other words, to balanced and unbalanced states. If the three relations are positive, there is a pleasant situation, and therefore per definition a state of balance between the three persons. No one will be forced to alter the situation. In daily language this situation is represented by the adage: 'the friends of my friends are my friends'.

Let us take as an example a family consisting of three persons[23]: father, mother and child. If the relations between the three of them are positive the state is pleasant and by definition balanced. Family life is unhappy, unpleasant and therefore unbalanced if one of the three relations is not positive but negative. If father and mother both love their child but father and mother cannot stand each other – better still, hate each other – a classical example of unhappy, even unstable, family life is provided. This state of unbalance, however, can be changed into one of balance by changing one of the positive relations in the triangle into a negative one.

If the child chooses the side of her mother and changes her positive relationship to her father into a negative one, we arrive at a stable or balanced state. The same holds true if the child chooses not the side of her mother but the side of her father and breaks with her mother. This state of two against one nevertheless is a stable one.

The state consisting of two positive and one negative relation is an unstable one, as familial experience in general demonstrates in a convincing way. Both father and mother may try, if they lack wisdom, to get their child on their side to arrive at stability and power: a situation of two against one.

Although in rather a simple way, the concept of balance has been operationalized. Even numbers of persons greater than three can be handled by combining these persons in as large a number of triangles as possible. For these sets of triangles a degree of balance or unbalance may even be calculated. According to Flament, for example, a complete algebraic graph is balanced if and only if all its triangles are balanced. From here to the definition of the degree of balance is but a step. It has turned out that the pleasantness or unpleasantness of a state of balance or imbalance corresponds perfectly with the results of multiplications of positive and negative integers, represented here by the signs on the sides of the triangles.[24]

The table of multiplication gives the following result:

	+	–
+	+	–
–	–	+

– If three persons have developed positive relationships between themselves, there is a state of balance. If we multiply the signs on the three sides we arrive at $+ \times + \times + = +$.

– If three persons have two positive and one negative relationship between themselves there is a state of imbalance. The multiplication of the signs on the three sides of the triangle is $+ \times + \times - = -$, and the sign of this unbalanced state is negative.

– If three persons have two negative and one positive relationship the multiplication of the signs on the three sides has a positive result.

All the possible combinations are shown in the following table:

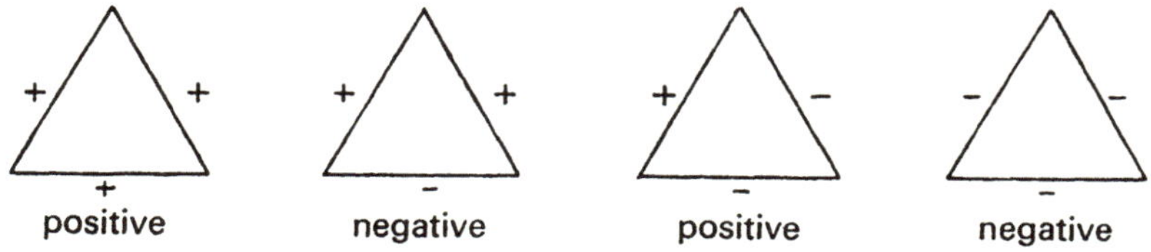

In practical research, however, we are confronted with a number of problems which cannot be solved, or better, which have not been solved up till now. The first problem is that the signs + and – are extremes on a continuum. How to handle relations which ought to find a place between the two extremes? There is a solution for only one point between the two extremes. It is the point which might be given the value 0, halfway between the extremes. In this case we arrive at a side, according to Flament, which can be given a sign 0 (zero), 'and it is assumed that a triangle having at least one zero edge is always balanced'.[25] If, however, he wants to apply his theory to human reality it would perhaps be a good idea to try to include these 'midway' sides in the system of triangles and handle them as 0 (zero)

relations, or relations of neutrality. As the basis of the theory is that unpleasant states change into pleasant ones in a triangle with a zero side, no influence from within the triangle can make itself felt; as such, a zero side is a '*sociism*' against change. In reality we are dealing not only with three persons and triangles, but with more persons. By introducing the sign zero, a number of real situations may be easily explained.[26]

But still there is no solution for the handling of relations lying between the zero point and the extremes on the continuum. In other words, the theory of balance cannot be applied to valued graphs. If only the empirical material can be produced, says Flament, mathematicians can handle it. Although of a very limited range, reality is hardly covered by three signs, +, –, and 0; this theory is applicable in cases of extreme conflict and in such circumstances seems to be a valuable instrument of analysis.[27] But even in a case where the conflict is more moderate the application is permissible if and only if the contestants can be divided into two parties, and plusses and minuses are correct representations of the existing relationships.

Before we are able to analyse the previously mentioned neighbourhood, consisting of the numbers 1, 5, 7, 8, 33, 3, 4 and 34 in terms of balance, we have to explain its composition.

1) 1, 5 and 7 belong to Nasseria and give full support to no. 12.
2) 33, 3 and 8 belong to 'black' Ramlia and give full support to no. 30.
3) 4 and 34 belong to 'white' Ramlia. They are anti-'black' and pro-12.

There are some important relationships in this neighbourhood:

1) 4 and 34 are father and son;
2) 33 and 3 are brothers;
3) 3 is the son-in-law of 4;
4) 8 is the son-in-law of 7.

If all the inhabitants of this neighbourhood acted according to their preferences we might *suppose* that:

1) 1, 5 and 7 would try to improve or maintain their mutual relationships;
2) 33, 3 and 8 would try to improve their mutual relationships, being 'black' in a pro-12 neighbourhood;
3) 4 and 34, being 'white', would improve or maintain their mutual relationships;
4) 1, 5 and 7 would improve or maintain their relations with 4 and 34 (in mutual support of no. 12 and being anti-black);
5) 4 and 34 (supporting no. 12) would devalue their relations with 33, 3 and 8.
6) 33, 3 and 8 would devalue their relations with 1, 5 and 7.

These suppositions are illustrated by the following matrix. By + is indicated an improvement in relationships, by – a deterioration in relationships and by 0 a stable relationship; improvement on a B relationship is impossible.

	1	33	3	4	34	5	7	8
1		–	–	0	+	0	+	–
33	–		+	–	–	–	–	+
3	–	+		–	–	–	–	0
4	0	–	–		0	+	+	–
34	+	–	–	0		+	+	–
5	0	–	–	+	+		0	–
7	+	–	–	+	+	0		–
8	–	+	0	–	–	–	–	

What really happened is shown in the following matrices.

	Before								After							
	33	3	4	34	1	5	7	8	33	3	4	34	1	5	7	8
33	.	F	P	B	B	B	P	P	.	F	B	B	F	B	B	F
3	F	.	B	B	P	P	N	B	F	.	F	B	F	F	F	E
4	P	B	.	B	B	P	N	B	F	B	.	B	B	B	F	B
34	P	B	B	.	P	F	N	P	B	B	B	.	B	B	B	E
1	B	P	B	P	.	B	P	P	F	F	B	B	.	B	B	F
5	B	P	P	F	B	.	B	B	F	F	B	B	B	.	B	N
7	P	N	N	N	P	B	.	B	F	F	B	B	B	B	.	F
8	P	B	B	P	P	B	B	.	F	E	B	E	F	N	F	.

In the next matrix is shown what really happened in terms of the symbols +, – and 0.

	1	33	3	4	34	5	7	8
1		–	–	0	+	0	+	–
33	–		0	0	–	–	–	–
3	–	0		–	0	–	+	–
4	0	–	0		0	+	+	0
34	+	+	0	0		+	+	–
5	0	–	–	+	+		0	–
7	+	–	+	+	+	0		–
8	–	–	–	0	–	–	–	

The results of a comparison of this last matrix with the matrix of suppositions are shown in the following table.

	suppositions	reality
+	8 times	7 times
0	5 times	8 times
–	15 times	13 times

– Suppositions nos. 1, 3, 4 and 6 (except the relation between 7 and 3, which has improved from N to F) are confirmed.

– Suppositions nos. 2 and 5 (except 34-8 and 4-33) are *not* confirmed, as is shown in the following sub-matrices:

Supposition 2 tested

	Before			After		
	33	3	8	33	3	8
33	.	F	P	.	F	P
3	F	.	B	F	.	B
8	P	B	.	P	B	.

Supposition 5 tested

	Before			After		
	33	3	8	33	3	8
4	P	B	B	F	B	B
34	P	B	P	B	B	E

Why did not all the inhabitants of this neighbourhood act according to their preferences? The answer is that if everybody had done so and the cases of deteriorated relationships had led to negative relationships, the neighbourhood would have split up completely into two exclusive, but spatially unseparated sub-groups. This is demonstrated by the following matrix.

	1	5	7	4	34	33	3	8
1		+	+	+	+	–	–	–
5	+		+	+	+	–	–	–
7	+	+		+	+	–	–	–
4	+	+	+		+	–	–	–
34	+	+	+	+		–	–	–
33	–	–	–	–	–		+	+
3	–	–	–	–	–	+		+
8	–	–	–	–	–	+	+	

The members of the neighbourhood seem not to prefer risking their system of cooperation, based on locality, descent and/or affinal links, which is *absolutely* necessary for the smooth running of daily life. But if necessary (*e.g.*, because they belong to Nasseria and are in contact with 'black' members of the neighbourhood) they are prepared at the utmost to adapt their relationships in accordance with the wishes or the interests of their leader or leaders. For instance, if they have to devalue from B or P they devalue to F, and not to N or E. That is why we notice, on comparing the two matrices, a growing number of F-relations. Before the conflict there were only 4 F relations, after the conflict 22!

All the hypotheses combined were tested statistically. First it was determined whether the difference between the situation before and after could be the result of the general trend of devaluing relationships. This hypothesis could be rejected ($p < 0.001$).

In the same way it was tested whether the result could be explained by the different situations existing within neighbourhoods. The trend of devaluation did not exist within neighbourhoods, and the changes within this particular neighbourhood could not be explained completely by this trend. The possibility of conditions in this neighbourhood being the same as those within the other neighbourhoods was fairly small: $p < 0.005$. There exist therefore good reasons for considering the fact that the hypotheses tested were generally confirmed as evidence for the rightness of the original assumptions behind the hypotheses. The hypotheses themselves could be confirmed ($p < 0.05$).[28] In total 28 predictions were made, while there was a choice amongst 71 possible predictions, for not all relations could improve. Of these 28 predictions 7 were false. Given the fact that 28 predictions could be correct, the probability of making a succesful prediction was $\frac{28}{71}$. Given this later condition one may test the null hypothesis as to whether the 21 successes obtained could be a matter of pure chance.[29]

Data		Actual		Total
	Pre-	21	7	28
	dicted	7	36	43
	Total	28	43	71

Test: Chi-square
Results: Chi-square = 24,5; df = 1; $p < .001$

Let us return to the relations between 3, 8 and 33. 8 and 3 had a relationship 'with good heart' before the conflict but became enemies during the conflict. This peculiar fact at least has to be explained. It is impossible to make graphs for the whole neighbourhood. Therefore we shall concentrate on some relations of strategical importance: those between 12, 11, and/or 13 on the one hand and 3 and 8 on the other. Now, supposing that 3 and 8 should continue their positive relationship 'with good heart', then the following graph, consisting of a set of triangles, may result.

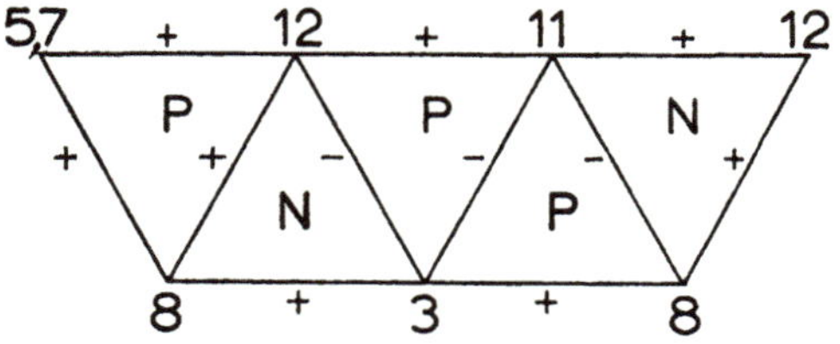

In the next graph the relation 3-8 will be given a negative value, the sign –, because 3 and 8 became enemies.

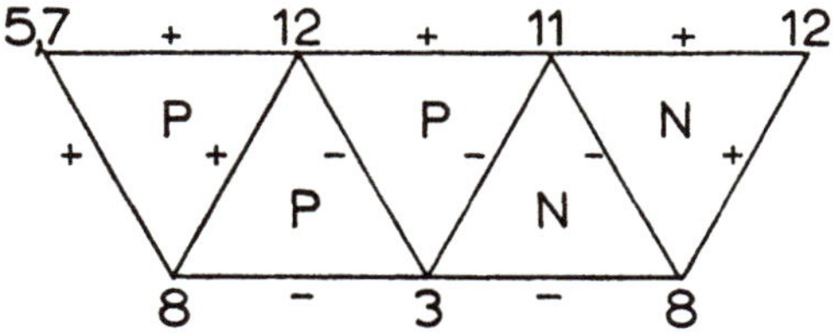

In the two graphs we find the same number of positive (P) and negative (N) triangles:

positive triangles: 3
negative triangles: 2

but – and this seems to be the most important phenomenon – two triangles changed places. The triangle 11-3-8, positive in the first graph, turned into negative in the second graph, and the triangle 12-8-3, negative in the first graph, became positive in the second graph. In the first graph 11 has a stable relationship (in a balanced triangle, for $- \times - \times + = +$) with 3 and 8, who are both enemies. 8 cannot succeed in attracting or winning over 11, nor has 12 a good chance of influencing 11 to establish a positive relationship with 8 (prevented by the positive, stable triangle consisting of 11, 3 and 8). The triangle 12-11-8 may become a positive one if 12 and 8 become enemies, but that is not what 12 is looking for. But if 3-8 becomes a negative relationship, 12 will be in a better position to create a positive relation between 11 and 8. For 8 at that time has the same enemy as 11, namely 3.

This way 8 invites the creation of a positive relationship between 8 and 11, and 12 is able to give a helping hand. Thus 8 is creating a better position for himself in the neighbourhood. At least after the conflict he will have the full support of 12 and 11.

8 accepts as a burden his presence in a number of negative triangles, all constructed on a negative 8-3 base. But he does not mind, because he is more interested in the future than in the pleasantness or stability of his position during the conflict.

This explanation is confirmed by what happened in the period following the conflict, when 8 and Nasseria established stable relationships (as can be illustrated with detailed ethnographical documentation).

There is a second negative relationship in the neighbourhood: 34-8. I think that this negative relationship may be explained in a similar way. In short, 13 devalued his relation with 34 from F to N. Now, if 8-34 turns into a negative relationship 8 will be in a more favourable position to establish a positive relationship with 13.

8 as an immigrant in the neighbourhood – almost a stranger – is seeking his own profit during the conflict.

The sub-group 15, 16, 10, 32, 41, 20, 21, 42, 22, 46, 17 and 18 provides another interesting field for the study of group dynamics. 15, 16, 17, 18 and 41 are 'black'; 10, 42, 46, 22 and 32 are pro-12 and anti-'black'. But 20 and 21 are fairly neutral. What is happening in this neighbourhood during the conflict is that 17 ('black') and 32 ('white', pro 12) are trying to better their position in this group. Though pro- and anti-12, they succeed in establishing a better relationship between themselves during the conflict: there is an improvement from P to B.

In this neighbourhood, too, not everyone acts in accordance with the interests of his leaders. It is clear that during the conflict between 12 and 30 there were local political processes in this neighbourhood. It may be worthwhile trying to analyse these processes and relating them to the conflict of 30-12 and other socio-political processes in the different neighbourhoods.

ACKNOWLEDGEMENTS

Apart from Abdullah ben Hellel, my invaluable field assistant, I have to single out for special thanks Mr. Rudo Niemeijer (see note 28), Mr. Wim van Binsbergen, who has shown a keen interest in this study, and developed my sense of testing, and Mr. G. W. Grootenhuis for the many services rendered by the Afrika-Studiecentrum.

NOTES

1. In the mountainous parts of north-western Tunisia anthropology students of the University of Amsterdam are receiving research training under the direction of the author, who in his spare time began research in Ramlia in 1964. Though unable to continue this research for long periods on end some disadvantages were overcome as a result of the activities of my research assistant Abdullah ben Hellel who in my absence observes what goes on almost daily.

Since 1964 Ramlia has been the object of a number of field studies. Miss I. A. Martin stayed here for two months in 1964. In 1966 she completed an unpublished M.A. thesis, 'Een proces van leren – voor de eerste maal in het veld bij de stam der Atatfa, Kroumirie, Tunesië.' H. A. Halbertsma stayed here for a period of six weeks, giving a helping hand to Miss Martin while himself doing research on affinal relationships. He continued his research during the summer holidays the next year. In 1968 and 1969 Miss M. L. Creyghton lived for more than four months in Ramlia studying folk illness. In 1969 she completed an unpublished M.A. thesis, 'Folk illness in an Tunesisch dorp'.

In 1967 I realized that the system of *meziaa's* provided an excellent introduction to the field of political structure and political process. In order to have a good, solid base we needed a conflict that shook the entire village. Although we studied this conflict in retrospection we had no difficulty in making the matrices, except that this constituted a wearisome, painstaking piece of research. The matrices were finished at the beginning of August 1969. In September a paper was presented to the Network Congress at Leiden. Then I returned to Ramlia, where I was able to analyze a number of 'apparent inconsistencies' in the matrices, which have provided a number of interesting partial cases. These cases have deepened my insight into the way the political game is played in Khroumiria. These cases have not been published in this paper.

In December 1970, no. 23 tried again to increase his fields by once more seizing part of the men's gathering-place. As rumours had been circulating for two months, and as we had some experience in working with matrices in the field we were fully prepared. For ten months we have been following the conflict on the spot. The process of mutual adaptation of interpersonal relations can now be placed in the context of time. A publication on political structure and political process in Khroumiria is forthcoming.

2. J. L. Moreno, *Who shall survive: Foundations of Sociometry, Group Psychotherapy and Sociodrama.* New York, 1953. Examples of networks can be found in articles published in *Sociometry.*

3. L. Festinger, S. Schachter and K. Back, *Social Pressures in Informal groups.* New York, 1950.

4. A. R. Radcliffe-Brown, *Structure and Function in Primitive Society: Essays and Addresses.* London, 1952. He defined social structure as a network of actually existing social relationships (p. 190).

5. B. Kapferer, 'Norms and the manipulations of relationships in a work context', in: J. C. Mitchell (Ed.), *Social Networks in Urban Situations.* Manchester, 1969, pp. 181-244.

6. J. C. Mitchell, 'The concept and use of social networks', in: J. C. Mitchell (Ed.), *Social Networks in Urban Situations.* Manchester, 1969, p. 49.

7. Harumi Befu, 'Network and corporate structure', in: R. K. Sakai (Ed.), *Studies on Asia.* Lincoln, 1963, p. 29.

8. 3.5 Dinar is roughly equivalent to 3 pounds sterling.

9. For dual organisation in Ramlia see: D. G. Jongmans, 'Le phénomène de bipartition tel qu'il se présente à Ramlia', in: *Cahiers des Arts et Traditions Populaires. Revue du Centre des Arts et Traditions Populaires* I, no. 2, 1968, pp. 99-113. Tunis, Institut National d'Archéologie et d'Arts.

10. For the system of *meziaa* relationship see: D. G. Jongmans, 'Meziaa en horma. Samenhangen tussen dienstbetoon, eer en welstand in een veranderde samenleving', in: *Kroniek van Afrika,* 1968/3, p. 1-34. French translation, published as: 'Mzia et Horma. Relations entre service, estime sociale et prospérité dans une société en transformation', in: *Cahiers des Arts et Traditions Populaires. Revue du Centre des Arts et Traditions Populaires.* Tunis, Institut National d'Archéologie et d'Arts.

11. In 1958, Homans, referring to Simmel and Blau, tried to sketch the outlines of a theory of exchange: 'Some of the statements of such a theory might be the following. Social behavior is an exchange of goods, material goods but also non-material ones, such as the symbols of approval or prestige. Persons that give much to others try to get much from them, and persons that get much from others are under pressure to give much to them. This process of influence tends to work out at equilibrium to a balance in the exchanges. For a person engaged in exchange, what he gives may be a cost to him, just as what he gets may be a reward, and his behavior changes less as profit, that is, reward less cost, tends to a maximum.' Quoted from: G. C. Homans, 'Social behavior as exchange. The problems of small group research', in: *Sentiments and Activities. Essays in Social Science.* New York, 1962, p. 278-293 (page 292). The theory has since been developed by Homans himself, Thibault and Kelly, and Blau. – G. C. Homans, *Social Behavior, Its Elementary Forms.* London, 1961. – J. W. Thibault and H. H. Kelley, *The Social Psychology of Groups.* New York, 1959. – P. M. Blau, *Exchange and Power in Social Life.* New York, 1964.

In describing authority in Ramlia and the relations between authorities and followers this model has proven to be a useful one.

12. Over and over again, in working with matrices in Ramlia, we were struck by the fact that partners, if asked, arrived in an independent way at identical answers in indicating the level of their mutual cooperation. This consensus has been the object of special research in Ramlia. A great number of inhabitants are even capable of indicating the level of cooperation – B or P or F – between a large number of partner-pairs in the village without making mistakes.

13. If the political process consists of numerous gradual reciprocal adaptations between partners reacting to the actions of other pairs of partners, with each partner acting in cooperation with persons who share the same interests, then the study of the political process in the form of *successive matrices* of interpersonal relations would be a powerful tool for arriving at a detailed insight into politics at the micro level.

14. I refer to L. A. Coser, *The Functions of Social Conflict*. New York, 1956. In Ramlia we seem to have group-binding functions between people who in reality do not seem to have anything to do with the conflict between 30 and 12. Conflict binds antagonists, the antagonists each forming cohesive structures with their own core members. But even outsiders, who have to defend their positions, are led into the way of greater cooperation, even if this is not cooperation on the highest level. If this is true, then for all the inhabitants of Ramlia belonging to the core of outsiders conflicts lead to the cohesion of groups.

15. The matrix of 1956 has been published in D. G. Jongmans, '*Meziaa en horma. Samenhangen tussen dienstbetoon, eer en welstand in een veranderde samenleving*'; see note 10. The other matrices will be published in an article entitled 'Networks and the perspective of time'.

16. Bourdieu has written an excellent article from a French structural point of view on the structural aspects of the notions of *hormaa* and shame in Algerian Kabylia. His study is, in my opinion and experience, applicable to wider regions in North Africa, the Khroumirian mountains included.
– P. Bourdieu, 'The sentiment of honour in Kabyle Society', in: J. G. Peristiany (Ed.), *Honour and Shame, The Values of Mediterranean Society*. London, 1965, pp. 191-241.

17. When I entered the field in northern Tunisia I was convinced that the model of the segmentary system could be applied in describing Khroumirian social structure and in explaining Khroumirian social processes. I was influenced by E. E. Evans Pritchard's *The Nuer* (Oxford, 1940), the Ph.D. dissertation of Emrys Peters on the Bedouins of Cyrenaica and M. Fortes, 'The structure of unilineal descent groups' (*American Anthropologist* 1953 (55), pp. 17-41). In the field however I soon realized that for explaining what was going on the model would not work on the village level. So I had to look for another tool and decided to start on the basis of interaction analysis. When later on I became interested in politics, I gradually became convinced that in this domain the model might be useful to a certain extent. While in Manchester as a visiting Simon Fellow in 1970, Prof. Gluckman and his assistants (among them Dr. G. K. Garbett, Dr. N. Long, D. Boswell, B. Samson and Dr. E. Marx (Simon Fellow from Israel)) helped me considerably in clarifying my points of view. The use of force has since long been placed in the hands of the government. The segmentary lineage system has been deprived of an essential function. Although the lineage system may have been there originally, afterwards its political function could be regarded as redundant. A number of students, while doing research in Tunisia, have published their M.A. theses. One of these, A. M. Hartong, started describing and analyzing the

history of the 'tribe' of the Atatfa. He has analyzed in terms of the segmentary lineage system and has not found any inconsistencies:
– A. M. Hartong, *De geschiedenis van het sjeikaat Atatfa op basis van de orale traditie* (1968).

Another student, W. M. J. van Binsbergen, in his M.A. thesis, *Verwantschap en territorialiteit in de sociale structuur van het bergland van Noord-West Tunesië*, denies that the model is applicable, however.

While the former discussed problems such as segmentation and political struggles, wars and conflicts, the second was looking for the process of interaction in daily life, which he could not place in the frame of relations between close agnates. I myself am of the opinion that there are two systems: 1) the segmentary system of the past, in a more or less ideal form (we must not forget that we are dealing with abstractions in model-building). This model does not work in modern political life, because the state has in a way taken the place of the old system. 2) the social system of daily life. It is here that ego-centered networks, kindred and locality are far more important moulds for social action than kinship and the moulds of lineages on different levels. The same may be true for daily interaction in the past. I have the impression that some anthropologists try to explain too much through the segmentary lineage system. If the model is applicable it is so in the first place in the field of power and politics. In my micro-research on the family level (the minimal lineage level) I think it is still working, though not smoothly.

18. R. W. Nicholas, 'Segmentary Factional Political Systems', in: *Political Anthropology* (eds. M. J. Swartz, V. W. Turner, A. Tuden), Chicago, 1966, pp. 49-59.

19. See page 178.

20. C. E. Russett, *The Concept of Equilibrium in American Social Thought*. New Haven & London, 1966. Since the days of Comte and Spencer this concept has formed an essential part of the way of thinking of sociologists, social anthropologists, social psychologists, economists, political scientists and workers in all other sciences in the social field. To stick to social anthropology, together with the concepts of functional integration, social solidarity and cultural uniformity the concept forms one of the basic assumptions of the structural-functional school and as such has led to a great deal of theorizing and more in particular to 'a way of looking at things',
– E. R. Leach, *Political Systems of Highland Burma. A Study of Kachin Social Structure*. London, 1964.

As the concept has never been operationalized, a balance could never be measured, nor could different states of imbalance be compared or identical states of balance or imbalance compared under different conditions. Nadel wrote some critical lines on the notion of equilibrium a long time ago. Leach and others have followed, and more and more critical comment is heard. Some other scholars go even further and express the opinion that the concept as such is heuristically misleading. Blok (p. 225) refers to Barth.
– A. Blok, 'Man as an entrepreneur', *Sociologische Gids*, 17, no. 3, 1970, pp. 225-234.

This opinion, without trying to penetrate the phenomenon of equilibrium in an exact way seems to me to be devoid of scientific meaning. Chapple and Coon, however, who must be considered as anthropological interactionists, have paved the way for measuring balance and imbalance. They define equilibrium in the following way: 'Equilibrium may be defined as a state in which if a small force is impressed on a system, the force will produce modifications to a greater or lesser degree within the

system, and when the force is removed, the system will tend to return to its previous state.'
– E. D. Chapple and C. S. Coon, *Principles of Anthropology*, New York, 1942, p. 14.

Nadel, in his *Foundations of Social Anthropology*, gave the following, in my opinion unsatisfactory, comment: 'There have been one or two attempts to reduce sociological or anthropological facts to basic units from which, by quantitative or quasi-quantitative combinations, the universe of culture and society can be built up. Brave though these attempts are, their hopelessness is, I think, only too evident'.
– S. F. Nadel, *The Foundations of Social Anthropology*. London, 1951, p. 192.

21. F. Heider, 'Attitudes and cognitive organization', *Journal of Psychology*, 1946, 21, pp. 107-112.

F. Heider, *The psychology of interpersonal relations*. 4th impression. New York, 1965.

22. D. Cartwright and F. Harary, 'Structural balance: a generalization of Heider's theory', *Psychological Review*, 1956, 63, pp. 277-293.

23. Flament gives the following example: 'Let A be a man, H a top hat and C a necktie. This man greatly likes to wear a top hat, and greatly dislikes to wear a necktie; but he knows that the top hat is worn with a necktie: his situation is very unpleasant. It can be said that a *positive relationship* exists between A and H, a *negative* one between A and C, and a *positive* one between H and C. By representing the positive relationships by full lines, and the negative ones by broken lines, we obtain Fig. 3.1 a.

In order to get out of this unpleasant situation, Mr. A has several choices: he can accept the wearing of a tie, then the negative relationship AC becomes positive (Fig. 3.1 b; or he can give up the idea of wearing the top hat, then AH becomes negative; or he can even convince himself that a top hat can be worn without a tie: HC becomes negative (Fig. 3.1 c).

Fig. 3.1

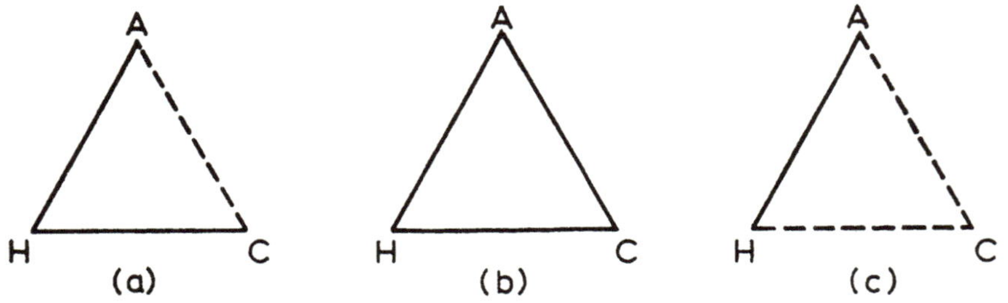

Now let A again be a man, and B his wife. A dislikes wearing a tie, but his wife B likes him to wear one. Finally let us suppose that husband and wife wish to please one another. This situation is formally identical to the preceding one; it is represented in Fig. 3.1 a, by deplacing H by B.'
– C. Flament, *Applications of Graph Theory to Group Structure*. Prentice-Hall Series in Mathematical Analysis of Social Behavior. Englewood Cliffs, 1963, p. 89.

24. Flament, *op. cit.*, pp. 92, 91.

25. Flament, *op. cit.*, p. 92.

26. In the following graph we have two balanced triangles. But the side AC cannot have two values at the same time. In such a situation a zero relationship may be a suitable one.

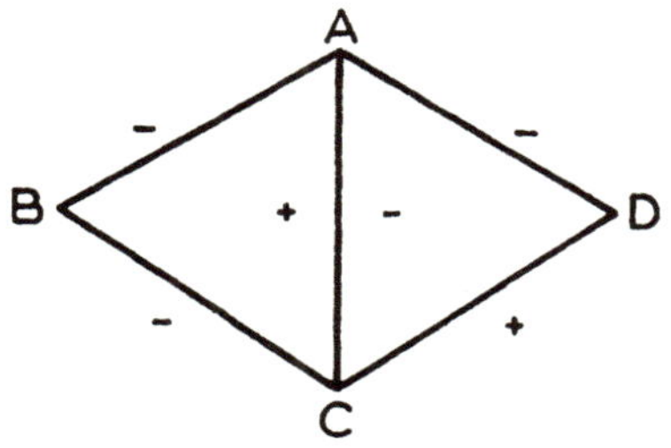

27. D. A. Sweetser, 'Path consistency in directed graphs and social structure', *American Journal of Sociology*, 1967, 73, pp. 287-293.

28. Likelihood ratio test for contingency tables.

A. Mood and I. Graybill, *Introduction to the Theory of Statistics*. New York, 1963. Sec. Ed., pp. 311-319. Calculations by Rudo Niemeijer.

Drs. Rudo Niemeijer has been of invaluable assistance in discussing my Leiden paper from a statistical point of view.

29. Calculations by Rudo Niemeijer.

Coalitions and network analysis

H. U. E. THODEN VAN VELZEN

'Politics makes strange bedfellows'

1. INTRODUCTION

The study of social networks has focused our attention on the more general problem of non-groups, the less crystallized forms of human interaction which are largely outside the scope of traditional group studies (*cf.* Boissevain, 1968). The major concern here is with one particular type of non-group: the coalition. A *coalition* is defined as *an alliance between social actors who adopt a common stand in conflict situations.*[1] The analysis of competitive interaction allows one to distinguish between two types of coalition which will be called the interest and the levelling coalition.

The aim of this paper is twofold. Firstly, to bring into focus the structural aspects of levelling and interest coalitions. Additionally, attention will be devoted to the role that coalitions play in the struggle for control of resources, a type of conflict which takes place in every society. Secondly, to investigate the use of the concepts of network analysis for the delineation of coalitions, and to discuss the relevance of the postulates which underlie modern network analysis for the study of conflict. The argument will be based on data concerning conflicts and coalitions gathered in a village in southwestern Tanzania.

The interest coalition

The interest coalition, better known as the *faction*, is the more exhaustively studied of the two, probably because its structure is of a more crystallized nature. Its features have often been indicated in literature, though considerable differences remain with regard to the importance attributed to the various characteristics. Nicholas (1965: 27-29), for example, lists the following five characteristics as essential for the faction:

1. Factions are conflict groups;
2. Factions are political groups;

3. Factions are not corporate groups;
4. Factions members are recruited by a leader;
5. Faction members are recruited on diverse principles.

The first three characteristics are not restricted to factions exclusively nor do they shed much light on the structure and functioning of these coalitions. The last two elements are of secondary importance: they do not bring the most important attribute into focus. Boissevain's definition presents a somewhat different and more useful emphasis: 'By "faction" I mean an exclusive coalition of persons (followers) recruited personally according to structurally diverse principles by or on behalf of a person in conflict with another person or persons within the same social unit over honour and/or control over resources' (1968: 551).

The most important feature of an interest coalition or faction[2] is a common fund of resources and honour. Its backbone is an *exchange circuit*, the particular system of paths through which goods and services circulate among members of the coalition. If this flow-system is asymmetrical (hierarchical), the common fund is controlled by only a small proportion of coalition members (the core). Other coalition members, the followers, hope to benefit through the channels of transactional linkage. Such coalitions have been called *teams* in the literature (Bailey, 1969: Chap. 3); a patron with his clients is an example of such a team.

The *raison d'être* of the interest coalition is to protect, consolidate and expand its fund. In order to realize this objective the core of a team mobilizes part or all of its followers (action-sets) for both defensive and offensive purposes. Members of the core act as entrepreneurs in the sense that they combine resources and manipulate persons to expand the coalition's fund (Barth, 1963: 6). These social entrepreneurs have the edge on other coalition members. This control of resources gives the entrepreneur the opportunity of stabilizing his relationships with others by creating an 'imbalance of obligations' (This concept is taken from Blau, 1964). Though the position of the entrepreneur is therefore relatively secure, other factors tend to weaken it. A lack of success in procuring benefits for the rank and file may cause the coalition to collapse. Internal strife and upheavals could and often do dislodge core members.

It is for these reasons that sociologists who analyzed the operation of teams – i.e. of coalitions with asymmetrical flow-systems – have devoted so much attention to management problems (*cf.* Bailey, 1969: Chap. 3 and Boissevain, in press).

Coalitions with symmetrical flow-systems have been given less attention in literature. Such alignments are less stabilized; successful mobilization is dependent upon complicated bargaining processes. On the whole, the structure and functioning of this type of coalition is very much akin to the team discussed above: both are coalitions managing a fund and both have an exchange circuit. As the partners in this coalition choose clients to help them secure their share of the spoils, teams evolve.

The levelling coalition

The interest coalition or faction, the two words are used synonymously, has been described as the basic unit of conflict (Boissevain, 1968: 551). However, quite another type of coalition exists which plays just as crucial a role in the struggle for resources in at least some societies. It is a much more loosely structured interaction pattern and often of a much more transient character. Its 'visibility' – the degree to which the actions of a social unit are observable or can be empirically studied – is lower than that of the faction. This, together with the characteristics mentioned before, might account for the small measure of attention it has so far received. This alignment between individuals who are united by their common feelings of hostility towards 'a target' will be called a levelling coalition. A 'target' is a social actor who poses a threat to the status quo: it could be a social climber, a reactionary,[3] or an innovator who breaks with traditional norms.

While interest coalitions are centered around a fund, and in the case of a team are also ego- or leader-centered, the levelling coalition is *target-oriented*. The aim of this type of alignment is not to protect or expand any fund, but rather to level that of the target. Interest coalitions also have targets, but their existence is not dependent upon an adversary as in the case of the levelling coalition. When the target disappears, the coalition collapses.

The levelling coalition lacks a skeleton of transactional ties, though some of its component units may be composed from such linkages. The levelling coalition functions in two different ways: (a) by inflicting losses on the enemy (target), denying him access to resources and undermining his reputation; (b) by forcing the owner of resources to convert his holdings into less dangerous commodities, i.e. into goods which will be less useful as a springboard to a greater share of power. This last process will not figure in the case study. A pertinent example of this type of levelling in recent literature is Whitten's account (1969: 233) of the timber work party in northwest Ecuador.

In the fifth section of this paper the features of both coalitions will be dealt with in a more systematic way.

Action-sets and coalitions

Existing terminology only partly fits the empirical data on coalitions. But as mentioned before, interest coalition and faction are concepts which cover the same ground and will therefore be used as synonyms. The closest thing to the levelling coalition in established terminology is the *quasi-group*. Ginsberg (1934: 40) defined it in this way: 'aggregates or portions of the community which have no recognizable structure, but whose members have certain interests or modes of behaviour in common, which may at any time lead them to form themselves into definite groups'. For a number of reasons, it does not seem advisable to use this concept. Boissevain (1971), for example, has rightly pointed out that the term 'quasi-group', as currently used, tends to create confusion and, if more precisely defined, becomes redundant. Moreover, the earlier definition of Ginsberg does include far more phenomena than levelling coalitions alone.

Neither the levelling nor the interest coalition will or can mobilize all their members in every conflict into which they are drawn. The particular set of persons which enter into the fray will be called an interest or levelling action-set, depending on whether they have been recruited by the leader of a faction (interest coalition) or whether they feel motivated to join forces with others in order to attack a target.

An *action-set* is defined as *a set of persons who have, for one particular purpose, attuned their actions to each other.*

The study of action-sets is closer to social reality than that of coalitions. An anthropologist observes social processes; he witnesses interaction between some people and knows for what purpose. This is the action-set. Now the question arises whether coalitions exist apart from the action-sets which we observe. The writer thinks they do, although the empirical basis for the two types of coalitions differs considerably. To start with the faction. Even if the leader of a particular interest coalition does not recruit any action-sets during a certain period of time, its flow-system can be detected and in this way the unit could be demarcated from other social units. The levelling coalition lacks an exchange circuit, but it has another kind of empirical reality. Those that have been the target of a levelling coalition certainly have some idea about the people who are conspiring against them, even if they have not yet collided with a levelling action-set. They refer to them as 'the enemies' or 'the people who are scheming to make life difficult for us'. Others in the community will also recognize the fact that a given set of people suspects that the status quo is being threatened and, moreover, that these people may be willing and capable of redressing the situation. Nevertheless, some measure of obscurity will remain; few people will have a completely accurate picture of the strength of the levelling coalition.

2. THE CONTEXT OF CONFLICT

The formation of coalitions and their competitive interaction will be studied on the basis of a series of conflicts which took place in Itumba between 1957 and 1968.

Itumba is an agrarian community in the southwestern part of Tanzania, close to the Malawi border. During my field work in 1967 the population of this village numbered approximately 1000 inhabitants. As Itumba is the headquarters of a division,[4] personnel of a few government services are resident in the village. The peasants call this group the 'staff people' (*Wasitafu*). Both peasants and staff people play a distinct role in the series of conflicts which will be described in the third section.

Distribution of resources: The peasants

There are three types of agricultural fields:

a) Fields used for ash cultivation in the hills and on the high plateau above the river valley in which Itumba is situated;
b) The dry area on the valley floor, intermediate between the area of shifting cultivation and the gardens;
c) River gardens which form the most important resource in this agricultural community. Yields from these fertile alluvial soils are on average three times higher than in the intermediate area. River gardens are either irrigated or they retain enough moisture to yield a second crop during the long dry season from the end of April to the middle of November. The main crops are: maize, bananas, sugar-cane, tobacco and vegetables.

As to the distribution of land the following facts are relevant:

1) Every peasant has enough land to satisfy his daily food necessities and to provide some surplus for sale or exchange at the local markets. The area lacks cash crops of any importance;
2) River gardens form closed resources which are unequally distributed among the peasants. Thus, 29 % of Itumba peasants have not been able to obtain any river land at all. Twenty peasants or 10 % of all heads of households own 45 % of the total acreage of river land.

About one third of Itumba's population consists of Ndali immigrants who settled in the area between 1910 and 1940. When the Ndali arrived in Itumba they took possession of some of the unoccupied reed and marshy land along the river that flows through Itumba. The indigeneous Nyiha, swidden cultivators, only later realized the value of these fields but the majority of the best places along creeks and river had already been occupied.

Distribution of resources: Staff people

All personnel of government services, whether paid by local or central government, are called 'staff people' by the peasants. A number of them are resident in Itumba. This group comprises the main representatives of the government in rural areas: the Divisional Executive Officer (D.E.O.); his treasurer and messengers; the Village Executive Officer (V.E.O.); the teachers of a primary school; the agricultural extension officer; a veterinary assistant; the magistrate of the primary court with his clerk and messengers; the medical dispenser and his sweeper; a community development officer; a mid-wife; a police officer with his constables.

In rural areas the staff form a social grouping with distinctive prestige symbols and prerogatives.[5] They consider themselves an elite grouping with a rightful claim so social esteem. The most important factor that sets this group apart from the peasants as a highly envied elite is the fact that they draw salaries. This regular and guaranteed income is in almost all cases higher than the income of the wealthiest peasants.[6]

There is a good deal of co-operation between staff. Occasionally, this co-operation is covert and aims at underpinning their position at the top of the rural hierarchy of prestige and power. Peasants are inclined to dramatize the collusion of staff and of staff and the wealthy farmers. Though the suspicions of the peasants are often without any factual basis they are nevertheless important enough to influence their actions and mould their strategy and thus form an integral part of the arena map.[7]

Staff people control access to several important resources. Because of their functions they dispose of goods and services (medicine, treatment, expertise in a number of fields, seeds, implements, insecticides). The staff are suspected of giving preferential treatment to rich peasants and in a number of instances which I saw they certainly confirmed these suspicions. They make some short-term employment available for their clients by giving them the opportunity of performing odd chores. Even more important is the fact that staff dominate the legitimate arenas, in other words arenas like the primary court and the 'council' – the D.E.O. with his staff. The decisions of these bodies are recognized by the government as authoritative and backed up by force.

Composition of the coalitions

The interest coalitions in the village centre around a few of the more wealthy farmers and some staff. These farmers are connected through transactional asymmetrical linkages with the peasants. The wealthy farmers give gardens on loan to some of the poorer peasants, who repay their debt by taking part in the patron's working parties and supporting the patron's prestige and political position. These sets of patron-client relations are in a number of cases connected with other sets of transactional relations to form larger coalitions. An example of the latter linkages is that between staff and wealthy farmer.

The interest coalition which would figure in the next section embraces a wealthy Ndali farmer named Chomo, some of his clients and some staff. Chomo owns 13 acres of river land apart from his holdings in the intermediate zone. He has given gardens on loan to about 15 farmers. Chomo's contacts among the staff include the medical dispenser, an extension officer (Mwakalinga) and some of the Divisional Executive Officers who have been posted in Itumba.[8]

The levelling coalition consists of most of the poorer peasants, the former Nyiha chief with his deputies,[9] some dignitaries of the community of Moravian Brethern and also a few wealthy farmers.

Compartments

For heuristic purposes it seems feasible and useful to separate the peasants of Itumba into *compartments*, i.e. into sets of persons who have more contact with one another than with persons outside their compartment. If conceptualized into dichotomies it appears possible to identify at least two important pairs of compartments: the tribal (Nyiha-Ndali) and the religious (Christians-Pagans) dichotomies.

The most important of these dichotomies in terms of the extent to which it restricts interaction is the religious one. Christians meet one another much more often than they meet Pagans. There are some fairly obvious reasons responsible for this communication schism. Firstly, Christian rites and social occasions (choir gatherings, the many meetings of the various Church organizations) restrict the possibilities of getting into contact with other villagers and greatly increase the level of interaction for the Christian group. Secondly, the taboos which tend to keep Christians and Pagans apart are just as important as the rites and the many social events of Church life. Christians are required by their pastor and elders not to participate in the funeral rites of the Pagans, except for a brief visit extending their condolences. Even more important are the restrictions imposed on the consumption of beer. Dignitaries (deacons, elders) of the Moravian Church are not allowed to drink beer while the other believers are discouraged from going to the beer halls. These beer halls or clubs (*kelábu*) are houses reserved or specially built for the drinking of locally produced finger-millet beer. Such clubs are important rallying-points for peasants who live scattered over many square miles of accidented territory and whose work tends to keep them apart during working-hours. With the exception of a few weeks during the peak of the agricultural season, peasants visit these clubs twice or thrice weekly and often spend several hours together before leaving again. The peasants intermingle to a great extent at these places and exchange the latest gossip. The beer halls function as hubs in a communication network. Thus, as the majority of the Christians observe the teachings of their elders and practise abstinence, a very tangible communication schism appears to exist.

Thirdly, territorial segregation of both groups tend to reinforce the compartimentalization of social life. The population of Itumba is distributed over 15 'ten house groups' or Party Cells.[10] Of the 50 Christian heads of households two thirds (34) live concentrated in four 'ten house groups'.

Summarizing, we might say that, *ceteris paribus*, Christians have greater chances of establishing exchange bonds with one another than with Pagans. In other words, Christians form a compartment.

The tribal compartments (Nyiha-Ndali) seem to be less important but they still do restrict contact to some extent. Peasants choose their friends mainly from among the members of their own tribal group. Owing to the high degree of territorial mobility, territorial segregation is not only a good indicator of compartimentalization but equally exhibits the voluntary element in it. If we call a 'ten house group' uniform where more than $^3/_4$ of the heads of households have the same tribal origin, then 13 of its 14 Party Cells have that character (one Party Cell, mainly consisting of government personnel, being excluded).

The exchange and communication schism which exists in a community like Itumba exhibits the following important consequences:

a) The span of a person's network tends to be restricted by the boundaries of a compartment;

b) Multiplex relations will grow and develop between persons within the same compartment rather than with persons outside these compartments.[11]

After having given an account of an extended case study in the following section, I will elucidate some of the implications involved in compartmentalization for network analysis.

3. CONFLICTS BETWEEN A LEVELLING AND AN INTEREST COALITION: A CASE STUDY

A number of conflicts in which the levelling coalition is mainly on the offensive will now be discussed. After relating the more important events in the dispute, the information on action-sets will be grouped together and presented in a brief summary and diagram at the end of each case. The aim of recounting this political drama[12] is twofold: firstly, to present a brief sketch of coalition fighting in a Tanzanian village, secondly, to distinguish on the basis of these data between two types of coalitions and to highlight their features.

A. *Banishment*

On a day in August 1957 most of the older men and some women from Itumba gathered for a secret meeting presided over by the chief of that area. This was the traditional village meeting (*ulubungano*) which is convened whenever the village community feels threatened. The subject discussed was the misbehaviour of Chomo, who was neither present nor informed by the village elders. Chomo was accused of a variety of offences, ranging from witchcraft to seducing the wives of other men. Not mentioned was the fact that Chomo with his 14 acres of river land is the wealthiest farmer in the whole village. People especially resented the aggressive way in which Chomo had managed to expand his original holdings. At the meeting the decision was made to banish Chomo from the village. That same afternoon the villagers gathered around Chomo's farm to bring him the verdict and to see to it that he would pack and leave before sunset.

Chomo had got wind of the intentions of his enemies and was well prepared for the encounter. He worked himself into a trancelike state by drinking beer and smeared ash over his face and chest to look fearsome. He knew that people feared his sorcery and that he was reputed to have trained his cows for his malevolent practices.

When the threatening mob of villagers had gathered around his houses, and began to shout that they would put fire to the thatched roofs, Chomo suddenly emerged from the byre chasing his cows in the direction of the mob. He followed behind spear in hand. People panicked at this sight and ran for safety. No more attempts to evict him with force were made.

Action-set diagram A

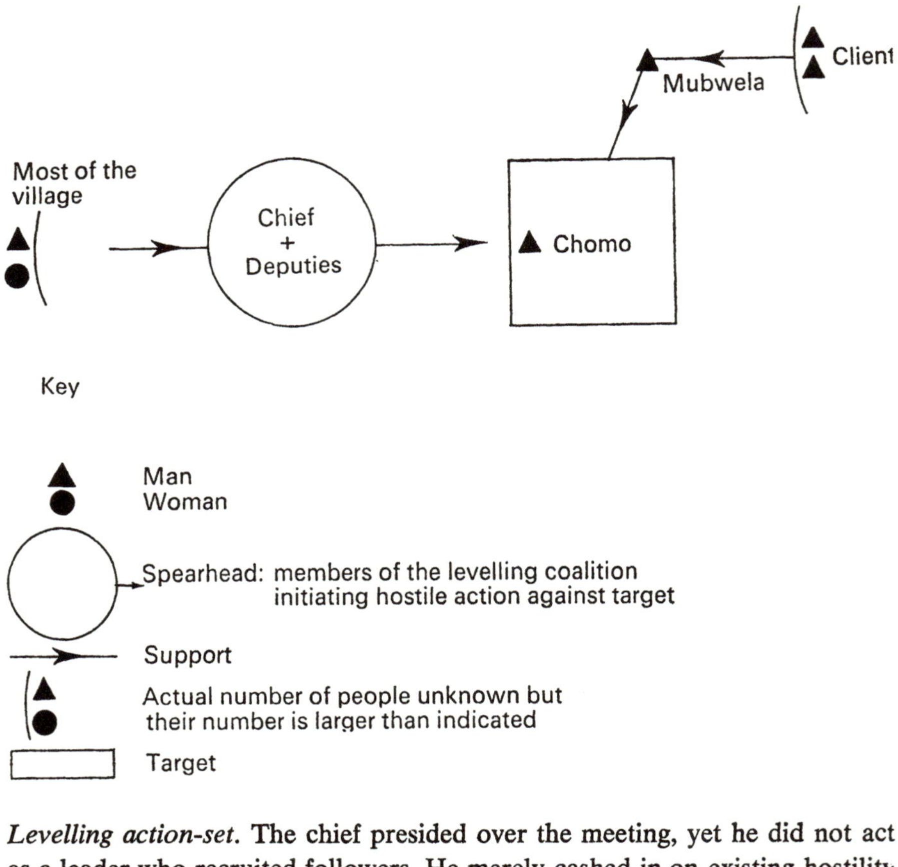

Levelling action-set. The chief presided over the meeting, yet he did not act as a leader who recruited followers. He merely cashed in on existing hostility and gave direction to it. Support came from various quarters within the village, as was clear during the village meeting when no one spoke out against the banishment and from the great number of people that went to Chomo's farm to chase him.

Interest action-set. Chomo was tipped off about the meeting by Mubwela, an 'affiliated' client (clients of Chomo belong to the same patri-group as Mubwela). The clients themselves remained neutral; they did not attend the meeting but neither did they come over to Chomo's farm. Though none of my informants mentioned any help for Chomo from the side of the staff people, it seems likely that their presence in Itumba acted as a restraint on the use of force. In the days following the mob action the staff people undoubtedly used their influence to prevent bloodshed.

B. *A tract of marshy land*

In September 1966 Chomo started opening a tract of marshy land in an area which had been closed some years before by a former extension officer to prevent erosion. The present extension officer was a friend of Chomo and pretended to be ignorant of what was going on. Chomo gave a piece of the newly opened plot to Joram, a man who had never been a client of Chomo before. A few days later he came to Chomo's plot accompanied by five other men and they started tilling the whole tract of marshy land. Two of these five peasants were generally known as enemies of long-standing of Chomo. An hour after their arrival Chomo received information on what had happened. He came running to the plot, swinging his spear. For a moment it looked as if a fight was about to erupt, but after insults had been exchanged both parties left the disputed plot and went over to the office of the Divisional Executive Officer (D.E.O.), the man who as the senior representative of the government in the area is 'justice of the peace'. The D.E.O. succeeded in cooling the tempers for that moment and promised a special meeting in which this case could be discussed. Two days later it was held. About fifty men from the village were present. Fifteen men, from various quarters within the village, both Christians and Pagans, denounced Chomo and asked the government for immediate and severe punishment. The D.E.O. at that time was generally known to be a friend of Chomo. He avoided taking sides. Later, however, when the chief made the careless remark that they had to chase not only Chomo from the village but also the other Ndali, the D.E.O. cleverly managed to exploit this slip of the tongue. He rebuked the gathering for 'tribalism' and shifted the focus of the discussion. The meeting ended with the decision by the D.E.O. that the whole area would again be closed for agriculture. Chomo was not punished for defying the orders of the extension service although these had been backed up by court rulings on other occasions.

The *levelling* spearhead consisted of six men, one of them was Joram who sided with the enemies of Chomo. Joram was subverted by S., who threatened that if he would not line up with the other villagers 'things' would happen to him. The core group received support from various quarters within the village

Action-set diagram B

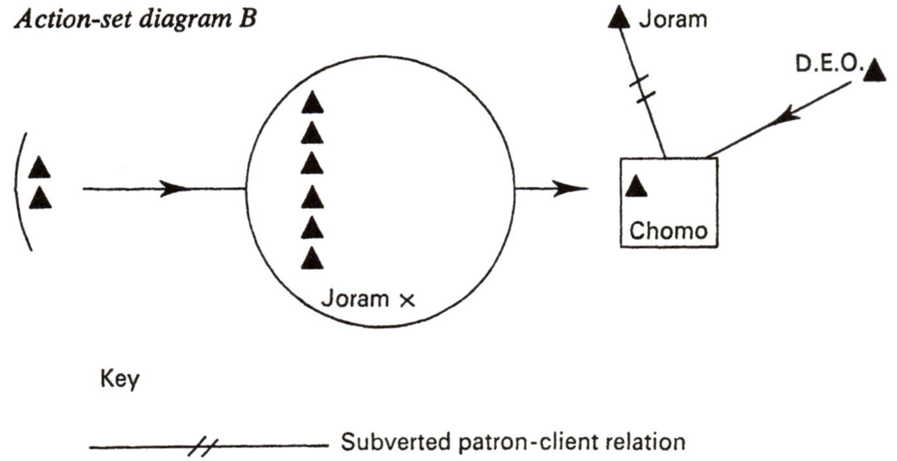

For the other symbols see p. 228.

during the special meeting arranged by the D.E.O. Both Christians and Pagans and both Ndali and Nyiha tribesmen spoke out against Chomo. No one of the villagers defended Chomo during the meeting.

Interest: Only one man, Chomo, became target for the levelling coalition. Chomo received support from the D.E.O. who prevented that the magistrate, another friend of Chomo's, would be forced to press charges against him.

C. *The death of John*

John fell sick on February 18, 1967, and died two days later. He was two and a half years old, the youngest of the eight children of Godfrey Mwakalinga, an agricultural extension officer, and Lena Nampamba. During the period of mourning for John it was Chomo who was in charge of the proceedings and received the gifts.

It was from Simon, Mwakalinga's eldest son, that I first learned of the social tensions which were simmering under the calm uneventful surface of everyday life and which now seemed to be erupting. About two weeks after the burial I had asked Simon to be my assistant in some activity in which I was at that time engaged. Simon replied gloomily that this would be impossible as his parents intended to leave Itumba on a transfer and that he would follow them. He added: 'seven years with these beastly people is long enough for anybody'. This answer came as a surprise to me since both Simon and his father had always emphasized that they lived on good terms with the peasants of Itumba. When I had pressed him for an explanation he told me that his little brother 'had not been killed by God but by the actions of people around here'. It was fear for the safety of his other children which drove Mwakalinga to ask for a transfer.

A few weeks after the burial Simon received an early warning that something was afoot. Cycling from his house to his parents' house, he was attacked by a swarm of bees. He saved his life by dropping the bicycle, running into a nearby house and throwing an armful of wet faggots on the fire. Later Donald (see *Genealogy*), a man who performs odd chores for the Mwakalingas, paid a visit to Simon's sickbed. Donald remarked, 'I must warn you, I have cast out feelers here and there and I know now for certain that this is only the start of people's revenge actions'. No further explanation was given. Note that Donald, while helping Mwakalinga by supplying him with information, served at the same time as an intermediary for the enemies of Mwakalinga and Chomo by conveying indications of unpopularity and threats to them.

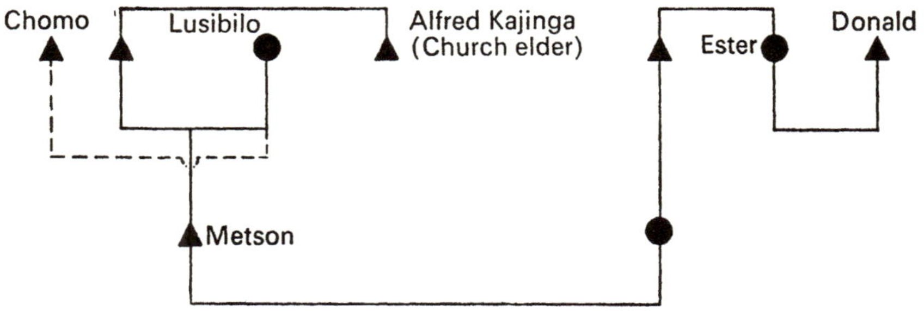

Genealogy

A few days later, at the end of March 1967, one month after the death of John, a friend told Lena Nampamba (wife of Mwakalinga) that people had started to speculate on the causes of her child's death. Rumour had it that some people in the village were actually claiming to have killed the boy. One of the names given was that of Metson Kajinga but there were other more powerful sorcerers who were backing him up, it was said. However, the identity of these sorcerers was not revealed. Two Christian women, both widows, were probably the ones most active in spreading the many rumours throughout the community.

Mwakalinga, after receiving this news, remained at home for more than a week. Lena, however, visited Alfred Kajinga, a church elder of Itumba's Moravian Church. He is a father's-brother of Metson (see *Genealogy*) who lives at variance with him. The church elder expressed his disapproval of

Metson's behaviour but made it equally plain that Mwakalinga and 'some people who are always in your house' had aroused the displeasure of deacons and elders of the church. Lena also visited some clients of the Mwakalingas. All these sources essentially confirmed the report of Lena's friend.

It gradually became clear to me that the resentment of many peasants against the Mwakalingas revolved round three complaints:

a) Simon had been playing things too low down when he and Metson were competing for the favours of Magdalena (1962-1964). This conflict has been reported elsewhere and will not be related here (*cf.* Thoden van Velzen, 1970).
b) Godfrey Mwakalinga had supported Chomo, the enemy of the Kajingas in the dispute over the sugar-cane garden (*vide infra*).
c) Mwakalinga and other staff people had colluded to reserve certain goods and privileges for themselves and some of the wealthy farmers with whom they associated (*vide infra*).

Action-set diagram C

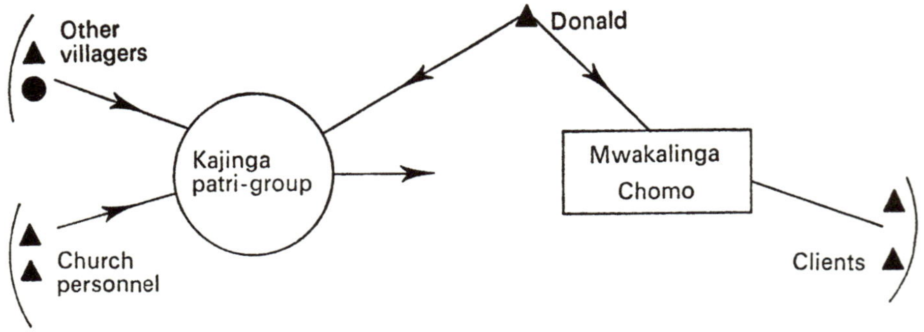

Levelling:

1. Metson Kajinga and other members of his patri-group;
2. Donald;
3. Church personnel;
4. A considerable number of other peasants in the village.

Interest:

1. Mwakalinga and Chomo (target);
2. Donald;
3. A number of clients of Mwakalinga who passed information on to him.

D. *The dispute over the sugar-cane garden*

The father of Kamasi was a court messenger, the father of Tonwell a medical dispenser; they had come to settle in Itumba in the thirties and they died at the end of the fifties. Some time after their death Chomo took one plot from each man and, as they were adjacent, made one garden of it. He irrigated it and planted sugar-cane. He was assisted in all these activities by Metson Kajinga who was staying with him at the time. This valuable garden consists of about three acres; it is fertile and well-irrigated. Chomo gave about one quarter of it on loan to Mwakalinga.

The relationship between Metson and Chomo started deteriorating in 1963. In 1965 Metson annexed a quarter of an acre of Chomo's sugar-cane garden to his own field which was adjacent to it. After Chomo instituted legal proceedings in Itumba's Primary Court, he was suddenly confronted with a claim to the whole garden. Kamasi and Tonwell (sons of the former owners, *vide supra*) in collusion with Metson, testified in court that they had inherited this plot from their fathers and that they had subsequently lent it to Metson. They asked the magistrate to give the whole garden to Metson. Metson claimed that he had let Chomo till this garden for a short period because the latter was married to his mother at that time. Most of the peasants of Itumba rallied to the support of Metson; they showed their interest in the case by crowding the small court building when the hearings started. The magistrate came under considerable pressure to pass a judgment favourable to Metson. Some told him that if he left the garden in Chomo's hands they would protest to Tanu[13] officials; others seem to have threatened him that they would set his (thatch-roofed) house on fire in the middle of the night.

The magistrate decided that the whole of the sugar-cane garden was to pass into the hands of Metson. In secret, he went to Mwakalinga, Chomo's friend, and apologised for his actions; he explained that he had been forced to make this unjust verdict because his life and that of his wife and children was in danger. The magistrate informed Mwakalinga that a court of appeal would certainly reverse the judgment and he asked the extension officer to instruct Chomo how and where to appeal. After he had borrowed a sum of money for legal and travel expenses from Mwakalinga, Chomo went to the District Court near Tukuyu and gave notice of appeal.

At the end of 1966 the District Court magistrate visited Itumba together with his assessors. Two weeks later the judgment of the Primary Court of Itumba was reversed. When this became known in Itumba people did not hide their disappointment. It was generally believed that Chomo would never have won his case without the vigorous support of Mwakalinga and that the latter had acted in connivance with the Primary Court magistrate. It was noted that this magistrate had been transferred a few months before the District magistrate visited Itumba. People alleged that Chomo had bribed the District Court magistrate with a cow. Mwakalinga and the wife of the medical dispenser were accused of helping Chomo to establish contact with the magistrate.[14]

Action-set diagram D

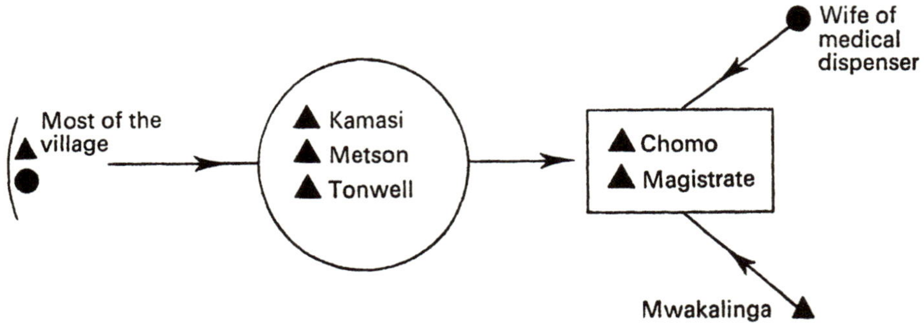

Levelling:
Kamasi, Metson and Tonnwell (core); support from many others villagers.

Interest:
Chomo and Magistrate Primary Court of Itumba; support from Mwakalinga and wife of medical dispenser.

E. *The divorced wife*

In 1966 and 1967 Itumba was rife with rumours about an alleged staff conspiracy. It was openly discussed in the local beer clubs 'that the reason why our children die while those of staff and "respected people" (*abagindikiwa*) stay alive is that ours do not get the medicines that their children are given'. They complained that the ordinary peasant never receives any good treatment and medicine; 'he is given a pill but never an injection'. Furthermore they alleged that when the stock of medicine in the local dispensary was depleted, the medical dispenser still had kept a secret stock for his staff friends: 'we have seen Mwakalinga and others of that group bring their children at night for treatment'.

In December 1966 Lusibilo (see *Genealogy* p. 231), the divorced wife of Chomo and the mother of Metson Kajinga, fell ill. There was talk of witchcraft and suspicion fell on Chomo; people remarked that Chomo had divorced her after a quarrel (1963). It was remembered that, even after the divorce, Chomo showed himself furious when he heard about the support Lusibilo gave to the Kajingas in the dispute over the sugar-cane garden. When she died the medical dispenser was accused of having withheld medicines from her at the request of Chomo so that she would not recover. People pointed out that like Mwakalinga, the medical dispenser also had an irrigated plot on loan from Chomo. Louise, wife of the medical dispenser, went to the mourning for Lusibilo, although her husband and Chomo did not go. When she sat down on the mat with her back against the mud wall of the house she overheard the mourners inside remarking: 'The one that has murdered her is not here and neither do we see his staff friends'. The acclaim that followed showed that peoples inside the house agreed; everybody knew that the insinuations were directed at Chomo and the medical dispenser.

When Louise went inside the house the conversation suddenly stopped. Later she told me, 'They knew I had overheard their backbiting, they were very much ashamed. Nobody dared to look at me'.

Lena Nampamba, Mwakalinga's wife, was informed by a church elder and some others that Metson had said, 'All the children of Mwakalinga lived thanks to the medicine of the medical dispenser while our children died. Mwakalinga has urged the medical dispenser not to give any medicine to my mother. Now the day of our revenge has come'.[15]

Action-set diagram E

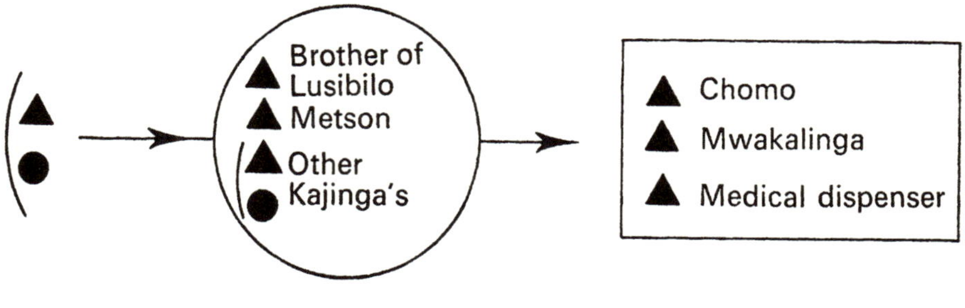

Levelling:
Brother of Lusibilo, Metson and a number of other Kajingas (core). Support was drawn from various quarters of the village but particularly from relatives of Lusibilo.

Interest:
Chomo, Mwakalinga and medical dispenser (target).

F. *Abuse*

During 1967 Chomo was summoned to appear before the local Primary Court. A former village headman had alleged that Chomo had openly threatened to murder him. The controversy took a critical turn when two clients of Chomo appeared to testify before the magistrate that such a threat had never been uttered, while they drew attention to the headman's own misbehaviour; according to them the headman had publicly discussed the condition of Chomo's mother's genitals. This is a standard type of abuse and one of the most provocative in this culture. The headman lost his case.

One of the two clients who rallied to Chomo's support had only recently settled in Itumba. This woman, Maria, had begged Chomo to help her. Chomo gave her a river plot.

Mwakalinga also testified in court in favour of Chomo. He threw doubt on some of the headman's statements, but he did not come up with new evidence.

Action-set diagram F

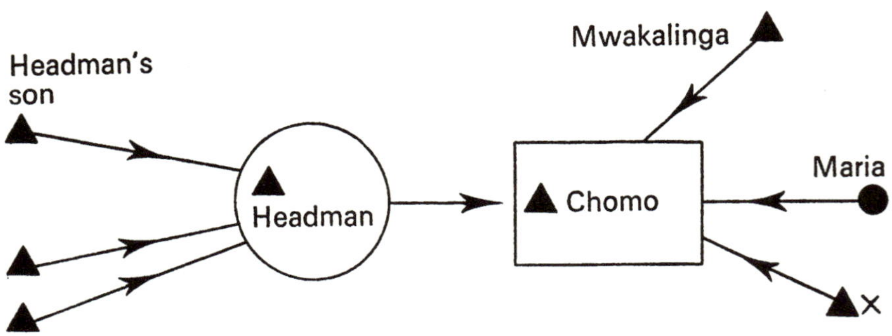

Levelling:
The headman was supported in court by his son and two unrelated men.

Interest:
Chomo (target). Support came from Mwakalinga and two clients of Chomo.

4. INTERPRETATION

At first glance this political drama is open to many interpretations. But a number of these apparent explanations should be eliminated.

Firstly, the least adequate explanation of this political drama is to consider it as a conflict between religious groupings, that is between Christians and Pagans. Though Chomo had been a member of the Moravian Church and most of his opponents were Pagans we should also note the following facts. Chomo left the Church when he married his second wife, long before 1950. Some of his fiercest opponents are Christians, for example, Metson Kajinga – to mention only one. It is equally true that a number of Christian dignitaries (a deacon and some of the elders) actively took part in the anti-Chomo campaign (*see The Death of John*). Furthermore, some of the gossips who spread rumours against Chomo and his 'staff contact' Mwakalinga were also devoted Christians.

Secondly, one could look upon the political drama as a series of collisions between the traditional political organization and the new party structure of Tanu at local level. The official position of the Chief was abolished by government decree in 1963: this meant that his official recognition was withdrawn and his salary withheld. Chomo had been a chairman of his 'ten house group', the party cell or smallest unit in Tanu's organization. Though the chief took an active role in only two of the cases, it is conceivable that he pulled the strings behind the scenes and urged his deputies to organize people in a campaign against Tanu. However convincing this explanation may sound, it does not stand up to closer examination. For one thing, there was no widespread dissatisfaction with Tanu. Quite apart from the fact that the conflict dates from the colonial time, long before Tanu came to this part of Tanzania, some of Chomo's most outspoken opponents themselves played leading roles in the local Tanu hierarchy. The son of the former chief who certainly belonged to the anti-Chomo coalition, though never among the most militant, climbed via the position of chairman of a 'ten house group' to the more important position of Tanu's branch chairman. Other spearhead members were also chairmen of Tanu cells in the village. Metson Kajinga at one time was Secretary of Bulambia's Tanu Youth League.

The tribal explanation seems more important. When the Ndali immigrated into this part of Bulambia between 1910 and 1940, they possessed superior agricultural techniques. While the Nyiha were practising slash-and-burn agriculture, the Ndali were familiar with ridging, making it practicable to till marshy soils, and they also knew how to water small plots along creeks. Therefore, when the first Ndali arrived and saw the fertile land along creeks and rivers unoccupied, they succeeded in bringing a good part of it under cultivation before the Nyiha realized the value of the land. Nowadays, 79 Ndali households own 67% of all river land while 126 Nyiha households have to make do with the remaining 33%.

Tribal jealousy is also aroused by the fact that the Ndali dominated the early Village Development Committees, became prominent in Tanu, occupied offices in the Moravian Church, and are among the more wealthy of the shop keepers in Bulambia. Thus the only two shops in Itumba, which deserve this name, are owned by Ndali.

It is therefore not surprising that stereotyped images of hostility are current among both groups with regard to each other. The Ndali are depicted as ambitious, greedy and bearers of new types of illness, while the Nyiha are accused of laziness and backwardness and are believed to be inclined to witchcraft.

In spite of undeniable tribal antagonism, I do not feel that it sufficiently explains the conflict. Take, for instance, the speech of the chief (*A Tract of Marshy Land*) in which he stated that he would not only chase Chomo from Itumba, but other Ndali as well. The Divisional Executive Officer immediately denounced the speech as 'a plea for tribalism'. Yet one wonders how much of the chief's speech was merely rhetorical: statements chosen as convenient slogans to which the majority of Itumba's population could rally in a drive against Chomo. It was interesting to note, for example, that none of the Ndali present at this meeting came to the rescue of Chomo. Though several of these Ndali used to be quite outspoken when facing an enemy, they remained reticent on this occasion. Metson, the most active opponent of Chomo in the case of the sugar-cane garden, was a Ndali. Equally, in other levelling action-sets some Ndali played a dominant role. It should be emphasized in this connection that Chomo on no occasion used a tribal rallying slogan to unite the Ndali behind him against the Nyiha.

While the tribal explanation cannot be wholly discarded – the Nyiha at least couched their arguments in the rhetorics of tribal identity – a class type of interpretation appears to be more relevant. There exists considerable antagonism between the mass of the peasantry on the one hand, and the wealthy peasants and staff people on the other (Thoden van Velzen, 1970). We could argue that Chomo as the wealthiest peasant of the village represents the enemy class better than anyone else did. However, this explanation is not entirely satisfactory: while much of the hostility between the poor and wealthy takes place behind the scenes in the form of slander, backbiting and the secretive destruction of property, the attacks on Chomo were often quite open. Moreover, the class theory leaves unexplained why it was that some wealthy farmers never came under attack from coalitions as formidable as the one that faced Chomo. In fact, the other wealthy farmers were either neutral or indirectly supported the levelling coalition.

Before giving an interpretation, one should first look at the gains which participants in the levelling coalition could hope for.

a) A few people would gain immediately from winning a dispute against Chomo. For example, Metson Kajinga, Kamasi and Tonwell would be able to occupy the sugar-cane garden; the six peasants (*A Tract of Marshy Land*) could then start to divide Chomo's illegally occupied plot in the closed erosion area.

b) Without giving such a central place to envy in the explanation of social behaviour as Schoeck (1969) does, it certainly plays an important role. Undoubtedly, there were many people in Itumba who joined the coalition in the hope that Chomo would be taken down a peg. They resented his wealth and well-being and envied the reputation he managed to build up. Most probably, they equally resented the wealth of others, but here at last was a golden opportunity of cutting one of them down to size.

c) Envious feelings on the part of the peasants cannot explain why Chomo regularly and openly became the target and not the other wealthy peasants. In order to give a more satisfactory interpretation, it is necessary to recognize the following facts. For the majority of the participants in the levelling coalition there was nothing to gain on a short-term basis. They realized, however, that a serious blow to Chomo could have entailed his departure from the village. In fact, during 1967 Chomo stated several times in public: 'if I lose that plot (the sugar-cane garden), I will leave this village, I cannot stand the idea of others going there to reap the fruits of my labour'.

The crucial point is that Chomo's departure would have brought a greater measure of security to many peasants who now felt, rightly or wrongly, that Chomo's presence endangered their control over their fields. They felt threatened in other ways (sorcery, adultery) and humiliated by his aggressive behaviour.

For an explanation of levelling and choice of target we need to take cognizance of the fact that a selection process is at work, for which probably two guidelines serve:

1) Individuals are selected who embody threats to the status quo. By *threat* I mean any recurrent pattern of signals which conveys the message that the target may change ego's control over his material or symbolic environment. An essential part of the symbolic environment is a set of rules which lay down the conditions of political competition. Chomo was a transgressor on

both scores: he was regarded by many as a clear and distinct threat to their control over their land (the material environment), while others believed that he harmed people with sorcery and inflicted too much damage on his opponents (symbolic environment). Thus, the peasants of Itumba tried to oust Chomo from their village in the hope that they would remove the greatest threat to their position in the local political field.

2) For any action to start people must feel that they have at least a fair chance of winning and that the consequences of losing will not be disastrous. However, in many societies the owners of resources are so solidly entrenched that any effort at overthrowing them is doomed to failure from the very beginning. The capacity of the establishment to retaliate works as an effective deterrent. Therefore, antagonistic interaction in such societies will be between interest coalitions rather than between interest coalitions and levelling coalitions.

5. INTEREST AND LEVELLING COALITIONS

Only six encounters between the two coalitions have been related here, while in reality many more took place during that period. Yet the trend is clear: on the one hand we have a coalition of a wealthy farmer, his clients and some government personnel; on the other we are confronted with an amorphous alignment of peasants coming from the various quarters within the community.

Features of the interest coalition[16]

a) The *fund of resources and honour* is the most important feature of the faction or interest coalition (p. 220). The fund is controlled by the core. Transactions take place between core and followers which serve two main purposes:
1) the benefits of coalition membership are made available to followers;
2) the transactions provide for the means to protect and expand the fund. The faction we took as an example is supplied with information, labour (e.g. work-parties), support and prestige signs and symbols. This flow 'upward' – from the rank and file to the leaders – buttresses the position of the core in competitive interaction. The input in labour – through work-parties – strengthens the economic position of the wealthy farmer.

b) The coalition is *leader-centred*. The fact that there is a fund to be managed requires this. Moreover, the leader (or leaders) have to weigh claims of other coalition members for a limited number of emoluments and to make authoritative decisions on them. Furthermore, the leader has to recruit followers and to give direction to the manoeuvres of the coalition.

c) The core mobilizes support through a number of well-known channels: the transactional linkages. *Recruitment essentially is a process of exchange,* a series of transactions between core and followers. A man will not give his backing to a coalition if he will not get anything in return.[17] As a minimum, prospects of future benefits must be held out to the followers because otherwise support will not be forthcoming.

d) The coalition is a *constructed social entity,* in the sense that linkages between persons and groups within the coalition are consciously created and maintained. The interest coalition has an architect.

e) This coalition is a *multi-purpose unit.*[18] Though initially the factions are formed for protection or support in conflict situations, at a later stage they often acquire other functions.

f) The interest coalition is a *bounded* social entity. Faction members are known to the core because they maintain transactional relations with them.

g. Its pictorial representation is a *star.* There is a more or less stable core (or spearhead) in the centre, from which transactional linkages radiate in several directions. The points at the end of these lines (the followers) are not necessarily connected with one another.

Features of the levelling coalition

a) The levelling coalition is *target-oriented* because (i) it becomes 'visible' through its actions against a target, (ii) the only basis for membership is shared aversion of this target. As a magnet changes the relative positions of iron particles from a distance, so the target patterns social relationships by causing the levelling coalition to arise. In its actions against the target the core can capitalize on existing sentiments of hostility and fear. The presence of a target creates favourable conditions for the spread of gossip. Interaction between the component parts need not immediately precede levelling actions. One incident is sometimes sufficient to generate a number of manoeuvres, independently undertaken by different persons in the coalition.

b) The levelling coalition is not leader-centred, at least not centred around an instrumental leader.[19] The reason is that there are no tasks to be performed which require authoritative decisions, such as managing a fund or dividing the spoils. The levelling coalition is *activated by social catalysts.* An example of the catalyst which plays an important role in our case study is the gossip-monger.[20]

c) Recruitment, if that name is applicable at all to the processes that take place in the formation of the levelling coalition, is not based on transaction. Support is seemingly spontaneous. It should be kept in mind, however, that the ground has been prepared by the social catalysts. This is the only plausible explanation for the fact that if one man takes the initiative, individuals from different groups and quarters of the village give their support to the core often simultaneously and in many cases independently of one another.

d) The *core* of the levelling coalition is *unstable.* A core in this type of coalition comprises all those persons who initiate actions against the target. The composition of the core is continually changing. While some members of the coalition may have for some time a more compelling reason to act as spearhead than others (the chief and Metson Kajinga, for example) seen in the long run the leading parts tend to be played by different persons.

e) The levelling coalition is a *single-purpose unit.* Its *raison d'être* is to minimize the danger and losses which those who threaten the status quo may cause, either because they have dangerously expanded their control of resources or because they do not conform to norms which are seen as essential by other group members.

f) The levelling coalition is *loosely structured.* Ties are tenuous because coalition members often have nothing more in common than a shared aversion of a social climber. In many cases core members will act from a feeling that others will back them up. But if this support does not materialize, there is no machinery to make coalition members toe the line nor are there sanctions to retaliate.

g) The levelling coalition is an amorphous grouping without any fixed membership criteria. It is hard to tell who will join the levelling action-sets.

h) Its pictorial representation is a *web.* In a series of successive encounters cores (spearheads) will emerge at different loci in the web.

6. THE RELEVANCE OF NETWORK ANALYSIS FOR MICRO-POLITICAL STUDIES

My concern in this section is with the relevance of network analysis for the study of conflict in general and the processes of micro-political mobilization in particular. For two reasons the discussion will be based on contributions of Kapferer (1969, and chapter of this book) in this field of study. Firstly, Kapferer explicitly draws a clear distinction between the set of concepts network analysts operate with and the theoretical propositions which underlie it.

Secondly, Kapferer's theoretical framework appears to have a relevance for other fields of sociological enquiry as well.

Regarding the concept of network, Kapferer gives a minimal working definition (1969: 182): '... the direct links radiating from a particular Ego to other individuals in a situation, and the links which connect those individuals who are directly tied to Ego, to one another'. Those links are then defined as representing *exchange* relations.

Network analysis as a technique for describing interaction patterns

The first question which seems pertinent from our perspective is can such a concept assist us in delineating the important groups which play a role in conflicts? Obviously, the answer depends on the extent to which existing exchange relations can be mapped by a field worker and whether conflict groups can be represented as networks of exchange relations in any meaningful way.

Two different types of exchange bonds can be mapped:

a) Relationships which are *asymmetrical*, i.e. one of the persons in a relationship offers his partner goods and services to which the latter cannot reciprocate sufficiently.
b) Symmetrical relationships with a pattern of exchanges between the two persons *differentiated* in volume and importance from other such relationships. For example, two persons are regularly exchanging goods and services at a rate which is markedly higher than for most other persons in that social unit.

Using these guidelines, we now focus our attention on coalition politics in Itumba. The interest coalition centered on Chomo is very easily mapped as a network of exchange bonds. The loan of plots by Chomo to other peasants of the village creates asymmetrical linkages of the patron-client type.

Additionally, with the help of our second criterion, more symmetrical links between Chomo and the staff people are differentiated from the 'ordinary' type of relationships between government personnel and peasants in terms of their volume and importance.

We encounter difficulties, however, when we try to apply the criteria outlined above to the levelling coalition. The levelling coalition which campaigned against Chomo did not have the asymmetrical backbone of exchange relationships on account of the fact that no distinct pattern of patron-client relationships between spearhead and other coalition partners emerged. Furthermore, coalition partners came from different compartments (see p. 245). This is important because it seems to reduce considerably the chance that these partners in the levelling coalition would be connected by exchange bonds. It seems to suggest that network analysis is fundamental for delineating the interest coalition, but has little, if anything, to contribute in getting the levelling coalition on the map.

Theoretical postulates of network analysis

From Kapferer's network analysis emerge two fundamental theoretical postulates which shed light on micro-political mobilization processes. These are derived from 'social exchange theory' as developed by Blau (1964) and Homans (1961). The first principle is that of the *imbalance of obligations* which Blau formulated in these words: 'By supplying services in demand to others, a person establishes power over them. If he regularly renders needed services they cannot readily obtain elsewhere, others become dependent on and obligated to him for these services, and unless they can furnish other benefits to him that produce interdependence by making him equally dependent on them, their unilateral dependence obligates them to comply with his requests lest he cease to continue to meet their needs' (1964: 118). Empirical evidence from Itumba fully corroborates the postulated consequences and functioning of this theoretical mechanism. A wealthy peasant like Chomo, for example, gives valuable plots on loan. The recipient places himself in an inferior position vis-à-vis the owner because, in most cases, the poorer peasant will fail to reciprocate in kind or in some other category of scarce goods. This failure to balance the scales will make the borrower dependent on the owner. An imbalance of obligations arises which enables the wealthy farmer to recruit the poorer peasant for his action-set. The way in which Chomo mobilized his action-sets could adequately be explained by means of this theoretical tool. Let us take case F (*Abuse*) as an example.

Chomo, without being in any way obliged to do so, had given Maria a fertile river plot. The goods that Maria returned were not on a par with Chomo's gift. Maria, for example, invited the wealthy farmer to several beer parties at her house, but this did not offset the considerable gift of the river garden. Thus, an imbalance in their relationship arose because Chomo obliged Maria without the latter being able to reciprocate. In this way an asymmetrical relationship was established. The fact that Maria came to the Primary Court to testify was seen by the peasants of Itumba as a direct consequence of her relationship with Chomo.

While the mechanism of unilaterality (asymmetry) in an exchange relationship satisfactorily explains some mobilization processes in the interest coalition, it fails to account for the forces that bring the levelling action-set together. As we had indicated before, no asymmetrical relationships between spearhead and other coalition partners were discerned.

The second important theoretical proposition in Kapferer's network analysis concerns *investments*, the postulate of which states: the more partners in an exchange relationship have invested in these relations, the higher the chances that they would join forces in a coalition when one of them gets involved in a conflict. To quote Kapferer: 'Persons will align themselves in a dispute in such a way as to incur the least loss to their investments in the total set of relationships in the situation' (1969: 243). For this author the concept of 'investments' refers to 'the amount of time and other resources individuals are prepared to expend in a social relationship in order to induce social rewards' (1972: p. 100). If a partner would not, at some later stage, discharge the obligations incurred then: '. . . the time and the energy alone which is expended in the support of another at a time of crisis would constitute a loss' (1972).

The mechanism which describes this type of mobilization may be formulated as follows: people will continue giving assistance to exchange partners – i.e. join their action-sets – because all of them realize that a refusal to support one another would mean jeopardizing their relationship and all their previous investments.

My objection amounts to the fact that both the theoretical postulate and the method used to record exchanges, instead of directing attention towards future transaction possibilities as seen by participants, directs attention towards past transaction (investments). While nobody will deny that transactions, as measured by present methods of network analysis, do give important clues to future behaviour, they could also lead us astray and cause us to formulate political predictions which are wide of the mark. There are several reasons for advocating a cautious use of network analysis.

1) Exchange partners try to ensure or safeguard their future dividends rather than past investments. At first glance this proposition may seem to coincide entirely with Kapferer's mechanism, yet the two propositions differ substantially.

When Chomo was about to lose his sugar-cane garden he was openly supported by Mwakalinga, the agricultural extension officer, and more indirectly by the medical dispenser and the magistrate. For Mwakalinga to have denied Chomo his support would have meant sacrificing a small but extremely fertile plot, from which he obtained all the vegetables his family consumed and some maize as well. Without his financial support and other forms of assistance Chomo would not have given notice of appeal. Consequently, the sugar-cane garden would have passed into other hands and

Mwakalinga would certainly have lost the part of it which he obtained from Chomo as a loan. The medical dispenser and the magistrate lent their support in a much more devious way and yet what they had in mind was much the same as Mwakalinga: they wanted to safeguard their future dividends.

2) This first proposition becomes important – and certainly not identical with Kapferer's mechanism – when we realise that political realities often change very quickly. Environmental instabilities, for example, regularly disturb the interaction patterns of small groups and affect the political fortunes of leaders and followers alike. In other words, the capability of exchange partners to fulfil their promises is influenced by a great many factors beyond the control of the persons concerned.

3) Participants in a political game continually assess one another's power position. If a leader's political prestige is high, people will clamber on his bandwagon, but if it is at low-ebb then they will leave him in the lurch and this, to some extent, takes place irrespective of past investments. A man may decide *to cut his losses* and opt out of a relationship when he feels that the political fortunes of his patron or exchange partner are dwindling. Bailey, in his reinterpretation of Barth's account of Swat Pathan society, has drawn our attention to such processes:

'No disgrace attaches to the man who changes sides. There is no thought that this is dishonourable: it is merely the sensible and rational thing to do. When shopping around to sell your allegiance where the best protection can be bought, no-one disapproves of a man who makes the best bargain. Presumably those who stay on the losing side when they had a chance to join the winners are written off as politically inept. Business is business'. (1969: 40).

Thus, what seems of crucial importance for any theory of political mobilization are the *expectations of the participants in a political game about emerging developments in the power distribution.* Their strategic coalition choice is based on this assessment: the preference for one exchange partner rather than another. This could, and often does, result in rather drastic changes of alignments which cannot be fully predicted from 'the structure and nature of his direct and indirect interpersonal relationships' (Kapferer, 1969: 209). Future expected benefits rather than past investments dictate political manoeuvring.

For all these reasons it seems hazardous to use the theoretical postulate of investments as a pillar for a theory of micro-political mobilization. While it would seem to be an important explanatory tool for a limited number of situations in small, face-to-face, groups with a stable environment, it appears highly unrealistic in predicting the many shifts and disruptions which occur in the political life of somewhat larger groups such as the local community.

By rephrasing Kapferer's theory of investments, we could make it more suitable for predicting mobilization:

'. . . *persons will align themselves in a dispute in such a way that it will bring them the optimal rate of exchange in future transactions in the total set of exchange circuits in which they partake.*'

Thus far, we discussed the relevance of the 'investments postulate' for the interest coalition. I now turn to the levelling coalition. Levelling action-sets which operated against Chomo do not seem to have emerged from any need to protect investments. As we saw before, the fact that partners in this type of coalition had come from various compartments made it highly unlikely that there was a framework of exchange bonds which kept this coalition working.

Furthermore, little or no recruitment, in the sense of active canvassing for support by spearhead members, ever took place. The existing resentment against Chomo allowed for a rapid and rather spontaneous build-up.

Summarizing, one may conclude that it is entirely feasible to map the interest coalition by means of the tools of network analysis because this pattern of interaction consists of both types of exchange bonds: the symmetrical and the asymmetrical. The levelling coalition, however, lacks the skeleton of transactional ties and, therefore, cannot be mapped in this way.

Two postulates which have been used by network analysts to explain processes of micro-political mobilization were discussed, namely, (1) the imbalance of obligations; and (2) the need for participants in exchange relations to protect their investments.

For the *interest coalition* the first postulate appears to be entirely valid. The second one, however, was reformulated in order to enhance its clarity for explanatory purposes. With reference to the *levelling coalition* none of the two postulates seems adequate to explain the processes of mobilization which give rise to the formation of levelling action-sets.

7. SUMMARY

Two types of coalition have been identified which play major roles in competitive interaction, and particularly in the struggle for the allocation of scarce resources. Both in structure and function substantial differences between the coalitions are apparent.

The first is the interest coalition or faction. The interest coalition manages a fund, is leader-centered, recruits members via transactional linkages, is a 'social construction', a bounded entity and a multi-purpose unit.

The levelling coalition is quite a different kind of 'non-group'. This coalition comes into existence as a reaction to the threat posed by the target. Social catalysts temporarily succeed in activating it.[21] Its core is unstable; it is a loosely-structured and a single-purpose unit.

But the main difference between the two coalitions lies in their principal objectives, their reason for existence. While it is the interest coalition's purpose to protect and expand a fund, the levelling coalition's purpose is to minimize the threat posed by the target. Both types of coalitions probably exist in all human societies.

The levelling coalition seems to be the type of 'non-group' least suited for study with the methods of network analysis. Furthermore, the postulates of modern network analysis appear to have little relevance, if any, for the study of the functioning of levelling coalitions. The study of the interest coalition on the other hand could very well proceed with the methods and from the perspective of network analysis.

Levelling coalitions belong to the most important interaction patterns as they determine to a large extent what obstacles a social climber or innovator would encounter. Yet these coalitions have not received the attention which they merit. The amorphous structure of the levelling coalition might be responsible for the lack of attention it has received, together with the fact that membership criteria are less fixed than in the interest coalition.

ACKNOWLEDGEMENT

This paper is based on field work in Itumba, an agrarian community in the southwest of Tanzania. It was part of a multidisciplinary project from the Afrika-Studiecentrum at Leiden to investigate factors hempering or stimulating the development of the rural economy. *The Netherlands Foundation for the Advancement of Tropical Research* (*Wotro*) financed this project.

I wish to thank Chris Baks and Jojada Verrips for their useful comments on an earlier version of this paper.

NOTES

1. Note that Boissevain (1968) is concerned with ego-centric interaction systems while one type of coalition to be discussed here does not have this cornerstone of ego-centric interaction. But Boissevain (p. 542) leaves the door open for other types of non-groups: 'These for *the most part* are social interaction systems centered on one person or a coalition of persons, the central ego' (my italics).

2. It would probably have been better to reserve the concept of *faction* for an exclusive coalition which can only exist in opposition to a similar unit within the same social entity. Thus, we might speak of factions when a social unit is polarized into two opposing camps. However, in view of its widespread use as a synonym for leader-centered coalition we are, for the moment, saddled with different notions for the concept of faction.

3. I am indebted to Paul Ten Have for drawing my attention to this point.

4. This is the headquarters of the Bulambia division of Rungwe District in Mbeya region. A 'division' was for a long time the smallest territorial unit used by the administration.

5. For a fuller account of the position of government personnel in a rural area, see Thoden van Velzen (1970).

6. The income of cash crop farmers in this district is considerably below that of the messenger, the lowest paid category in government bureaucracies. The average coffee and pyrethrum farmer's income per annum, will not exceed 750 and 500 shs respectively. The income of a messenger will in most cases be around 2000 shs per annum.

7. *Arena map* comprises the perceptions of a particular participant concerning the position of others in a arena or political field (Thoden van Velzen, 1970: 37).

8. The Divisional Executive Officers, as is the case with other government personnel as well, are regularly transferred. During a stay of 13 months in Itumba the post of D.E.O. was filled by three different persons.

9. Soon after independence the government of Tanzania decreed that hereditary succession to offices was to be abolished. This put an end to the official recognition and payment of the chiefs. In many rural areas a de facto recognition of the authority of the chief over some spheres of influence has emerged. For the political composition of former Nyiha chiefdoms, see Brock (1966).

10. The 'ten house group' or Party Cell is the smallest unit in *Tanu,* Tanzania's political party. As is well known Tanzania is a one-party state.

11. *Span* is defined by Kapferer (1969: 224) as 'the number of links out of the total viable links operating between actors . . .' *Multiplexity* is operationally defined by Kapferer (1969: 226) as a characteristic of relationships having two or more exchange contents.

12. A *political drama* is a set of antagonistic interactions triggered off by a crisis situation, i.e. by a state of marked or extreme insecurity among actors in a political field (van Hekken and Thoden van Velzen, 1972: 59).

13. The political party of Tanzania.

14. It should be pointed out that there is no evidence at all to conclude that the magistrate had been bribed. In fact, such statements are the stock-in-trade of peasants to explain unfavourable attitudes of government officials and staff in general. There is little doubt, however, about the part played by Mwakalinga; he told me personally that

he had instructed Chomo how to appeal 'after receiving a visit of the magistrate', as he chose to express himself.

15. I should like to add here once more that I have no reason at all to believe all the rumours that were circulating. I do not, for example, think that the medical dispenser really withheld medicines from the peasants or that Chomo had asked him to do so in the case of Lusibilo.

16. Interest coalitions with a symmetrical exchange circuit are not discussed here. They seem to represent only a transient form which evolves into the leader-centered coalitions. As the original group of equals gradually enlists the help of weaker partners as a result of this process the unit is transformed into a core-centered hierarchical coalition.

17. Here one is reminded of a terse 'Mailerism' (1968: 106): '*Politics is property*': 'Everybody in the game has a piece, and that piece is workable, it is equivalent to capital...'

18. This implies that I do not agree with Nicholas' (1965: 23) assertion that factions have no important social functions outside politics. Empirical data suggest that factions are like tools in the hands of leaders. They can be put to good use in a wide variety of contexts.

19. This concept of Parson's has been 'translated' by Zelditch (1955: 317) in some 'designation rules' which comprise the operational definition. Zelditch mentions the 'managerial complex' as consisting of '... direct responsibility for the solution of group tasks, for the skills and information prerequisite to the role in its adaptive aspects, and for the authority required to make binding managerial decisions...'

20. Attention should be drawn to the important role played by gossip. As we have seen in this case-study hostility is expressed through gossip: it is clearly a weapon in the war-of nerves between the coalitions. Gossip is also a form of communication (Paine, 1967: 278), which makes it feasible for people who have otherwise little or no contact – for example the church elders and the chief – to reach a *communis opinio* on the selection of a target. Furthermore, through gossip one gets a notion of the measure of support to be hoped for in case of conflict.

24. For the role that gossips play as social catalysts, see Paine (1967).

Bibliography

Aldous, J. and Strauss, M. A., 1965-1966, 'Social networks and conjugal roles: a test of Bott's hypothesis', *Social Forces, 44*: 576-581.

Anderson, J. A., 1970, 'Personal intermediation, network and transactionally generated social organization in the Philippines'. Paper presented at the symposium Developments in the study of network organizations, 6th Annual Meeting of the American Anthropoligical Association, November 1970, San Diego, California.

Aronson, Dan R., ed., 1970, 'Social networks', *The Canadian Review of Sociology and Anthropology*, Special issue, *7*: 221-286.

Barnes, J. A., 1954, 'Class and committees in the Norwegian Island parish', *Human Relations, 7*: 39-58.

— 1969a, 'Networks and political process'. In Mitchell, J. C., ed., *Social networks in urban situations*. Manchester: Manchester University Press for Institute of Social Research, Zambia, 51-76.

– 1969b, 'Graph theory and social networks: A technical comment on connectness and connectivity', *Sociology, 3*: 215-332.

– 1968, 'Networks and political process'. In Marc J. Swartz, ed., *Local-level politics: Social and cultural perspectives*. Chicago: Aldine Publishing Company, 107-131.

Bailey, F. G., 1969, *Stratagems and spoils: A social anthropology of politics*. Oxford: Basil Blackwell.

Barth, F., 1966, *Models of social organization*. Occasional papers of the Royal Anthropological Institute, 23, London: Royal Anthropological Institute.

– 1963, *The role of the entrepreneur in social change in Northern Norway*. Oslo: Universitetsforlaget.

– 1967, 'On the study of social change', *American Anthropologist, 69* (6): 661-69.

Befu, Harumi, 1963a, 'Network and corporate structure: A structural approach to community interrelations in Japan'. In Robert K. Sakai, ed., *Studies on Asia*, IV, Lincoln: University of Nebraska Press, 27-43.

– 1963b, 'Classification of unilineal-bilateral societies', *Southwestern Journal of Anthropology, 19* (4): 335-55.

Beum, C. and Brundage, E. G., 1950, 'A method for analysing the sociomatrix', *Sociometry, 13*: 141-145.

Blau, P. M., 1964, *Exchange and power in social life*. New York: Wiley.

Blok, Anton, 1966, 'Land reform in a West Sicilian latifondo village: The persistence of a feudal structure', *Anthropological Quarterly, 39* (1): 1-16.

– 1969a, 'Mafia and peasant rebellion as contrasting factors in Sicilian latifundism', *Archives Européennes de Sociologie, 10* (1): 95-116.

– 1969b, 'South Italian agro-towns', *Comparative Studies in Society and History, 11* (2): 121-25.

– 1969c, 'Peasants, patrons, and brokers in Western Sicily', *Anthropological Quarterly, 42* (3): 155-70.

– 1971, 'The mafia of a Sicilian village (1860-1960): An anthropological study of political middlemen'. Ph. D. thesis, University of Amsterdam.

– in press, 'The peasant and the brigand: Social banditry reconsidered' (with a comment by E. J. Hobsbawm). *Comparative studies in society and history*. Cambridge: Cambridge University Press.

Bock, R. D. and Husain, S. Z., 1950, 'An adaptation of Holzinger's B-coefficients for the analysis of sociometric data', *Sociometry, 13*: 146-153.

Boissevain, J., 1968, 'The place of non-groups in the social sciences', *Man* (3): 542-556.

– 1965, *Saints and fireworks: Religion and politics in rural Malta*. London: Athlone Press.

– 1969, *Hal-Farrug: A village in Malta*. New York: Holt, Rinehart and Winston.

1968, 'The place of non-groups in the social sciences', *Man, 3* (4): 542-56.

– 1971, 'Second thoughts on quasi-groups, categories and coalitions', *Man*.

– in press, *Friends of friends: Networks, manipulators and coalitions*. Oxford: Basil Blackwell.

Bobek, Hans, 1962, 'The main stages in socio-economic evolution from a geographic point of view'. In P. L. Wagner and M-W. Mikesell, eds., *Readings in cultural geography*. Chicago: The University of Chicago Press, 218-248.

Bott, E., 1957, *Family and social network*. London: Tavistock.

Bradley, J. V., 1968, *Distribution-tree statistical tests*. New Jersey: Prentice-Hall.

Brock, Beverly, 1966, 'The Nyiha of Mbozi', *Tanzania Notes and Records*. March, *65*: 1-31.

Chomsky, Noam, 1957, *Syntactic structures*. The Hague: Mouton.

Cohn, B. S. and Marriott, McK., 1958, 'Networks and centres in the integration of Indian civilization', *Journal of Social Research* (Ranchi), *1*: 1-9.

Coleman, James, Katz, Elihu, and Menzel, Herbert, 1957, 'The diffusion of an innovation among physicians', *Sociometry, 20*: 253-270.

Collins, B. E. and H. Guetzkow, 1964, *A social psychology of group process for decision-making*. London: John Wiley and Sons.

Dahrendorf, R., 1965, *Homo sociologicus. De categorie van de sociale rol*. Hilversum: Brand. First German edition: 1959.

Davis, J. A., 1962, 'Structural balance, mechanical solidarity, and interpersonal relations', *The American Journal of Sociology, 68*: 444-462.

Davis, K., 1952, *Human society*. New York: The Macmillan Co.

Eisenstadt, S. N., 1965, *Essays on comparative institutions*. New York: John Wiley and Sons.

Ekeh, P., 1969, 'Issues in exchange theory', *Berkeley Journal of Sociology*, July: 42-58.

Elias, Norbert, 1969, 'Sociology and psychiatry', In S. H. Foulkes and G. Stewart Prince, eds., *Psychiatry in a changing society*. London: Tavistock Publications, 117-144.

– 1970, *Was ist Soziologie?* München: Juvenat Verlag.

Elias, Norbert and Scotson, John L., 1965, *The established and the outsiders. A sociological enquiry into community problems.* London: Frank Cass.

Elias, Norbert and Dunning, Eric, 1966, 'Dynamics of group sports with special reference to football', *British Journal of Sociology, 17* (4): 388-401.

Epstein, A. L., 1961, 'The network and urban social organization', *Rhodes-Livingstone Institute Journal, 29*: 29-62.

– 1962, 'Immigrants to northern Rhodesian towns', Paper presented to Section of the British Association for the Advancement of Science, August 1962.

– 1969, 'Gossip norms and social network'. In J. C. Mitchell, ed., *Social networks in urban situations.* Manchester: Manchester University Press for Institute of Social Research, Zambia, 117-128.

Firth, R., 1951, *Elements of social organisation.* London: Watts.

– 1956, 'Introduction', *Two studies of kinship in London.* London: The Athlone Press.

– 1963, 'Bilateral descent groups. An operational viewpoint'. In I. Schapera, ed., *Studies in kinship and marriage.* London: R.A.I. Occasional Paper, 16: 22-37.

Garfinkel, Harold, 1967, *Studies in ethnomethodology,* New Jersey: Prentice-Hall.

Ginsberg, M., 1934, *Sociology.* London: Butterworth.

Gluckman, M., 1967, 'Introduction'. In A. L. Epstein, ed., *The craft of social anthropology.* London: Social Science Paperbacks.

Gross, N. C., Mason, W. S., and McEachern, A. W., 1958, *Explorations in role analysis: Studies in the school superintendency role.* New York: John Wiley and Sons, Inc.

Gutkind, P., 1968, 'The energy of despair: A study of unemployed in Lagos and Nairobi', *Civilizations,* December.

Harary, F., 1969, *Graph theory,* New York: Addison-Wesley.

Harrell-Bond, B. E., 1969, 'Conjugal role behaviour', *Human Relations, 22* (1): 77-93.

Harris, M., 1968, *The rise of anthropological theory.* London: Routledge, Paul and Kegan.

Harsanyi, J. C., 1969, 'Rational-choice models of political behaviour vs. functionalist and conformist theories', *World Politics, 21,* (4): 513-539.

Hobsbawn, E. J., 1969, *Bandits.* London: Weidenfeld and Nicolson.

Homans, G. C., 1961, *Social behaviour: Its elementary forms.* New York: Harcourt, Brace and World.

Homans, G. C., 1951, *The human group.* London: Routledge, Paul and Kegan.

Jay, E., 1964, 'The concepts of "fields" and "network" in anthropological research', *Man, 64*: 177-178.

Kapferer, B., 1969, 'Norms and the manipulation of relationships in a work context'. In J. A. Mitchell, ed., *Social networks in urban situations.* Manchester: Manchester University Press for Institute of Social Research, Zambia, 181-245.

– 1964, *The population of a Zambian municipal township.* Communication 1, Lusaka, Zambia: Institute for African Research.

Kephart, W. M., 1950, 'A quantitative analysis of intragroup relationships', *American Journal of Sociology, 55*: 544-550.

Klein, J., 1965, *Samples from English cultures,* London: Routledge, Paul and Kegan.

Kuhn, Th. S., 1970, *The structure of scientific revolutions,* 2nd ed. International Encyclopedia of Unified Science. Chicago: University of Chicago Press.

Lancaster, Lorraine, 1961, 'Some theoretical problems in the study of family and kin ties in the British Isles', *British Journal of Sociology, 12*: 317-333.

Lee, Nancy Howell, 1969, *The search for an abortionist*. Chicago: Chicago University Press.

Lemarchand, P., 1970, *Rwanda and Burundi*. London: Pall Mall Press.

Levy, Marion J., 1949, *The family revolution in modern China*. Cambridge, Mass.: Harvard University Press.

Ruel, M., 1968, 'The opportunist society and social change'. Paper read at meeting of the British Association for the Advancement of Science.

Mailer, Norman, 1968, *Miami and the siege of Chicago*. New York: Signet Books.

Mayer, Adrian C., 1966, 'Quasi-groups in the study of complex societies'. In M. Banton, ed., *The social anthropology of complex societies*, A.S.A. 4. London: Tavistock Publications, 97-123.

Mayer, P., 1964, 'Labour migrancy and the social network'. In J. F. Holleman, J. Knox, J. W. Mann and K. A. Heard, eds., *Problems of transition: Proceedings of the Social Science Research Conference held in the University of Natal, Durban, July 1962*. Pietermaritzburg: Natal University Press, 21-34.

Meehan, E. J., 1968, *Explanation in social science*. Homewood, Ill.: Dorsey Press.

Mitchell, J. Clyde, ed., 1969, *Social networks and urban situations*. Manchester: Manchester University Press for Institute of Social Research, Zambia.

– 1966, 'Theoretical orientations in African urban studies'. In M. Banton, ed., *The social anthropology of complex societies*, A.S.A. 4. London: Tavistock Publications.

– 1959, 'The study of African urban social structures', In *Housing and urbanization: Inter-African Conference*, 2nd Session. Nairobi Publication No. 47, CCTA.

Merton, R. K., and Rossi, A., 1957, *Social theory and social structure*, Glencoe, Illinois: Free Press.

Mori, Cesare, 1933, *The last struggle with the mafia*. London: Putnam.

Nadel, S. F., 1962, *The theory of social structure*. London: Cohen and West Ltd.

Nagel, Ernest, 1961, *The structure of science problems in the logic of scientific explanation*. New York: Harcourt, Brace and World.

Nelson, J. I., 1966, 'Clique contacts and family orientations', *American Sociological Review, 31*: 663-673.

Nicholas, Ralph W., 1965, 'Factions: A comparative analysis'. In *Political systems and the distribution of power*. A.S.A. Monograph 2, London: Tavistock.

Noble, Mary, 1964, 'Family structure and social network among the Yoruba'. Colloquium on the conditions of life of the African child in urban environment, Centre International de l'Enfance Dakar, December.

Nye, F. Ivan and Berardo, Felix M., 1966, *Emerging conceptual frameworks in family analysis*. New York: Macmillan.

Paine, Robert, 1970, 'Lappish decisions, partnership, information management, and sanctions – a nomadie pastoral adaptation'. *Ethnology, 9* (1): 52-67.

– 1967, 'What is gossip about? An alternative hypothesis', *Man, 2* (2): 278-286.

Pehrson, Robert N., 1964, *The bilateral network of social relations in Könkämä Lapp district*. Oslo: Universitetsforlaget.

Reader, D. H., 1964, 'Models in social change, with special reference to Southern Africa', *Journal of African Studies, 23*: 11-33.

Radcliffe-Brown, A. R., 1952, *Structure and function in primitive society*. London: Cohen and West Ltd.

Redfield, R., 1955, 'Societies and cultures as natural system', *Journal of the Royal Anthropological Institute, 85*: 19-32.

Schoeck, Helmut, 1969, *Envy: A theory of social behavior*. New York: Harcourt, Brace and World.

Schneider, Jane, 1971, 'Of vigilance and virgins: Honor, shame and access to resources in Mediterranean societies', *Ethnology, 10* (1): 1-24.

Siegel, S., 1956, *Nonparametric statistics for the behavioral sciences*. New York: McGraw-Hill.

Southall, A., 1959, 'An operational theory of role', *Human Relations, 12*: 17-34.

Srinivas, M. N. and Beteille, Andre, 1964, 'Networks in Indian social structure', *Man, 64*: 165-168.

Susser, M. W. and Watson, W., 1962, *Sociology in medicine*. London: Oxford Medical Publications.

Thoden van Velzen, H. U. E., 1970, 'Staff, kulaks and peasants'. *Mededelingen van het Afrika-Studiecentrum*, 3, Leiden.

Trouwborst, A. A., 1961, 'L'organisation politique entant que système d'échange au Burundi', *Anthropologica* N.S., *3* (1): 65-81.

– 1962, 'L'accord de clientèle et l'organisation politique au Burundi'. *Anthropologica* N.S., *4* (1): 9-43.

– 1970, 'Quelques aspects symboliques des échanges de bière au Burundi (Afrique Centrale)' *Anniversary contributions to anthropology. Twelve essays on the occasion of the 40th anniversary of the Leiden Ethnological Society W.D.O.* Leiden: E. J. Brill, 143-152.

Turner, C., 1967, 'Conjugal roles and social networks', *Human Relations, 20*: 121-131.

Udry, J. R. and Hall, M., 1965, 'Marital role segregation and social networks in middle-class, middle-aged couples', *Journal of Marriage and the Family, 27*: 392-395.

Van Velsen, J., 1964, *The politics of kinship*. Manchester: Manchester University Press.

– 1967, 'The extended-case method and situational analysis'. In A. L. Epstein, ed., *The craft of social anthropology*, London: Tavistock Publications, 129-149.

Wilson, G., 1940-1941, *An essay on the economics of detribalization in Northern Rhodesia*, Parts 1 and 2. Rhodes-Livingstone Institute Papers 5 and 6. Livingstone, Eng.

Whitten, Norman E. Jr., and Wolfe, Alvin W., in press, 'Network analysis'. In J. Honigmann, ed., *The handbook of social and cultural anthropology*. Chicago: Rand McNally.

– 1969, 'Strategies of adaptive mobility in the Columbian-Ecuadorian Littoral', *American Anthropologist, 71* (2): 228-243.

Wolf, Eric R., 1966, *Peasants*. Englewood Cliffs, N.J.: Prentice-Hall.

Young, Michael and Willmott, Peter, 1959, *Family and kinship in East London*, London: Routledge, Paul and Kegan.

Zelditch, Morris Jr., 1955, 'Role differentiation in the nuclear family: A comparative study'. In M. W. Bell and E. F. Vogel, eds., *Family, socialization and interaction Process*. Glencoe, Ill.: Free Press, 348-354.

Biographical data of authors

Banck, Geert A., Research Fellow, Center for Latin American Research and Documentation (CEDLA) 16 Nieuwe Doelenstraat, Amsterdam, Netherlands.

Blok, Dr. Anton, Lecturer, Department of Anthropology, University of Amsterdam, 397 Keizersgracht, Amsterdam, Netherlands (1972-73 Associate Professor, University of Michigan, Ann Arbor, USA). Publications: *The mafia of a sicilian village, 1860-1960: An anthropological study of political middlemen* (in press). Contributor to: *Anthropological Quarterly, Archives Européennes de Sociologie, Comparative Studies in Society and History, Sociologica Neerlandica.*

Boissevain, Dr. Jeremy, Professor of Social Anthropology, Department of Anthropology, University of Amsterdam, 397 Keizersgracht, Amsterdam, Netherlands. Publications: *Saints and fireworks: Religion and politics in rural Malta* (1965); *Hal-Farrug: A village in Malta* (1969); *The Italians of Montreal: Social adjustment in a plural society* (1970); *Friends of friends: Networks, manipulators and coalitions* (in press).

Cubitt, Dr. Tessa, Lecturer in Social Anthropology, Department of Geography, Portsmouth Polytechnic, 111 High Street, Portsmouth, PO1 2HL, England.

Jongmans, Dr. Douwe Geert, Research Fellow, Department of Social Research, Royal Tropical Institute, 2a Linnaeusstraat, Amsterdam, Netherlands. Publications: Editor, with P.C.W. Gutkind, *Anthropologists in the field* (1967). Forthcoming: 'Meziaa and Hormaa. The Connections between Services, Honour and Prosperity in a Changing Society', in *Culture, structure, process: Dutch contributions to anthropology and sociology of non-western societies.*

Kapferer, Dr. Bruce, Lecturer in Social Anthropology, Department of Sociology, University of Manchester, Dover Street, Manchester, M13 9 PL, England. Publications: *Cooperation, leadership and village structure* (1967); *Strategy and transaction in an African factory* (1972); 'Norms and the manipulation of relationships in a work context', in *Social networks in urban situations* (1969).

Mitchell, Dr. J. Clyde, Professor of Urban Sociology, Department of Sociology, University of Manchester, Dover Street, Manchester, M13 9PL, England. Publications: *The Yao village* (1956); *The Kalela dance* (1957); Editor, *Social networks in urban situation* (1969). Contributor to: *Rhodes Livingstone Journal, African Studies, Africa, International Journal of Comparative Sociology, Sociology, Journal of Asian and African Studies, British Journal of Sociology*, and to twelve books of collected essays.

Niemeijer, Rudo, Research Fellow, Afrika-Studiecentrum, 10 Stationsplein, Leiden, Netherlands.

Noble, Dr. Mary, Lecturer in Social Anthropology, Department of Social Anthropology, University of Edinburgh, Adam Ferguson Building, George Square, Edinburgh, EH8 9LL, Scotland. Contributor to: *Colloquium Centre International de l'Enfance, British Journal of Sociology, The Journal of International Nursing Studies, Africa*, and to the book *The conditions of life of the African child in urban environments* (1964).

Thoden van Velzen, H. U. E., Professor of Cultural Anthropology, Department of Cultural Anthropology, University of Utrecht, Utrecht, Netherlands. Publications: With P. M. van Hekken, *Land scarcity and rural inequality in Tanzania. Some case studies from Rungwe District* (1972).

Trouwborst, Dr. A. A., Professor of Social Anthropology, Catholic University of Nijmegen, 43 Verlengde Groenestraat, Nijmegen, Netherlands. Publications: *Vee als voorwerp van rijkdom in Oost-Afrika* (1956). Contributor to: *Les anciens royaumes de la zone inter-lacustre méridionale Rwanda, Burundi, Buha* (1962); *Liber amicorum E. M. A. A. J. Allard* (1970); *Anniversary contributions to anthropology* (1970).

Subject index

Abagindikiwa 234
Abatare 116
Abatererezi *see* Beer friends
Abezi 116
Abigeato *see* Raid
Absence of State control 156
Absentee estate owners 154
Abstract society VIII
Acquaintances 142,145
  differences in circle of 128
Action
  aim-oriented 163
  social 21, 28
Action-set 111, 116, 117, 220, 222 def.
  activation of 147
  aim of 117
  complex 11, 117
  composition of 117
  interest 222, 228
  inward base of 117
  levelling 222, 228, 245
  and network *see* Network
  outward base of 117
  simple 11, 117
  size of 117
Activities
  extra-household 92
  household 92
Activity field XI, 134, 137, 138, 140, 152
Activity situations 88
Adultery 239
Age and expectations of behaviour 28
Age-group as source of bandits 165
Agrarian reform 153
Agricultural season 226
Agricultural cooperative association 18
Agro-town 152
Ain Draham 169
All-channel net 87
Alliances 26
  composite 152
  equivocal 158
  impermanent 152
Alteration of the formal rules 122
Ancestor spirits 28
Anthropological present 11 def.
Arena map 249 def.
Ascent social 161
Association
  religious 151
  voluntary 20, 82
Assumptions
  of anthropology XI
  basic to the concept of network 6
  of Bott's network analysis 88
  exchange theoretical 105
  of game theory 90
  about nature of the family 16, 17
  about nature of the interaction VIII
  about nature of man 6, 7
  about nature of society 6, 7
  of neo-classical economic theory 90
  of stimulus-response school 90
  structural functional VIII
  of symbolic interactionism 90

Balance VIII
  definition of the degree of 205
  theory IX, 204
Bana Multima 93, *see also* Sacred Heart of Jesus Church
Band
  built-in tensions of 160
  changing structure of 160
  composition of 157
  core of 157
  membership of 157
  support of 157
Bandits X, 156, 165
Bargain(ing) 221, 246
Beer friends 111, 113, 119, 120
  and network *see* Network
Behaviour
  actual 92
  deviant VII
  standardized 31
Belief
  as cognitive phenomenon 35
  system VIII
Bethal Green 70
Bilateral kinship structure 127
Binary classification of relations 49, 53, 64
Binar interval scale 62
Birkirkana 131, 132
Bonds *see* Lines
Bott's assumptions IX, 85, 88, 106
Bott's hypotheses IX, 71, 91

Boundary
fixed 161
of network *see* Network
structural VII
traditional 152
Bridewealth 119
Brigandage 165
Broken Hill 25
Broker 40, 51
Brokerage 40, 51
Bulambia 237
Burundi 111, 116
royal family of 116

Capitalism
and ecosystem 165
rent 155, 165
Caste 25
Catalyst
social 241
Catholic Action 129
Cattle clientship 121, 122
Cattlemen 154
Centalized State 154
Ceremonies
baptismal 127
bethrothal 127
kinship 142
wedding 127
Change (social) VII, XI, 4, 20, 83, 122, 164
in the content of relations XI
in corporate groups 39
directions of XI
dysfunctional VIII
forces of XI
in groups IX, XI
process of XI
situational 10
in the social system 10
technical 154
Channels of communication 87
Character
differences in 133
Charting of network 11
Chief 122, 177
informal 171, 174
sub- 122
Choice 168
personal 7, 15
problem 50
rational 90
Christians 225
Circle 87
Circle (social) 92
Circulation of personnel 21
Civili *see* Status of gentlemen
Class(es)
business 131
differences 73, 79, 132
division 131
landed 154
social 17
theory 239
upward mobile government 131
Client 112, 119, 220, 221, 224
affiliated 228
personal 118
Clientship 111, 113, 123
Clientship agreement 112, 121, 122, 123
Clientship relation
asymmetrical character of 112, 115
vertical character of 112, 115
Climber
social 248
Clique 23, 54 def., 81, 94
Clubs
political party 131
rival 128, 129, 130, 131
Cluster
analysis 57, 62, 64
and network *see* Network
Clusterability 107
Coalition(s) X, XI, 19, 39, 115, 155 def., 219
built-in tensions of 160, 163
choice of 246
competing X
composition of 158
as constructed social entity 241
core of 220
core centered hierarchical 250
of entrepreneurs 156
of entrepreneurs and bandits 163, 164
fund of 220
genesis of 156
interest X, 219, 240, 241
leader-centred 240
levelling X, 219, 221, def., 241, 242
of mafiosi 161
as multi-purpose unit 241
temporary 153
Coalition of members realignment of XI
Commercialization 154
Communication
chain 147

content 23
of information 87
theory X
potentia 138
Community
industrial 147
moral 144, 146
rural 147, 152
stratified 131
Compartment 60, 64 def., 143, 144, 225 def., 243
boundaries of 226
tribal 226
Compartimentalization
of social life 226
and territorial segregation 226
Complementary opposition VIII
Complex society
and friendship 9
and kinship 9
and patron-client 9
and right and obligations 13
Concept
of action-set 111, 117
of boundary 46
of cluster IX, 46
of 'content' 123 def.
of corporate groups 151
of degree 46
of density IX, 46
egocentric 163
of network 219, 243
of rationality 109
Configurations XII, 65, 164
inherent tensions of 165
of links 34
of W. Sicilian Society 155
Configurational Sociology 165
Configurational theory XII
Conflict 133, 162, 168, 195, 243
basic forms of X
between religious groups 237
dysfunctional VII
functional VII
group 243
group binding functions of 195
Confraternity of the Blessed Heart 129, 130
Confrontation with rival 159
Congregation 7
Conjugal behaviour 17
and network *see* Network
Conjugal role relationship 5, 71, 82, 93
Conjugal role segregation 50, 71, 104
Connectedness 109
degree of 106
of network *see* Network
Consensus, degree of normative 106
Constraints
moral XII
normative 90
structural XII
Contact
first order 117
indirect 116
informal 127
international 94
second order 117
social 74 def.
Continuity VIII
Continuum 38
of relationships 19, 20
Contractual relationships 21
Control
absence of State 154
over land 160, 161
of resources 219, 220
social 40, 43, 146
Cooperation
forms of 160
Cosca 161, 165
Cosche 160, 162, 163
Cost (social) 100
Council
of the elders 193, 196, 200
Court
District 233
Primary 233
session 119
Culture VIII, 144, def.
Cultural
conditioning 7
ecology XI
Custom 105

Decision making process 120
Degree
and network *see* Network
of person 49 def., 56
Density
degree of 106
and network *see* Network
of person 49 def., 64 def.
Direction of change IX
Division of labour
in large scale societies 16

in small societies 16, 17
Division Executive Officer 224, 239
Differences
in character 133
in circle of acquaintances 128
Djemaa see Council of elders
Dominant norms and values 12
Dual organization 213
Dyadic
bonds 152
relationship 31
framework 123
Dynamic
inherent VIII
model 151
process XI

East London 20
Ecological
conditions 161
constraints 161
Economic relations XI, 57
Ecosystems and rent capitalism 165
Edinburgh 72, 74
Egocentred relations 5
Egoism 171
Egotism 194, 198
Election 128
Electoral
field 156
supporters 25
Elite 24, 224
category 24
rural 128
Emancipation XII
Employment opportunities 171
Entrepreneurs 146, 154, 169, 220
violent 161, 165
peasant 153, 154, 155, 162
Environment X, 125 def., 126, 132, 133, 146
and content of network 126
and the individual 4
material 239
and network 125
personal 125, 126
and prestige 133
and structure of network 125, 126
total 125
town 143
urban 93
Envy 239
Equilibrium
approach 9, 11
dynamic 203
social 203, 215 def.
static 4
system in VII
Estate
landed 153, 155, 161
owner 153, 154, 159, 163
Ethnicity
as perception 28
Evolutionary
doctrine and dynamic approach 9
theories VIII
Exchange (social) XII, 99 def.
of beer 112, 113, 118, 119, 122
circuit X, 220, 221
content of 113, 138, 147, 243
of good 118
of gossip 226
individual 112
of information 145
of meziaas 198
nature of 90
partners 246
rate of 247
relationship 26, *see also* Relationship
theory X, XII, 34, 177, *see also* Theory
Expectations
of normal behaviour 27
normative- 30
in political game 246
role 41, 42
sets of 33
Extended case 167

Faction 19, 25, 39, 116, 167, 219, 220 def.
characteristics of 219, 220
as exclusive groupings 201
festa- 133
formation of 184
labour 131
obligations towards 194
political 117
rival 195
struggle 177
theory 201
Family
and total society 16
developmental cycle of 73
elementary 17
in small-scale societies 16
middle-class 68
nuclear 16, 17

of origin 80
patronominal 155
urban 17
Farrug 127
Fascism 163
Fascist intervention 163
Feasts
annual 128
religious 127, 142
Festas *see* Feasts
Feud 172
Feudal jurisdiction 154
Feudi *see* Landed estates
Force
use of 197

Gabella 153
Gabelloti *see* Peasant entrepreneurs
Game
cooperative 194
non-zero sum 194
zero sum 194
Gentry 154
Genuardo 152
Gossip 23, 24, 95, 226, 237, 250
and network *see* Network
monger 241
Government personnel X
Gozo 127
Grand Harbour 126
Graphtheory X, 64
Group VIII
age 165
analysis X
bounded 4, 7, 21
of brothers 195
conflict 219, 243, 249
core 119, 229
corporate 18, 19, 31 def., 39
criterion of membership of 33
cult 7
demarcated 160
descent 165
dynamics of 165
enduring 20, 152
interactional 19
institutionalized 5
kin 16, 165
local 16
managerial 73
non- 19, 38, 67, 219
organization of the 32
organized 16, 17
patri 228
play 19
political 219
professional 73
quasi 19, 31, 222 def.
reference 5, 38
strongly and weakly structured 164 def.
temporary 151, 164
tribal 226
Groupings 50
Group characteristics
objective existence of 21
Guerilla warfare
stratagems of 156

Hal-Farrug 128
Homo-sociologicus 41
Honour 220
attack on 183, 198
blow to 185
Hormaa *see* Prestige

Ideological cleavages 128
Illness and differences in network structure 146
Imbalance
of obligations 220, 244 def. 173, 202, 211, 233
Impact of the State and market 152
Indicator of the relative strength of a boundary 51 def.
Individual
choice 12
and configuration 165
and environment 4, 7
as focal point of a network 96
freedom of 163
motivation 12
and network *see* Network
and self interest 90
and social structure 152
and the social units he forms 163
and society as aspect of man 152
units of interdependant 160, 161
Individual manipulation XII
Individualism 171, 196
Influence 112, 116
political 199
Information 23, 116, 130, 133, 145, 240
actual flow of 138
exchange of 145
Inherent dynamics VIII
Innovation 122, 146

Innovator 221, 248, *see also* Entrepreneur
Institution XI
  of marriage 29, 30
Institutional
  complexes 19
  factors 16, 19 def.
  fields XI
Interaction
  analysis 214
  antagonistic 240
  competitive 24, 219
  convivial 95
  form of 89
  patterns of 89, 246, 247
  sociable 94, 95
Interactional structure 89
Interdependence of human beings XII
Interest
  opposed- 112
Interest coalition
  features of 240, 241
Intermediaries 11
Intermediary 231
Intermediate peasantry 154
Internal process VIII
Interval scale 62, 64
Intrigue 159
Investment 100 def., 102, 107, 247
  degree of 107
  index of 95
  and network *see* Network
  in relationships 121, 125 def.
  of resources 120
  postulate 246, 247
  social 143
Itumba 223

Japan 18
Jealousy 198
Jehovah's Witness 94
Joint interest 109

Kabende tribe 89, 93, 100
Kabwe tribe 93
Kebir douar 176, 197, 200
Kelábu 226
Khroumiria 169
Khroumirian
  political theory 184
  values 193
King 122
Kinship XI, 5, 119, 144, 147
  bilateral- 19, 127, 152
  and circles of intimacy 13
  density of 80
  and division of labour 16
  fictive 152
  and moral evaluation of conduct 6
  and network *see* Network
  obligations 127
  and process of socialization 6
  ritual 25
  and symbols 6
Kinsmen 134, 140, 141, 142, 143, 144, 158, 160, 163
  and network *see* Network
  as social investment 143
Kingroup 16, 152
  and network *see* Network
  strongly structured 164
  weakly structured 164

Laazem 176
Labour
  migrant 153
  menial 121
  skilled 142
  unskilled 142
Labourers
  casual 159, 161
  industrial 131
  land 153
  landness 161
  skilled 128
  unskilled 128
Lala tribe 93
Land tenure 153
Land and labour as market commodities 154
Latifond *see* Landed estates
Latifondisti *see* Estate owners
Leaders X
  of extended family 196
  of faction 52, 220
  instrumental 241
  political 52
  potential 117
  village X
Levelling coalition (features of) 241, 242
Lease-holders 16, 154, 155
Lineage 7, 19, 21
  local 114
  system 214
Linguistics
  and 'deep structure' 12
  and social structure 151

and 'surface structure' 12
Links
content of 23
dyadic 152
exchange 243
multiplex 141
non-transactional 12
transactional 12, 221, 247
Lintonian tradition 41
Local favour 156, 157
Local administration 160, 163
Luapula Province 93

Mafiosi X, 155, 159, 161, 162, 165
Malta 126
Malta Labour Party 128
Man as interacting social being VIII
Manipulation 8, 39, 116, 197
of environment 9
individual XII
of network structure 146
Many-stranded relations *see* Relations
Marabout 175
Market development of 154
Mandante 159
Mandatario 159
Marriage
agreement 119
arrangements 196
Masseria 153, 155
organization of 163
Mathematical theory of balance 187, 203
Matrix 23, 81, 195
analysis 195
use of IX, 168
Men's meeting place 176
Membership
ascribed 144
criteria for 56
family 134
trade union 25
to tribal categories 25
village 147
Methodological problems VIII
Methodology of network analysis IX
Meziaa 174 def.
associates 176
characteristics of 175
kinds of 175, 176
partnership 199, 200
relation 175, 193, 200, 213
Mobility
geographical 8, 133, 142
outward 154
social- 105, 116
Mobility
teritorial 226
vertical 154
Mobilization 89
micro-political 242
potential 89
support 89
Model
of group dynamics 160
normative consensus 83
of segmentary system 214
Moiety
anti-establishment 128
establishment 128
ritual 128
rival 128
Moral
code 128
corporation VIII
order VIII
Moravian Brethern 225
Multiplex relations *see* Relations
Mwakalinga 225

Nairobi 84
Nationalist Party (of Malta) 128
Neighbourhood 18 def., 112, 113, 114, 119
density of 80
Naola 24
Network 243 def.
and action-set 10, 11
acquaintance 24
activity field of 69 def.
and age 134, 141, 142
and age distribution 134
aims of 111
ambiguity in the term 10
and amount of interaction 5
analysis VII, VIII, X, XII, 146
and analysis of human behaviour 6
approach 118, 147, 151
ascribed segment in 141
of assistance 158, 161
as basis for the recruitment of action-sets 116
of beer friends 113, 116, 117, 118
and behaviour X, 125
of blood relatives 127
bounded 5, 10, 11, 114
boundary of 53, 59, 60, 62, 64 def.
centre-point of 31

as chain of dyadic relationships 152
change in 122
and change 7
characteristics of 21 def., 37, 126
and children 10, 134
class 5
clientship 113, 116, 118
close-knit 10, 40, 67, 68, 71, 85, 88, 91, 104, 105
cluster 54 def., 84, 94, 97, 110
and communication 23, 26
communication 226
communication content of 23
and compartment 143, 144, 227
composition of 111, 134, 137
concept of 6, 219, 243
as conceptual tool 4
connectedness of 10, 17, 67, 68 def., 69 85
connectivity 10, 67
consensus 40
content of partial 24, 117
core of 113, 115
and corporate group X, 27, 30, 31, 33, 34
and corporate structure 18
of countrymen X
degree of 47, 48 def., 58
degree of clustering of 97, 99, 101
degree of cross-linkage of 97, 101, 102
degree of interconnection of 143
density 10, 11, 12, 46 def., 47, 49, 58, 67, 68, 71, 72, 73, 84, 85, 88, 89, 91, 93, 96, 101, 102, 106, 107, 109, 111, 113, 115, 138 def., 143, 144
density areas of 68
density of extended 72, 75
density and geographic mobility 71
density index of 138
density 'knots' of 68
density score of 143
density sectors of 73
differences between 14, 111, 112, 116, 141, 146
and differences between town and country 132
directedness of 111
and duration of contact 13
and economic factors 11
and education 134, 141, 142
effective 5, 69, 72
effective zone of 97 def., 109
egocentric VII, 97, 164
as egocentric structure 125, 151
egocentred partial 111 def.
and environment 125
exchange 25, 26
of exchange bonds 243
exchange content of 25
extended 5, 72
extended zone of 97 def., 110
family 10, 91 def.
and family 8, 9, 11, 13
and family cycle 73
family interaction 5
and family studies 40
as a field of social relationship 4
first zone of IX, 45, 110, 140
first order star of relation of 115
first order zone of 125, 126, 144, 147
focus and the family 10
formations 168, 169
and friendship 18, 19
and frequency of contact 11
and geographical distance 11
and geographical mobility 8
geographical spread of 137
and gossip 5
and the individual 37, 38, 40
individuals 74
individual aims and 6
influential 5
and informal contact 67
information 20, 24
and initiation of contact 12
and institution X, 19
interactional characteristics of 126
interconnection of partial 147
intimate 69, 141
intimate category of 140
intimate cell of 140
intimate personal 115 def.
intimate zone of 97 def., 99, 102, 109, 140, 141
and investments 245
kin 142, 144
and kinship 18, 19, 70
kinship segment of 144
and kinsmen X
local core of 111, 114 def.
loose-knit 10, 45, 67, 68, 75 def., 85, 91
and lower class 72
and manipulation 9
of married couples 81, 82
as a metaphor 23, 37, 45, 68
middle-class 70, 73

and middle-class populations 8
moral 144
moral sanctions of kin 144
multiplexity of 111, 113
and neighbourhoodliness 18, 19, 70
Newbolt family 104
non-intimate zone of 141
normative 26 def.
normative content of 26, 27
and norms X, 5, 10
number of people in 80, 113
objective characteristics of 22
objective structural characteristics of 126
open 17
overall 104, 160
of parents 10
partial XI, 22, 28, 29, 30 def., 113, 118, 120, 122, 123, 125, 147, 152
and peasant communities 8, 9
personal 16, 18, 122, 126, 152, 164
and personality 125
of personal links 10
and place of contact 12
political 5, 22
and political studies 40
primary zone of 125, 138, 143, 144, 147 def.
quality of 111
and quality of relations 12
and quasi-group 10
radiating character of 52
and rate of stability and unstability 198
of relatives by marriage 127
religious 22
and residence 134, 136, 141, 142
and roles X, 30
rural 73
rural-based 136
second zone of 140
section of 67
sectors of 70 def.
segment of 50, 60, 62, 64 def., 67, 69, 137, 144
and self-progress 9
as series of relations VIII
and sets of people 119
and sex 134, 141, 142
size of 47, 49 def., 58, 91, 133, 141, 143
and social categories 134
and social control 40
and social equilibrium 7
and sources 111, 116
span of 89 def., 96 def., 226
spread of 142
star 164
star cross-linkage of 97, 110
and structural approach 9
structural aspects of 84, 89
structural characteristics of 69
structure of 17, 94, 108, 122, 132, 146
structure and environment 125
subjective characteristics of 22, 126
as system of relations VIII
and time 11
total family 10
total personal IX, 22 def., 140
of townsmen X
and transactions 122
and tribal communities 8, 9
unbounded 5, 10
urban 73
and urban family 16, 17
and urban mobile societies 7
and working class communities 8
zones of 97, 134, 164
zone cross-linkage of 9 def., 110
and zones of intimacy 140
Network analysis
and compartimentalization 227
methodology of IX
and psychiatry X
and psychology X
Niche 141, 165 def.
exploitation of 155
residential 133
social 133
village 143
Norms 168
as cognitive phenomenon 35
dissemination of 5
formation of 5
general 29
interconnectedness of 30
kinship 144
and process of interaction 123
traditional 146
transmission of 17
Norm of reciprocity 90
Normative consensus 86, 88
degree of 106
Normative content of
friendship 26
kinship 26
neighbourliness 26
Normative pressure 88
Nuer 21

Nyha 224
Objective variables 50
Obligations 88
  kinship 127, 144, 145
  one-sided 194
  two-sided 194
One-class milieu 132
Opportunist Society 9
Opposition 26
Order 20
  categorical 20
  moral VIII
  personal 20
  of relationships 20
  structural 20
Ordinal measurement 62, 63
Ordinal scale 64
Outlaw 156, 161, 162

Paese 153
Pagans 225
Palermo 153
Parameter of continuum 19
Partnership of leaseholdings 159
Party Cell *see* 'Ten House Group'
Pastoralists 169
  organizational flexibility of 165
Patriotism
  parochial 131
Patron 61, 112, 119, 121, 159, 220, 246
  working parties of 225
Patron saints 128, 142
Patronage 25, 119, 152, 154
Patronymic 165
Patterned interaction 19 def.
Pauperization 171
Peasant
  cluster of 160
  cultivator 153
  entrepreneur 153, 154, 155, 162
  intermediate 154
  order 154
  ordinary 234
  poor 244
  proletarianized 154
  wealthy 153, 224, 225, 227, 238, 239, 240, 244
Perception 90, 138
  actor's 20
  and density index 138
  and norms and belief 27
  race as 28
Personal
  choice 7, 15
  degree 62
Personality
  basic 145
  differences in 133, 143
  reserved 146
  structure 146
'Point of anchorage' 123
Political
  career 200
  competition 239
  conflict 169
  cooperation 196
  dispute IX
  drama 227, 249 def.
  fortune 246
  game 246
  help 121
  manoeuvring 246
  mobilization 246
  party 20, 133
  prestige 246
  process 174, 194
  process as game 194
  reality 246
  structure 174
Population increase 154
Postulate of network approach VIII, 12
Power IX
  distribution 246
  position 246
  and resources 197
Pressure
  to conform the expectations 25
  normative 88
Prestige 112, 176, 199, 200, 213, 246
  ladder 132
  personal 133
  political 246
Priest 130
Priority of individual to group
Process
  of bargaining 40, 221
  of change 9, 39, 151
  of creation 39
  historical 153
  of individual interactional behaviour 83, 88, 90
  of interaction 6, 42
  internal VIII
  of social action 90
Process
  of decision-making 120

micro-political mobilization 244
political 57, 194, 195
transactional 43
Processions 127
Prohibition of goats 170, 171, 200
Public image 144, 176, 199, 200
Public property 172

Qdar *see* Respect
Qrende 129
Quasi-group *see* Group

Race
as perception 28
Raid 157, 161, 162
Ramlia 169
'black' 173, 185, 189, 201, 202, 203, 206
'white' 173, 180, 191, 202, 206
Random mesh 50 def.
Rational Choice 90
Rational behaviour 194
Rebellion 154
Reciprocal pattern of relationship 13
Reciprocity between patrons and clients 112
Recruitment as process of exchange 241
Reference group 5, 38
Reform
agrarian 163
Registrar General's classification 73
Relation(ship)
anonymous 145
with close skin 198
content of III, 138
exchange X, 138, 139, 140, 143, 243
impersonal 145
many-stranded XI, 95, 144
meziaa 175, 176, 177, 178, 192, 193, 194, 195, 200, 213
of neutrality 206
nominal 139
patron-client 114, 225, 243
to personalize 133, 141, 145
quality of 112, 137 def.
single-stranded 114, 145
transactional X, 94, 110, 225
Relation
asymmetrical 64, 243, 244
actual 49
between bandits and entrepreneurs 159
'blood' 199
between brothers 196
bureaucratic 122
clientship 114, 117
composite 22
cross-linking 51
devalued 180
directed 67
directedness of 112
economic 57
free 198, 201
horizontal 112, 115, 116
indirected 67
joint 102
key 101 def.
kin 127
'milk' 195, 199
multi-bonded 22
multiplex 95, 114, 227
multi-stranded XI, 22, 29, 33
non-actual 49
obligatory 198
orders of 20
reciprocal pattern of 13
religious XI
set of XI
sociational content of 95 def.
symmetrical 64, 243
vertical 115, 116
Rent capitalism 155, 165
Resources 120
distribution of 122
human 160, 197
material 197, 198
reallocation of 122
Respect 197, 199
Revolution XII
'Right of man' 20
Rival 159
Role VII, XI, 30 def., 41, 42, 134, 195
achieved 4
ascribed 4
behaviour 31, 89
concept 119
double 177
dyad 42
of employee 159
expectations 92
formal teaching 133
and heterogeneous societies 4
kinship 133
occupational 141
opposite 195
performer 42
segregation 17, 86

theory 119
Role-set 30, 87
occupational 137, 138, 140
Role-relationship 91, 92 def., 93
complementary 93, 102
conjugal 130
occupational 139
Roman Catholic 93, 94, 128
Royal Family of Burundi 116
Sacred Heart of Jesus, Church of 93
Saint Martin 128
Saint Rocco 128
Sample 58, 59, 60
Sampling distribution 58
Sampling procedure IX
Sampling technique 147
Sanction 185, 200, 201
of the Church 128
negative 42
positive 42
segment of network 60, 62, 64 def.
Segmentation
degree of 102
Self-interest 8, 109
Sex and expectations of behaviour 28
Shinto institution 18
Sharecropper 153
Shepherds 153
cluster of 160
Sheik 176, 177
Shifting cultivation 223
Sicily IX, X, 154
Western 152
Sliema 127, 132
Small holder 153
Società 155
Society
complex VII
large-scale 16, 34
simpler VII
small-scale 16, 34
static 38
tribal VII
Sociism 206
Sorcery 123, 231, 239
Span 109 def., *see also* Network
Spearhead
levelling 229
members of 237
Staff People 223, 229
Star *see* Network
first order 117
State 163
Statistical procedures 13
Status 122
civilized 154
of gentlemen 154
in public life 199, 200
seignorial 154
Status occupant 82
Strangers 145
Strategy of individual 120
Struggle for power 116
Structure (social) 213 def.
built-in tensions of 164
and fixed boundaries 4
and the individual 151
as static model 151
of network *see* Network
Radcliffe-Brown's definition of 14
Structure
administrative 18
corporate 18
educational 18
of interpersonal relations 16
Structural-functional approach VII, XII, 151
and change 4
and the individual 4, 108
and network *see* Network
and non-literate societies 4
static quality of 4
and study of complex societies 4
Subjective variables 50
Supernatural forces 200, 201
Support X, 167
electoral 159
network of 159
political 116, 117, 118
Symbols 6, 30, 32
Swat Pathan society 246
Swidden-cultivation 224

Tanu 233, 237
branch chairman of 237
Youth League of 237
Tanzania IX, 219
Target of levelling coalition 221
Team 220
management problems of 220
Teleology
functional 4
Tenant peasant 153
'Ten House Group' 226
Territorial
mobility 226

segregation 226
Theft of animals 161
Theory
contract 50
exchange 34, 41, 43, 50, 90, 109, 213, 244
on faction 201
game 4, 43
interaction 41
network 151
role 41
triangle 204, 205
Ties *see* Links
Time 120
perspective XI
Trade Union 151, 163
Transaction XII, 25, 107, 122, 240
between core and followers 240, 241
and network *see* Network
Transactional linkages 241
Transfer of wealth 154
Tribes
matrilineal 93
Tribal antagonism 238
Tribalism 229
Triangle theory 204, 205
Trust 100, 107
Tukuyu 233
Tunisia IX, 167
government of 197

Ubugabire 111, 120
Ukuterera 111, 115, 116, 119, 120
Ulubugano *see* 'Village meeting'
Urban situation 16, 105
Use of force 197, *see also* Force
Use of violence *see* Violence
Ushi tribe 93

Valletta 127, 131
Values 26, 105
as cognitive phenomenon 35
Variables
objective 50
subjective 50
Viddanu 154, 155
Village
Development Committees 238
elders 227
Executive Officers 224
as highly interconnected community 145
meeting 227
as moral community 144
politics 130
rival 142
situation 16
subculture of 144
Violence
use of 154, 155
Visibility
social 133

Wage employment 99
Wasitafu *see* Staff People
Wealthy peasants 227, *see also* Peasants
Wheel communication 99
Witchcraft 227, 235
Workers
religious 134
semi-skilled 73
skilled 73, 135
unskilled 135
white collar 134
Working parties 225, 240

Xhosa migrants 20

Zambia 25, 85, 89
Central Province of 93
Zone
first order IX, 68, 74
of network *see* Network

Bei Fragen zur Produktsicherheit wenden Sie sich bitte an:
If you have any questions regarding product safety,
please contact:

Walter de Gruyter GmbH
Genthiner Straße 13
10785 Berlin
productsafety@degruyterbrill.com